W. ing.

LANGUAGE IN SOCIAL LIFE SERIES

Series Editor: Professor Christopher N Candlin
Chair Professor of Applied Linguistics
Centre for English Language Education & Communication Research
Department of English
City University of Hong Kong, Hong Kong

For a complete list of books in this series see pages *v* and *vi*

Writing Business:
Genres, Media and Discourses

Edited by

Francesca Bargiela-Chiappini

and

Catherine Nickerson

LONGMAN

Pearson Education Limited,
Edinburgh Gate,
Harlow,
Essex CM20 2JE,
United Kingdom
and Associated Companies throughout the world.

*Published in the United States of America
by Pearson Education Inc. New York*

First published 1999

ISBN 0–582–31984–6 CSD
ISBN 0–582–31985–4 PPR

Visit our world wide web site at
http://www.awl-he.com

' ⸱ing Resources
'entre

12929433

British Library Cataloguing-in-Publication Data

A catalogue record for this book is available from the British Library

Library of Congress Cataloging-in-Publication Data

Writing business : genres, media, and discourses / edited by Francesca
  Bargiela-Chiappini and Catherine Nickerson.
    p. cm. — (Language in social life series)
  Includes bibliographical references and index.
    ISBN (invalid) 0–582–31984–6 (csd). — ISBN 0–582–31985–4 (ppr)
    1. English language—Business English. 2. English language—
Discourse analysis. 3. Business writing. I. Bargiela-Chiappini,
Francesca. II. Nickerson, Catherine. III. Series.
PE1479.B87W73 1999
808'.0665'014—dc21   98–49111
                                                            CIP

Set by 35 in 10/12pt Palatino
Produced by Addison Wesley Singapore (Pte) Ltd.
Printed and bound by Antony Rowe Ltd, Eastbourne

LANGUAGE IN SOCIAL LIFE SERIES

Series Editor: Professor Christopher N Candlin
Chair Professor of Applied Linguistics
Centre for English Language Education & Communication Research
Department of English
City University of Hong Kong, Hong Kong

Language and Power
Basil Hatim and Ian Mason

Planning Language, Planning Inequality
James W Tollefson

Language and Ideology in Children's Fiction
John Stephens

Linguistics and Aphasia
Ruth Lesser and Leslie Milroy

Language and the Law
John Gibbons (ed.)

The Cultural Politics of English as an International Language
Alastair Pennycook

Literacy Practices: Investigating Literacy in Social Contexts
Mike Baynham

Critical Discourse Analysis: the Critical Study of Language
Norman Fairclough

Fictions at Work: Language and Social Practice in Fiction
Mary M Talbot

Knowledge Machines: Language and Information in a
Technological Society
Denise E Murray

Achieving Understanding: Discourse in Intercultural Encounters
Katharine Bremer, Celia Roberts, Marie-Thérèse Vasseur,
Margaret Simonot and Peter Broeder

The Construction of Professional Discourse
Britt-Louise Gunnarsson, Per Linell and Bengt Nordberg (eds)

Mediated Discourse as Social Interaction
Ron Scollon

To Andrzej and Geoff,
who know all
about the negotiation of shared meaning
with members of a different discourse community

The centripetal forces of need, labour and science
which are pulling us together as a species
are counter-balanced by centrifugal forces,
the claims of tribe, race, class, section, region and nation,
pulling us apart.

Michael Ignatieff (1984) *The Needs of Strangers*

Contents

Publisher's acknowledgements

We are indebted to the following for permission to reproduce copyright material:

Communication Research Institute of Australia for sample letter from 'Safe Insurance Co'; Elsamprojeckt A/S for extracts from introduction of *ENERGIEKONZEPT* from a German Town, May 1993; the author, Marcia Hanson for extracts from her speech to AmerUs Bank; the author, Professor Andrew M. Lister for example emails from database of emails used by administrative staff at University of Queensland; the author, Dr. Eugene Loos for transcripts of conversations recorded in the Grandorado Leisure NV company. Transcripts copyright Utrecht University; Wm H. Muller & Co for the article 'Can we count on your bookings of potatoes to Madeira? Corporate Context and discourse practices in direct sales letters' by Miriam van Nus; Yhhteisviejat Tames Oy for example faxes; Shell Chemical Company for tables 2.1 & 2.2 reproduced from data supplied by Shell Chemicals in Amsterdam; the author, Nora Slattery for an extract from a speech to Ogilvy & Mather; KAREKS, Deri Sanayi ve Ticaret Ltd. Şti of Istanbul, Turkey for the use of commercial correspondence in Chapter 10.

Notes on contributors

Didar Akar holds a PhD in Linguistics from the University of Michigan. She is Assistant Professor at Bogaziçi University and Koç University, both in Instanbul. Her research interests include discourse analysis, business communication and language teaching. She has worked as a senior writing consultant in the Communication Department of the University of Michigan Business School and has taught Turkish as a foreign language.

Leila Barbara is Professor of Linguistics at the Catholic University of São Paulo and attached to the Graduate Programme in Applied Linguistics. She is the editor of *DELTA*, the journal of the Brazilian Linguistic Association. Her main research interests are related to corpus linguistics, in particular the analysis of business genres with special reference to the lexicon.

Francesca Bargiela-Chiappini is Research Fellow in the Department of English and Media Studies, Nottingham Trent University. She has been engaged in work on inter- and cross-cultural business discourse for a number of years. Her publications include the monograph *Managing Language: the Discourse of Corporate Meetings* (with Sandra Harris) and the edited collection *The Languages of Business: An International Perspective* (also with S. Harris).

Carol David is an Associate Professor in rhetoric and professional communication at Iowa State University, Ames, IA, where she teaches undergraduate and graduate courses in professional communication and composition. She has published articles on organisational communication and first-year composition in a variety of professional journals.

Florence Davies is Senior Research Fellow in the Department of English Language at the University of Glasgow. She was Director of the Applied English Language Studies Unit at the University of Liverpool from 1986 to 1992 and has held posts in English and Education departments at the Universities of Birmingham, Nottingham, Sheffield and Bristol and Homerton College, Cambridge, and has worked extensively abroad. In Brazil she was co-founder of the DIRECT (Developing International Research in English for Commerce and Technology) project and at Bristol, Director of the Effective Writing for Management project. Her publications in the fields of applied linguistics and education include books and articles on the teaching of reading, reading in the sciences, text analysis and the language of the workplace.

Gail Forey is Assistant Professor in the Department of English at the Hong Kong Polytechnic University. She has taught in England, Hungary, Australia, Japan and Hong Kong. She is presently studying for a PhD in Applied Linguistics in the area of Business English, at the University of Glasgow.

Pamela M Homer is Professor in the Marketing Department at California State University, Long Beach. Dr Homer's primary research interests include advertising effects, the role of emotion in advertising, information processing, values, and structural equation models. Her research is published in numerous academic journals across multiple disciplines, most notably, the *Journal of Marketing Research*, the *Journal of Consumer Research* and the *Journal of Personality and Social Psychology*.

David Hyatt is the Course Director for the MEd (ELT) by Distance Learning at the University of Sheffield. He has worked as a teacher, teacher trainer, researcher and lecturer in the UK, Spain and Hungary. His research interests include language and power, language and the media, ESP English for Politics, textual and discourse analysis and academic literacy.

Scott Koslow is Senior Lecturer in the Department of Marketing and International Management, at the Waikato Management School (Te Raupapa) of the University of Waikato (Te Whare Waananga o Wiakato) in Hamilton, New Zealand. Dr Koslow studies cross-cultural issues in advertising, consumer behaviour and marketing research. His work has appeared in a number of journals, including the *Journal of Consumer Research* and the *Journal of Advertising*. He has also received the *Journal of Advertising*'s 'Best Article Award'. He has a PhD in Marketing from the University of Southern California, and an MBA and BA from the University of Michigan.

Eugène Loos holds a first degree in French Language and Literature and Public Relations and a PhD in International Business Communication from Utrecht University (the Netherlands). He is currently a lecturer in the Centre for Policy and Management Studies (Centrum voor Beleid en Management) at the same university, where he also conducts research in international business communication. He has written several articles on intercultural communication.

Leena Louhiala-Salminen, LicPhil, MSc (Econ) is a lecturer of English Business Communication in the Department of Languages and Communication at the Helsinki School of Economics and Business Administration in Finland. She has also worked as a consultant and trainer in several Finnish companies and has edited a Finnish–English/English-Finnish banking and finance dictionary. Her academic publications include contributions to Finnish and international books and journals, such as *English for Specific Purposes* and the *Journal of Business Communication*.

Joan Mulholland is Associate Professor of Communication Studies in the English Department, University of Queensland. She has published monographs and articles on business language, on rhetorical tactics and genres.

Catherine Nickerson worked for five years as a language trainer for the Dutch business community before joining the Business Communication department at the university of Nijmegen in 1993. Her publications have appeared in ESPJ and Language Sciences, and her research interests include the use of written genres in multinational corporate contexts and the interface between local languages and International Business English. She is co-editor, with Martin Hewings, of *Business English: Research into Practice*, also published by Longman (1999).

Karl-Heinz Pogner holds a PhD from Odense University (Denmark) which will be published under the title *Schreiben im Beruf als Handeln im Fach* (1999). He has lectured at Odense University and at the Southern Denmark Business School in Sonderborg (Denmark). In 1998 he joined the Department of Intercultural Communication and Management, Copenhagen Business School, as Associate Professor. His main research and teaching interests are in the areas of text production, foreign language interaction and corporate and intercultural communication.

Mike Scott taught EFL, ESP and Applied Linguistics in Latin America for many years. He now lectures in the Department of English of the University of Liverpool. He has published in ESP and corpus linguistics and is the author of the lexical analysis software Word-Smith Tools (1996). His current research centres on the analysis of key words.

David Sless is Research Director and co-founder of the Communication Research Institute of Australia. He is also Professor in Science Communication at the Australian National University. Among his recent publications are numerous articles and books on visual communication, visual literacy, information design, semiotics, communication theory, technology in the workplace and communications policy.

Ellen Touchstone is president of Touchstone Language Management, a Los Angeles-based consulting firm which advises organisations on their language services delivery systems. She is also a Visiting Assistant Professor of Business Administration at Whittier College in Los Angeles. She received her Master of International Management degree from the American Graduate School of International Management – Thunderbird – and her PhD in Applied Linguistics from the University of Southern California.

Sonja Vandermeeren gained a PhD in German linguistics in 1992. For the past six years she has been working at the University of Duisburg (Germany) from which she received the *habilitation* in German linguistics. She has recently published her third book, entitled *Fremdsprachen in europäischen Unternehmen* (Foreign Languages in European Companies).

Miriam van Nus is a Lecturer in Business Communication Studies at the University of Nijmegen in the Netherlands. She is currently researching the effectiveness of persuasive tactics in sales offers. Her main research interests include intercultural communication in business and academic settings, in particular concerning job application letters and research papers.

ONE

Business writing as social action

Francesca Bargiela-Chiappini and Catherine Nickerson

1. ON THE TITLE OF THIS VOLUME

Giving a book its final title is equivalent to calling it into being, bestowing on it a unique identity that distinguishes it from other books and giving the potential readers an indication of what they may expect to find in it. This creative act takes on further significance when it attempts to capture the collective effort of a group of authors who have agreed to share in the adventure of writing 'under one title'.

A discussion of what distinguishes and unites three well-established descriptive labels that resonate in the title of this volume seems an appropriate starting point. These are 'professional discourse' (Gunnarsson *et al.* 1997), 'institutional discourse' (Agar 1985; Drew and Sorjonen 1997) and 'business discourse' (Bargiela-Chiappini and Harris 1997). In their introduction to *The Construction of Professional Discourse*, Gunnarsson and colleagues refer to the legal, medical, social welfare, educational and scientific fields as distinctive 'professional areas' or 'domains', each characterised by 'a unique set of cognitive needs, social conditions and relationships with society at large' (1997: 5). Although the role of their language and discourse will vary, too, they argue that beyond the specificity of individual professional discourses there are common underlying processes which the various chapters set out to explore. Institutional discourse as intended by Agar (1985) – i.e. an interaction between an expert and a lay person – is described as 'a major type of professional discourse' by Gunnarsson *et al.*, thus implying that 'professional discourse' is a hyper-category that encompasses several others, or, rather, it is a collective category where discourse is intended in the singular and towards which other institutional genres converge by virtue of sharing in some of its characteristics. If this reading is correct, then 'business discourse' (Bargiela-Chiappini and Harris 1997) can also be seen to be sharing in many of the general characteristics of professional discourse, not only through *intertextuality*, but also through *interdiscursivity*; that is, through constitutive linguistic features which can be found in various business discourse genres.[1]

The status of the interactants could be seen as a decisive element in the distinction between professional and business discourse: as already mentioned above, in the former (but not in the latter) a lay person is often involved and the professional discourse is therefore of an institutional nature. In contrast, 'business discourse' is dominated by talk and writing between individuals whose main work activities and interests are in the domain of business and who come together for the purpose of doing business. In addition, an active corporate dimension is implied in the identities of these interactants, which may supersede or, at most, co-exist with the interests of any professional group to which they may also happen to belong (Barabas 1990). The majority of the studies included in the present volume report on aspects of writing by and for business individuals and groups, and they therefore constitute 'business' rather than 'professional' discourse. The remaining chapters blur the distinction between the two, however, as exemplified in the contributions by Bargiela-Chiappini and Pogner, who both explore the consequences of hybrid membership of business and professional groups, and in the chapters by Touchstone *et al.* and Loos, where the interaction is between business and non-business interactants. In the latter studies, although the discourse is more similar to professional (i.e. institutional) discourse it may also be viewed as being distinct from it, since the primary social roles involved are those of buyer and seller rather than those of expert and lay person.[2] Business writing, therefore, always involves or facilitates doing business. In addition, it encompasses not only intra-group communication within a business organisation (or a unit within a business organisation), but also inter-group interaction, both with other organisations and private individuals, where the purpose of the texts produced as a result is to buy or sell goods or services, or to facilitate the buying and selling of goods and services.

In this volume, writing *at* work and *for* work is equivalent to writing *as* work; that is writing is seen as an activity that shapes organisational and social structures (see section 4 below). We will argue that social constructionism provides an ideal background for the study of writing as a social activity, on which we will project Miller's construct of written and spoken genres as 'typified social action' (Miller 1984) (see sections 2 and 3 below). Furthermore, in a constructionist perspective, the analytically useful dimensions of context (local, organisational, regional, national and so on) adopted in many situated approaches to language analysis are subsumed within the all-encompassing process of 'contextualising', resulting from the interactional activities of social actors, which include the production of written and spoken texts. Contextualising, which employs the social conventions and cultural assumptions brought to bear on the texts by the actors themselves, is also signalled in the unfolding discourse through intertextuality and interdiscursivity (see section 3 below). Many chapters in this book, despite using different methodological approaches, have identified the phenomenon of interconnectedness of texts in the social context, its realisation in real-time and its vital contribution to the dynamics of the interaction.

The concern of the authors in this volume is not only with *what* actors write and *how* they write it, but also, and perhaps more importantly, with *why* they write the way they do, and what the effects of their writing on inter-firm and inter-group relations are (see Bhatia 1993). Although not all authors take an openly constructionist view of social activities (e.g. David, Touchstone *et al.*, Vandermeeren) and therefore of writing, it is clear that the findings of their research reveal the inherently social nature of writing, its relatedness to other social activities and its power to shape the way human life unfolds through purposeful, personal acts of intervention (see section 5).

2. SOCIAL CONSTRUCTIONISM

Embracing a social constructionist approach to the understanding of writing in and for business implies adherence to the tenets of a theoretical orientation that has been instrumental in the development of some of the critical and radical alternative disciplines that have emerged in the humanities and the social sciences during the last two decades (Burr 1995). Although no single feature characterises social constructionism, there are some underlying assumptions which represent its epistemology:

1. a rejection of the taken-for-granted stance of positivism and empiricism;
2. the cultural and historical relativity of all forms of knowledge;
3. the processual and interactional nature of knowledge;
4. the interdependence of knowledge and patterns of social action.

These tenets underpin an understanding of society and human nature that refutes any definable and discoverable feature in the world and therefore also excludes the existence of objective facts. Moreover, all knowledge is seen as culture- and time-bound. For social constructionism, language is the vehicle for thought in that concepts and categories are passed from one group of people to another through its medium. Language is social action and a means through which the 'construction of the world' is effected. Cognitive or sociological explanations of social phenomena are not acceptable: explanations are to be found in social practices and interpersonal interactions. In other words, reality for the social constructionist is a matter of social definition: 'entities we normally call reality, knowledge, thought, facts, texts, selves, and so on are constructs generated by communities of like-minded peers' (Bruffee 1986: 774; see also Grabe and Kaplan 1996).

The focus on language as social action and the central role attributed to it in the construction of reality is undoubtedly an attractive starting point for any research that seeks to bridge the gap between the researcher and the researched, and between the actions of the researched and social structures. According to constructionism, people 'construct' organisations through daily interaction, and it is therefore there that researchers must place themselves as observers and interpreters of those historically and culturally important happenings as they unfold.

In this volume, the first six chapters and the epilogue acknowledge, to a greater or lesser degree, a debt to moderate constructionism based on the following assumptions:

1. that writing is a social activity that creates and maintains organisations;
2. that the analysis of social practices in general, and language in particular, is a means towards gaining an understanding of the world; and
3. that culture affects the construction of the world through language.

It is against this broad social constructionist perspective that the concepts of genre and structure(s) are discussed in sections 3 and 4, respectively.

For researchers concerned with communication in professional or organisational communities, and with written communication in particular, social constructionism has proved a useful framework in accounting for how a social group comes to recognise certain actions as germane (e.g. Rubin 1988; Barabas 1990; Orlikowski and Yates 1994).

Among research applying social constructionism to the study of written communication in institutional settings, the edited volume by Rafoth and Rubin (1988) is of particular relevance to our discussion, because it represents an attempt to bridge the gap between the social and the cognitive forms of constructionism. The introductory chapter presents four dimensions, each describing a type of social constructive process, which are illustrated through the relationship between social context and written discourse; thus, 'social contexts and written discourse stand in a reciprocal, mutually constructive relationship, one to the other', and 'the participants . . . negotiate the definition of their relationship; discourse has constructed social context' (Rubin 1988: 1). Rubin's description of the four constructive processes involved covers many of the concerns of the research in the present volume:

1. writers construct mental representations of the social contexts in which their writing is embedded;
2. writing as a social process or system can create or constitute social contexts;
3. writers – in some senses *all* writers – create texts collectively with other participants in discourse communities;
4. writers assign consensual values to writing and thus construct a dimension of social meaning. (Rubin 1988: 2)

First of all, writers construct a mental background for their writing including features such as audience, purpose and topics for discussion. The analysis of ceremonial speeches by Carol David (this volume) maps this process in the rhetorical choices of two female CEOs. Although the mechanism writers use to do this is a cognitive one, the actual composition of the mental representation is a consensual one which is determined through a process of social negotiation.

The second assumption relates to the reciprocal relationship between the social action constituted by written communication and the context in which it takes place.[3] It is this dimension of social construction that is involved in the process of structuration (see section 4 below), as Rubin demonstrates by using the US Constitution as an example of the production and reproduction of social structures through the creation of, and reference to, a written document (see also Pogner, this volume).

The third assumption explicates the collaborative nature of writing production, and the fourth the consensual nature of its interpretation. Therefore, texts such as a corporate report or a business letter are collectively constructed, either directly through multiple authorship, as in the construction of a legal brief, which Rubin describes – where several lawyers may be involved in drafting one document – or indirectly, through a process of intertextuality. In turn, intertextuality may occur through several different mechanisms such as direct reference to other texts, as is frequently the case in business correspondence, or in the incorporation of what Rubin refers to as linguistic shells or 'boilerplates' (i.e. sections of text which are copied over from previous texts as is common practice in legal discourse), or similarly, in direct reference to other pertinent texts, such as the reference to tax regulations identified by Devitt (1991) in correspondence written by tax accountants. (Intertextuality is discussed in detail in section 3 on Genre below.)

Rubin's third assumption implies the concept of discourse community, as the social group for whom a text has social relevance, and which 'may be roughly understood as a consensus about . . . what is worth communicating, how it may be communicated, what other members of the community are likely to know and believe to be true about certain subjects, how other members can be persuaded, and so on' (Faigley 1985: 238, quoted in Rubin 1988: 13). Further insights into the workings of discourse communities as social groups formed around shared use of genres emerge from Orlikowski and Yates's (1994) social constructionist research on organisational settings, where 'the notion of community . . . broadly includes identifiable social units such as groups, organizations, and occupations (as in Van Maanen and Barley 1984) or communities of practice (Brown and Duguid 1991; Lave and Wenger 1991)' (Orlikowski and Yates 1994: 542). In this approach to the investigation of organisational communication, each social community is seen as having its own set of shared communicative practices, or genres, which the community recognises and uses, and through which it is constituted. A genre such as a memo or business letter may therefore be recognised and used by 'most advanced industrial nations', whereas a genre such as an audit report may be 'specific to transorganizational groups such as occupations and industries' (Yates and Orlikowski 1992: 304). This is discussed in more detail in section 3 below.

Consensus is the principle governing the attribution of values to writing from which social meaning is constructed, in Rubin's fourth assumption (Rubin 1988). This includes the value which is socially assigned to the written medium in general, as opposed to the spoken medium, by a social group. For example, Rubin refers to the veto on note-taking by jurors in the US legal system; Yli-Jokipii (1994) identifies a British preference for written communication in initiating a business contact with a foreign customer, and Rogers and Swales (1990) describe a US corporation where the use of writing is actively discouraged as a medium of internal communication. In each case, the value assigned to the written medium is socially constructed by the group involved, and as several of the contributors in the present volume suggest, this may also extend to the selection of an appropriate medium within the general category of written communication; e.g. Nickerson (this volume) on e-mail communication and Akar and Louhiala-Salminen (this volume) on fax communication.

In business settings, discourse communities are likely to be characterised by 'hybrid membership'; that is, communities composed of individuals with dual, or even multiple, membership. Management consultants are a good example of a hybrid discourse community where the combination of academic and private practice requires mobility across discourses. Tensions within the dual membership of the scientific community and the corporate community and the effect which this has on organisational discourse has been investigated in terms of the relationship between the writer's intention, the reader's expectations and the text itself, and the effect which corporate culture may have on all three (Barabas 1990). Barabas's work explores the social construction of language and the context-dependency of meaning, and exemplifies this with reference to the social constructs inherent in, and constitutive of, both national and organisational cultures and their effect on business discourse.[4] What emerges from her research is that the sense of community and culture in organisations is established and maintained by written and spoken communication, as demonstrated in the texts produced by technical writers who acknowledge that their writing is shaped both by audience expectations and by general company expectations. The contributions by David, Pogner and Davies *et al.* (this volume) confirm these findings and further investigate the consequences of membership in more than one discourse community.

3. GENRE

The 'relatively stable'[5] forms of communication which develop in the course of the production and reproduction of communicative practices within a community, and which are recognised by the members of that community, may be referred to as genres. The term genre has been used in a number of different fields, including linguistics, literary studies and rhetoric, as the overviews by Swales (1990) and Grabe and Kaplan (1996) indicate. It is, as Swales suggests, a word which is 'highly attractive – even to the Parisian timbre of its normal pronunciation – but extremely slippery' (1990: 33). In this introduction to the construct of genre, we begin our discussion from an understanding of genre as 'typified social action', as expounded in Carolyn Miller's (1984) seminal work 'Genre as social action', which has been the subject of much discussion and application in research on scientific, professional and organisational discourse (e.g. Swales 1990; Devitt 1991; Yates and Orlikowski 1992; Bhatia 1993; Berkenkotter and Huckin 1995; Bazerman 1988, 1994, 1995).[6] Our understanding of genre within a social constructionist perspective will also draw on intertextuality as understood by Bakhtin (1986) and, more recently, Fairclough (1992a, 1992b). In particular, intertextuality is seen to account for the relationship between genres in the formation of genre repertoires, or sets of genres (Bakhtin 1986; Orlikowski and Yates 1994) and also for the relationship which exists between sets of genres in the structuring of a genre system, as proposed by Devitt (1993) and elaborated by Bazerman (1995).

Miller (1984: 151) warns that 'a rhetorically sound definition of genre must be centred not on the substance or the form of discourse but on the action it is used to accomplish'. Furthermore, her account envisages genre as a system which classifies discourse not on the basis of similar rhetorical action, but on the basis of 'typified rhetorical action'; that is, action related to a typified recurrent

situation which also includes typifications of participants (*ibid.*).
'Typification'[7] is based on the premise that a social community has
a 'stock of knowledge' which is determined by the recognition
of types. In turn, the recognition of a type and its reproduction
are socially constructed processes through which a community can
carry out its business. A community's stock of knowledge remains
relatively stable, but it may change if the community identifies a
situation as a new situation for which it requires a new rhetorical
response. This response will evolve from existing types through a
process of intertextuality (Bakhtin 1986; Fairclough 1992b) so that
'if a new typification proves continually useful for mastering states
of affairs, it enters that stock of knowledge and its application
becomes routine' (Miller 1984: 157).

The concept of 'typification' – and its implicit contention that
(successful) communication is facilitated through the shared (socially created) recognition of type, including type of situation, type of
participants and type of rhetoric – indicates that the types of communication used by the members of any social community have
the potential to constitute a genre.[8] This suggests that genre, as a
discourse classification system based on typified forms of communication invoked in situations recurring in a particular social context, can be usefully applied to investigating the communicative
practices of any social group, including professional groups and
business organisations (see Yates and Orlikowski 1992 for further
discussion on this point). Understanding the use of language by a
community in the form of a genre will ultimately lead to a greater
understanding of the way in which that community operates as a
social group (see Mulholland, Nickerson and Sless, this volume).

The social constructionist perspective within Miller's conceptualisation of genre lies in her definition of genre as social action in
response to recurrent rhetorical situations which are recognised as
of one type within a community. These recurrent, rhetorical situations present an exigence, or social motive, for that social action
to be invoked.[9] According to Miller, the recognition of a rhetorical
situation and the exigence which it presents are both social constructs, as is the genre invoked as a result.[10] Therefore, if a genre is
defined through reference to a specific recurrent rhetorical situation
– although genre is an open class of discourse; i.e. an indeterminate
number of text types may constitute a genre – an individual genre
may not be in a hierarchical relationship with another genre. In other
words, whereas genres may have similar discourse characteristics,

a sub-genre within a genre cannot exist since, by definition, each genre is associated with a different rhetorical situation. This does not, however, preclude the role played by existing typifications in the evolution of a new genre (e.g. Miller 1984: 163), nor does it rule out the possibility of referring to one genre while using another. In both cases, the evolution of a new genre and/or reference to an existing genre takes place through intertextuality and interdiscursivity (see Sless, this volume, for a discussion of a possible engineered hyper-genre; and Mulholland, this volume, for her definition of e-mail as an 'ancillary genre').

According to Bakhtin, intertextuality exists since a speaker 'presupposes not only the existence of the language system he is using, but also the existence of previous utterances – his own and others' – with which his given utterance enters into one kind of relation or another (builds on them, polemicizes with them, or simply presumes that they are already known to the listener). Any utterance is a link in a very complexly organized chain of other utterances' (1986: 69). In addition, a distinction may also be made between primary and secondary genres, where primary or simple genres such as conversation take place in real time, and secondary or complex genres such as a scientific research article do not. Between primary and secondary genres an additional form of intertextuality operates, in the evolution of secondary genres by a social community through a process that Bakhtin describes as absorption and digestion of the community's existing primary genres.[11] (A similar process is described in Sless, this volume.)

More recently, Fairclough has drawn on Bakhtin (1986) and, in particular, Kristeva (1986) for his analysis of the recursive role played by discourse in changes affecting society as a whole. In his critical discourse analytic approach, Fairclough (1) situates genres within a range of available discourse practices, and (2) he elaborates the concept of intertextuality and its role in the analysis of discourse. Like Miller, Fairclough reiterates the concept of genre as a conventional category of discourse, which is meaningful as social action within a given social context and which may co-exist with other conventionalised discourse practices which do not, or do not yet, constitute genres. He proposes the concept of 'orders of discourse', which are 'the particular configurations of conventionalized practices . . . available to text producers and interpreters in particular social circumstances' (1992a: 194). Genre, in this account, is one possible conventionalised practice which Fairclough uses to refer to a 'socially ratified type of linguistic activity with specified positions for subjects (e.g. interview, television news)'. Other conventionalised practices include 'discourse', which is used to refer to 'domain of knowledge or experience from a particular perspective (e.g. Marxist political discourse, feminist discourse)' and 'narrative', which is a 'socially ratified story type' (1992a: 215).

Fairclough's stance is that a distinction should be made between text analysis, where the concern is with vocabulary, grammar, cohesion and text structure, and the analysis of discursive practice, which involves the speech acts occurring in the texts, the coherence of texts and, finally, their intertextuality. Intertextuality becomes an analytic construct applied to the investigation of the relationship between genres as important forms of social action, and the social structures within which they are in use. Furthermore, intertextuality can be 'manifest', where specific reference is made to other texts within a text, or 'constitutive' (i.e. 'interdiscursivity'), which refers to the constitution of texts from the conventionalised practices within the available orders of discourse (Fairclough 1992b). It seems plausible that both of these types of intertextuality are involved in the formation of genres, and in the evolution of complex genres from simple genres, described by Bakhtin, and equally, in the evolution of new genres out of existing typifications within a community, as proposed by Miller. (See also Akar and Louhiala-Salminen, Van Nus, Mulholland and Loos, this volume, for related discussions on intertextuality.)

A further example of intertextuality between genres relevant to business writing is provided by Devitt (1991) in her research on the communicative practices of the tax accounting community. She proposes a three-dimensional concept of intertextuality – referential, functional and generic – which collectively account for the interaction between texts which the community needs in order to carry out its work.[12] Referential intertextuality refers simply to the use of or reference to other texts; e.g. a reference to a client's tax return in a letter to the taxing authorities, or an IRS regulation included in an opinion letter to a client. Functional intertextuality describes how a network of texts is formed within the community, such that past texts create the need for future texts and also influence their form and content; e.g. a request for information from a client creates the need for an opinion or response letter, which may in turn be influenced by previous correspondence held in the client's file (see also Gunnarsson 1997 for a description of a network of communicative events including spoken and written texts). Generic intertextuality refers to the types of texts available to the profession, their evolution into genres from recurrent rhetorical situations, and the subsequent formation of these genres into a set of established genres which are recognised as germane by the profession concerned. Therefore, 'in examining the genre set of a community, we are examining the community's situations, its recurring activities and relationships. The genre set accomplishes its work' (Devitt 1991: 340). Incidentally, it is possible to perceive the influence of Giddens's 'duality of structure' (see section 4 below) behind Devitt's conceptualisation of the relationship between the profession's genre set and the recurrent situations with which it is associated. She writes: 'this genre set not only reflects the professions' situations; it may also help to define and stabilize those situations' (1991: 340).

The concluding part of this discussion on the rhetorical, socially constructed nature of genres addresses the notion that different types of intertextuality and interdiscursivity may operate not only between genres *within* a community, but also between genres *across* communities. The multi-functional nature of intertextuality and interdiscursivity explains relations between individual genres, which form sets of genres, and between sets of genres, in the formation of genre systems. Following Bakhtin's (1986: 60) observation that 'each sphere of activity contains an entire repertoire of speech genres that differentiate and grow as a particular sphere develops and becomes more complex', Orlikowski and Yates use the term 'repertoire' to refer to a community's set of genres, or indeed the set of organising structures, which therefore constitute a vital part of that community's established communicative practices. Indeed, their observation of organisational life reveals that 'members of a community rarely depend on a single genre for their communication. Rather, they tend to use multiple, different, and interacting genres over time' (1994: 542).

A further elaboration of the concept of 'systems of genre', which combines Devitt's account with Giddens's structuration theory, emerges from the study of the historical development of the patent system by Bazerman (1995). Bazerman's contention is that, like Devitt's tax accountants, it is possible to identify a genre set for every occupational group, 'from hod-carrier to philosopher', consisting of the limited number of genres through which that group needs to structure their social relations, and, therefore, to carry out their work. As in Devitt's account, part of the maintenance of the structures of the genre system in which these genre sets operate – i.e. the contribution made by the genre sets to the patterns of social relations – involves intertextual interaction within the genre set. However, as Bazerman points out, each individual occupational genre set only accounts for the work of one occupational group. The extended notion of 'genre system' is needed to account for the intertextual interaction which occurs *between* genre sets when more than one occupational group is involved.

Bazerman's concept of 'systems of genres' is particularly useful in the investigation of business discourse in that it envisages the very real situation of interaction between different social groups contributing their own sets of genres; e.g. Head Office–subsidiary, supplier–customer and so on (see Loos and Vandermeeren, this volume). Communication will be possible as long as some of those genres are mutually recognisable to both sets of participants, in which case they will become shared in the process as organising structures. Intertextuality and interdiscursivity across genre sets would explain how different parts of a large organisation are able to communicate with each other, and foster the patterns of social relations necessary within the corporate social system as a whole, while at the same time maintaining their individual group identity, as represented, or structured, by their own genre set.

4. STRUCTURE(S)

Sections 2 and 3 above have suggested that while social constructionism provides the main theoretical assumptions for an understanding of business writing as social action, genre, intertextuality and interdiscursivity are appropriate constructs in referring to the conventionalised practices and their dynamics which realise that social action within the social environment. Business organisations, which are constructed and maintained through conventionalised social practices such as genres, are examples of structures that constitute a social system.

Giddens's structuration theory posits that the structures of social institutions both shape and are shaped by the social practices carried out by those working within them, and that our view of the world and our presentation of knowledge are not absolutes but social constructs. In Giddens's words, 'structure is both the medium and the outcome of the human activities it recursively organizes' (Giddens 1987: 61) and 'all social life has a recursive quality to it, derived from the fact that actors reproduce the conditions of their social existence by means of the very activities that – in contexts of time-space – constitute that existence' (1987: 221). If 'structure' consists of 'rules and resources, recursively implicated in the reproduction of social systems', then 'structures' are definable as 'rule-resource sets, implicated in the institutional articulation of social systems' (Giddens 1984: 377). The social system refers to the patterns of social relations which may be identified within a given group (e.g. a multi-national corporation), and the structures facilitate the generation and maintenance of those relations, i.e. the system (Poole and DeSanctis 1990). The recursive nature of the relationship between social structures and the social practices which both produce and reproduce them is accounted for by what Giddens refers to as 'the duality of structure' (1979), or, in other words, 'the rules and resources drawn upon in the production and reproduction of social action are at the same time the means of system reproduction' (Giddens 1984: 19).

This concept of the 'duality of structure', and the link which it allows between social groupings and social action, have been a powerful influence on the work of a number of researchers in organisational communication and discourse analysis since the beginning of the 1990s. The principle that language constitutes social action, which in turn both constitutes social structures and is constituted by them, has been embraced by the critical discourse analysis tradition (e.g. Fairclough 1989, 1992a, 1992b, 1992c). In his earlier volume, Fairclough writes that 'as well as being determined by social structures, discourse has effects upon social structures and contributes to the achievement of social continuity or social change' (1989: 37), while more recently he refers to language use as social practice, and comments that 'it is socially shaped, but is also socially shaping – or socially *constitutive*' (1992c: 55). His suggestion that textual analysis should be included in social science research is based on a structurationist understanding of society and texts. Social structures, Fairclough argues, are constituted by social action, and since texts are one important form of social action they should therefore be studied by researchers (1992c) – we would add, in collaboration with practitioners and users (see Sless, this volume).

The small, but growing, body of research in organisational communication employing ethnomethodology and conversation analysis

(CA), convincingly demonstrates that within organisations, structuration or 'structure-in-action' (Boden 1994: 58) is achieved through talk; i.e. the social structure generates talk and is itself produced by talk. Combining ethnomethodology and CA with Garfinkel's notion of human agency in an empirical study of different organisations, Boden's work demonstrates the power of a language-based approach to the understanding of the nature of organisations and of work. Still on the micro-level of intra-group action through talk, and concerned with its dependency on the social context, discourse analysts have also looked at the organisation of an archetypal form of business interaction, negotiation, the way its discourse is organised, and the nature of the relationship between actors. There are, it is suggested, 'particular ways in which the extralinguistic business context shapes negotiation discourse, and thus creates a mutual interdependency' (Charles 1996: 20). Charles observes this both in New Relationship Negotiations (NRNs), and in Old Relationship Negotiations (ORNs), where the common aim is to create or maintain patterns of social relations (the business relationship), which is in turn achieved through social interaction – i.e. the organisation of the discourse of the negotiation (Charles 1996).

Alongside the works discussed above, where structuration is seen to be achieved through the social practices of language use, interest among social scientists has grown in the effects of a specific form of social action; i.e. the interaction with computer-based technologies, producing and re-producing social structure and thus sustaining a social system (see Nickerson and Mulholland, this volume). Such research analyses the effects of the introduction, or increased use, of a technological medium as social action, and assesses the recursive impact of this action on the system. Although technologies may be adopted to achieve a specific aim, such as an electronic mail system to improve efficiency, the new medium may have other unforeseen effects on the organisation, such as the acquisition of more prominence by individuals proficient in the use of the system, or an overall increase in internal communication (Contractor and Eisenberg 1990). Giddens's definition of a social system in terms of the patterns of relations, maintained or generated through structures in a social group, has also been applied to the prediction of the possible effects of computer-based technologies on decision-making processes within an organisation. Therefore, certain computer support systems have been predicted as facilitating the resolution of conflict within a group, while other media may be less effective than conventional methods;

similarly, the response of a group leader to a computer support system has been shown to affect directly the response of the group as a whole (Poole and DeSanctis 1990) (see Mulholland, this volume, on the effects of e-mail on interpersonal relations).

A structurational approach to organisational communication which considers *both* language use and the use of media as social action, characterises Yates and Orlikowski's work (1992). They propose the concept of genres of organisational communication[13] as communicative practices through which the process of structuration is achieved. According to Yates and Orlikowski, members of the organisation draw upon certain sets of rules – i.e. structures – through which they produce and reproduce social action – i.e. genres – and in doing so, they reproduce the social system which constitutes the organisation; that is, they achieve structuration. Language use and medium are identified by Yates and Orlikowski as two of the formal properties which conventionally characterise a genre of organisational communication, and which therefore allow it to be recognised as legitimate social action by the members of an organisation (for a more detailed discussion of this model, see Nickerson, this volume).

5.   LANGUAGE AND METHODS

Since the early eighties, there has been a growing body of research on writing in institutional and organisational settings that has acknowledged the existence of several theoretical perspectives on the phenomenon of writing. These can be grouped under three broad headings: textual, cognitive and social. The seminal collection *Writing in Non-Academic Settings* by Odell and Goswami (1985), for example, embraces a social perspective on writing, regardless of the methodology used by individual authors (text analysis, survey or interviews). From this perspective, Faigley (1985) re-examines the significance of concepts such as 'discourse community' and 'context', and proposes a model of researcher inspired by the ethnographic tradition – i.e. the interpretative anthropologist, equipped with a corrective self-reflexive attitude.

The follow-up to Odell and Goswami's work, Spilka's (1993) collection entitled *Writing in the Workplace*, shows the remarkable advances made in the increasingly interdisciplinary field of professional writing. The original social perspective on writing appears enriched and diversified in the novel applications, and critical examination, of the range of qualitative methods exemplified in the collection. The contribution of 'discourse community', 'genre', 'context' and 'intertextuality' are finally established as pivotal in the theoretical debate on the social nature of writing. More recently, reviews of the two complementary disciplines of 'institutional dialogue' (Drew and Sorjonen 1997) and 'critical organisational discourse analysis' (Mumby and Clair 1997) significantly point not only to a growing interest in the language of organisations but also to the wealth of perspectives and methods available to researchers from the humanities and social sciences who are interested in an interdisciplinary agenda on business discourse, including reference to written and spoken modes. Some important aspects of the socially orientated research on business writing are represented in the chapters in this volume: the inherently social nature of writing that incorporates the contributions from cognitive and linguistic research; the awareness of the need to look at individual texts as components of intertextual and interdiscursive networks that cut across communication modes (writing, speaking, graphics, sound and so on); the usefulness of the concept of genre, and sets and systems of genres, emanating from and embedded in the wider socio-historic context; the depth of insight that a multi-method approach can contribute to the study of writing, without losing sight of a future where methodological integration will strengthen the discipline and contribute to a robust theoretical interdisciplinarity.

This volume is concerned with the language of written business not only in terms of electronic and more traditional text types (Parts I and III) , but also in relation to the role that language fulfils in the construction of the professional identities of members of a discourse community from which they partly derive their personal rhetorical styles (Part II). On a societal scale, some of the studies in this volume address the question of the impact of corporate language choice and use, and micro language planning on intra-firm and firm–society relations (Part IV). Therefore, to varying degrees, all chapters contain a 'linguistic component', although the emphasis of the analysis may vary: language is examined as a product of the social activity or writing; or as a means to achieve certain aims, or as a process through which social actors construct their discursive personalities. In other words, language is analysed as derived from, leading to, or representing social action, where these three dimensions are not mutually exclusive and do, in fact, overlap. The social nature of language at work is exemplified in business writing practices, both as processes and as products. Writing in business contexts is often, generically speaking, *hybrid* in that many texts display signs of inter-textuality and interdiscursivity ; *collective*, in that texts are often the products of a multiple authorship process; *structure-dependent and structure-shaping*, in that writing always takes place within a cultural and historic context by which it is influenced and which, in turn, it influences.

6.   THE CHAPTERS

6.1.   Part I: Electronic media and writing in organisations

Catherine Nickerson's discussion of the use of media and electronic mail in a multinational company aptly sets the scene for this section, being based on Yates and Orlikowski's (1992) framework for organisational communication discussed in section 3 on Genre. Nickerson demonstrates how the three factors that determine the use and characteristics of organisational genres in monolingual settings (recurrent situations, communicative purpose and form) all come into play in the multilingual environment of the Dutch corporation which is the object of her study. Her analysis of a sample of 100 electronic messages chosen from a database of several hundreds demonstrates that the specific practices of the company are directly responsible not only for the choice of code (English rather than Dutch) but also for the layout and lexical parameters of the messages. Moreover, based on textual evidence, she concludes that the use of English, rather than Dutch, is determinant in structuring the organisation since there is 'widespread circulation of and reference to English electronic communication and, in particular, electronic messages containing official information relating to the organisational processes are always written in English' (p. 53). Findings from this strand of research show that the application of Giddens's structuration theory in the investigation of the interplay between writing and organisational structure well warrants the systematic and concerted efforts of linguists, as well as social scientists.

The influence of media on structures also comes under close scrutiny in Joan Mulholland's study of electronic mail use in an organisational setting with which all of our contributors and most of our readers will be familiar: the university. Referring to culture-specific features of use, attributable to the location of the organisation (Australia) as a background, Mulholland concentrates on the interplay between internal work procedures and conventions and computer technology, and its effects on electronic communication. The language and distribution processes of messages related to the preparation of committee agendas are examined, paying special attention to the manifestation of minimalism in language which, the author warns, may damage interpersonal relations. Noticeable examples are the disappearance of politeness markers, or the 'un-adorned' presentation of subject matter. In relation to the medium, efficiency of use of electronic communication is shown to be directly related to users' computer skills. The author suggests that attempts at optimising processes to suit the needs of specific groups might create interpersonal problems, while, at the same time, the heterogeneity of the intertextual environment to which the e-mail messages contribute is shown to be the cause of confusion and of potential misuse. On this point, Mulholland details the opportunity that e-mail presents for circulation of documents beyond the author-ised committee membership, thus compromising the authority of the chair and of the committee itself. Ethical considerations aside, the research shows that electronic mail is not a neutral medium, and that lack of proficiency in its use may impinge on interpersonal relations, too, with effects that may be felt throughout the organisation.

An original example of interventionist research that has been instrumental in the creation of a new genre of automatically–produced letters is reported in the last chapter of Part I. David Sless is Research Director of the Australian Institute of Communication where the approach to document production on behalf of many corporate and public sector clients has embraced an openly constructionist agenda. The creation of the new genre that Sless calls 'mass-produced, personalised letters' has been made possible by the interaction of researchers, clients and users responding to the needs of the latter category, and by the application of the latest computer and laser printing technology. The characteristics of the 'new letter' concern (1) the modality of its production, in that it is not written by a single author; (2) its performance, i.e. improved usability and accessibility; and (3) its form and content, which are completely different from those of a conventional business letter. The detailed analysis of a sample of the new genre reveals how the pragmatics of text usage (as suggested by surveyed end users) are mapped closely onto the formal and functional features of the document. Thus, the adoption of three visually distinct zones, matched by purposeful typographical choices and the preference for a user-orientated temporal sequencing of events, subverts the categories of conventional business letter writing. Linguistically, the new genre has disposed of perhaps the most enduring and distinctive features of traditional letters, the opening and closing salutations, despite some strong resistance from both private and public institutions. As Sless observes, end users in Australia seem not to mind the changes; it would be interesting to assess the role that cultural preferences play on reactions to the new genre elsewhere.

6.2. Part II: Identities, discourse communities and rhetorical styles

The section opens with a study of professional identities and discourse communities and, indeed, the rhetorical choices and conventions that construct these two categories and are in turn interactively constructed by them. Karl-Heinz Pogner examines the process of production of a complex technical document written in German, a contract between a Danish private business and a German municipal authority, jointly constructed in several stages by members of two distinct discourse communities: an engineer for the business community, and a senior executive for the governmental agency. A decisive indicator of the social nature of writing is the effect, verbalised in successive revisions of the contract, that the changing context has on the writers' expectations, which in turn shape the nature of the planning task that is the object of the document. Pogner also demonstrates how text expectations, negotiated interactively, may not only be linked to the values and conventions of the discourse communities to which the social actors belong but also to their (national and corporate) cultural background.

The complexity of the socio-political and cultural environment which shapes the writing activity and is shaped by it prompts Pogner to put forward a research agenda based on the construction and self-perception of the interactional identities of professionals who operate across discourse and cultural communities. Its realisation is dependent on abandoning de-contextualised textual studies in favour of a situated, socio-cognitive approach to writing as an activity through which members of communities, whether professional or national, construct the 'social' interactively.

Power may indeed be 'naturally' attributed to business managers as one of the distinctive traits of a senior position, but the predicament of one class of individuals whose role in organisations could (potentially) be much more influential tells quite a different story of a profession beset by a persisting identity crisis. The competing discourses in the official magazines for personnel managers in Britain and Italy construct corporate identities torn apart by expectations of loyalty to contradictory values. The human resources managers (in Britain) and personnel managers (in Italy) struggle to reconcile the demands imposed upon them by the 'control–care' paradigm that governs the profession.

Francesca Bargiela-Chiappini argues that the socially constructed figure of the HR manager is the collaborative effort of the discourses of the triad 'reader, writer and practitioner', where the practitioner is often the writer and/or reader of a professional magazine. Therefore, paradoxically, discourse production and consumption converge into the *personae* of the HR managers or personnel officers, who, in turn, are constructed and de-constructed in the discourses of their professional magazines. A socio-constructionist understanding of genre is invoked, through which Bargiela-Chiappini defines 'professional magazines' as 'tokens of management', and subjects them to a structural and functional analysis that takes selected linguistic and layout choices into account. She concludes that an investigation of all the features that characterise professional magazines (including graphics, use of colour, photography and so on) is needed for a deeper understanding of how linguistic and non-linguistic elements are drawn upon in the semiotic construction of a written genre.

Carol David demonstrates that gender-related preferences distinguish the rhetorical strategies adopted by American female CEOs in the composition of their ceremonial speeches, a genre 'written to be spoken' and therefore possibly sharing the features of both spoken and written texts. The almost exclusively male domains of rhetoric and business public speaking have left senior businesswomen in a double bind: they are expected to display powerful persuasive rhetoric while fulfilling a feminine role through relational and collaborative verbal behaviour. David concentrates on two epideictic speeches (written to be delivered at ceremonial occasions) and analyses the rhetorical strategies, the choice of evidence, the metaphorical language and the tone employed by two female CEOs.

The rhetorical identities that emerge are predominantly feminine but they also employ traditional strategies attributed to (business) men, such as the promotion of traditional business values of hard work and company loyalty, and risk-taking. Alongside these strategies, distinct feminine rhetorical devices are identifiable, such as the use of personal experience and the metaphorical language of nurturing and stewardship, connectedness and psychological growth and development. In both cases, the text of the speeches shows that professionalism and legitimacy to speak are not attained through strong style and an authoritarian voice but through honesty and commitment. In other words, they persuade but do not coerce; they teach rather than argue.

6.3.   Part III: Business genres and their language

Miriam van Nus elaborates a model of corporate context based on Fairclough's dimensions of 'situation' and 'intertextuality', within which she uses a concept of genre defined as 'a sequence of communicative acts that realises moves'. Following Mauranen (1993) and Van Leeuwen (1993), her detailed functional and structural analysis of letters supplied by the Dutch subsidiary of an international ship's broker firm, confirms earlier findings for a very similar genre but with a different language and cultural background (see Bhatia 1993 on sales promotion letters by Singaporean companies and Western multi-nationals). Significantly, all the studies in this section identify similarities across languages in the case of three very different genres, regardless of the analytical approach employed.

The second study identifies genre-distinctive features in fax communication, through the structural and functional analysis of texts in English, accounting for corporate as well as cultural influences. Didar Akar and Leena Louhiala-Salminen start by asking the question whether documents sent and received by fax in two companies in Finland and Turkey actually constitute tokens of a distinctive genre. In addition to the main focus of the chapter on the structural features of fax messages (following Swales and Bhatia), the authors find Bakhtin's notion of intertextuality (particularly in its application by Fairclough) useful in exploring the linguistically hybrid nature of faxes, where features of the written and spoken modes seem to co-exist. Besides well-documented borrowings from spoken language conventions, the generic distinctiveness of the fax messages, the authors argue, is probably the consequence of the medium itself, which relies on efficiency and speed rather than formality. The chapter that follows exemplifies how manual and automated techniques may be combined in the analysis of an unfamiliar genre, invitations for bids (IFBs), which are shown to share structural and lexical features across two languages (English and Portuguese) and four countries (England, Brazil, Jamaica and India). Leila Barbara and Mike Scott find that Hoey's (1986) concept of 'colony text' usefully characterises the nature of invitations for bids as texts, in that all structural components can operate with a high degree of independence. Interestingly, one of the features of IFBs that the authors add to Hoey's list of parameters which define a colony text is intertextuality, an indicator that the genre, however distinctively identifiable cross-culturally, is part of a set of genres. A computer analysis of keywords (KWs) determines the 'aboutness' of the genre; i.e. its propositional meaning. KWs are found to match across the two languages (and four cultures), which indicates a commonality of function and also signals 'common membership of an international discourse community'. Moreover, keywords reflect both the structural properties of the genre and the actions described in it, leading the authors to conclude that IFBs are a metalinguistic genre.

6.4.   Part IV: The business of relating: effectiveness, adaptation and emotion in writing

In the fourth section, the research focus is shifted from the individual to the corporate dimension of writing as a group activity which affects relations between and beyond organisations. Corporate language choices are shown to shape relations within and between firms and between the business world and consumers.

Ellen Touchstone *et al.* explore the effects of Spanish use in billboard advertising in Long Beach, California where 70 per cent of the population is English-speaking and 20 per cent Spanish-speaking. An experiment was conducted on a sample of 220 participants to measure advertisement-induced emotions and attitudes (brand attitudes, alienation, anger, racism, target of the advertisement and threat) and stereotyping (linguistic assimilation and social assimilation). The results show that the choice of Spanish on billboards does affect non-Hispanic viewers. In particular, bilingual (English and Spanish) and monolingual (Spanish) billboards are likely to increase the feeling of alienation of non-Hispanics from their community. Racism-related attitudes are also significantly affected by monolingual advertisements (but not by bilingual advertisements) but such negative emotions appear not to be transferred to the brand. These findings justify the need for more sensitivity in micro-language planning by business organisations which have great influence in a consumer society and therefore also an obligation to assess critically the effect of their language choices on large sections of the population, especially when advertising language is potentially damaging to intercultural relations.

Back in Europe, interest in the role that language choice plays in inter-firm relations received an expected boost from '1992 fever', when the urgency of foreign language awareness affected by the Single Market move reached its peak. One of the many European-based projects that saw the light on the wake of economic union was based at the University of Duisburg in Germany and spanned four years and five countries. Sonja Vandermeeren reports on the findings of this project related to language choice, and in particular English as a lingua franca, in external communication in 143 German companies trading with France and the Netherlands. The survey shows that companies in the different countries select between the two main strategies of 'standardisation' – that is, use of a lingua franca (English) – or 'adaptation' – that is, adoption of the customers' language (and its variant, i.e. 'reciprocal adaptation', or use of each other's language). Such corporate choices are not neutral and, according to Vandermeeren, they affect the export performance of the companies in question.

Therefore, if the findings show that adaptation leads to increased export volumes, Vandermeeren asks whether the alternative strategy of standardisation should not be regarded suspiciously by business practitioners. To illustrate, she points to the case of some French companies which opt for extensive standardisation when exporting to Germany and which are less successful in their trade in terms of volume. However, the overall picture is more complex. Again from the French–German example: the survey records examples of adaptation and standardisation in French companies, which indicate that hybrid strategies can co-exist and are dictated by the nature of the specific tasks. Therefore, in pre-sale documents, such as brochures and catalogues, the tendency is to 'adapt', which seems to indicate awareness of the potential role of language choice in attracting new customers, whereas in post-sale documents the tendency is to 'standardise'.

If there were still doubts about the importance of writing as a managerial activity, the findings of the survey of 200 British managers reported by Davies *et al.* go a long way to dispel them. Contradicting the alleged trend towards a 'paperless office', over 80 per cent of the respondents agreed with the statements that 'writing is an essential part of the organisation' and, somewhat unexpectedly for the sober-minded (textbook) manager, 'it is an opportunity to impress'. A concern with the effectiveness of writing, arising within academic and business circles, requires a deeper understanding of what managers actually write, as do how often, with whom and for whom they write. While the findings of Davies *et al.* show that some dimensions of writing practice are more amenable to quantitative representation – e.g. the time spent by managers on writing and the number of documents written during a working week – other aspects elude the precise categories of the survey approach, and are captured in follow-up interviews with the respondents. Interestingly, managers' feelings about writing can be both positive and negative at the same time, while the beliefs expressed in interviews appear to contradict observed practice. The conclusion implicitly answers this conundrum: the interplay of corporate goals and activities is often far from clearly discernible to managers, and is reflected in the complexity of the writing tasks to which they are called daily. Therefore, although the survey found that they seem to have an intuitive notion of 'effective writing', it is hardly surprising that managers none the less struggle with the operationalisation of the academic concepts of 'conciseness' and 'structure'. One can only wholeheartedly agree with the authors' concluding call for continuing research into writing employing different methodologies and approaches.

6.5. Epilogue: At the intersection between writing and speaking

Intertextuality is referred to, or dealt with, to a greater or lesser degree, in many of the preceding chapters. In this last study by Eugène Loos, it is finally given full prominence and illustrated with examples from spoken and written texts. Loos supports our view that future research in business language, whether written or spoken, will have to contend with the realisation, borne out by the research reported in this volume, that, in society at large, and in organisations in particular, texts do not occur in isolation from each other, and the written and spoken mode of text production are often symbiotically connected. Loos builds his framework on the two constructs of 'tyings' (actions that build sequential context – Firth 1991, 1995), and 'cues' (linguistic features that signal contextual presuppositions and therefore ensure cultural contextualisation – Gumperz 1978, 1982), and anchors his concept of intertextuality to Giddens's structuration theory.

It is interesting to note that the construction of meaning within interactions taken from two sets of intercultural data (Firth 1995 and Loos 1997) appears to happen *despite* the different cultural backgrounds (and languages) of the actors. However, business values can, on occasion, override cultural norms and expectations. The concept of 'social and strategic utility of communicative mode selection' quoted by Loos with reference to the decision of a Danish supplier to use the telephone instead of the fax as instructed by an Arab customer, is one such value to which practitioners appear to adhere in (apparent) contradiction to expectations. We are not told whether, in the end, the 'mode switch' achieved the supplier's aim, but the incident illustrates that intertextuality is not realised following rules which pre-exist the interaction but that it takes place in the multi-dimensional 'construction' of business, sometimes even in contradiction to expectations and conventions. And while this may also be true of social action in general, the implications for non-prescriptive research into the realisation of business through written and spoken texts must be far-reaching.

NOTES

1. We are indebted to Christopher Candlin for drawing our attention to the notion of interdiscursivity and for his helpful comments and suggestions on this and other chapters in this volume.
2. We acknowledge the fact that at times the two may overlap as in the case of professional services such as tax or legal consultancy.
3. Rubin uses several examples of business correspondence to illustrate this, such as in the opening line of a memo, 'Pursuant to the agreement we reached in our conversation of January 15th . . .', in which the writer constructs a social context for the written communication (1988: 3) and also in the use of forms of address contained within the salutation of a business letter, where 'Dear Herb' is likely to replace 'Dear Mr X' as the social relationship changes (1988: 11). It is important to note in the second example that the change in salutation both reflects the change in relationship as well as reinforces it; i.e. the context both shapes and is shaped by the discourse.

4. For example, she refers to the work of Varner (1987) and Manekeller (1980) who report considerable variation in the openings and closings used in business correspondence in different ethnolinguistic cultures (see also Jenkins and Hinds 1987; Nickerson 1994; Akar 1998), and she illustrates the reciprocal – socially constructed – relationship between organisational culture and organisational discourse using examples of corporate slogans and the discourse of corporate takeovers (Hirsch and Andrews 1983).

5. See Bakhtin (1986) for further discussion on this point.

6. Bazerman (1994: 82) summarises recent developments in genre theory as follows:

> Genre theory as elaborated by Carolyn Miller (1984), John Swales (1990) and myself (1988) has been concerned with the development of single types of texts through repeated use in situations perceived as similar. That is, over a period of time individuals perceive homologies in circumstances that encourage them to see these as occasions for similar kinds of utterances. These typified utterances, often developing standardized formal features, appear as ready solutions to similar appearing problems. Eventually the genres sediment into forms so expected that readers are surprised or even uncooperative if a standard perception of the situation is not met by an utterance of the expected form.

7. Originally introduced by Schutz and Luckmann (1973).

8. As both Swales, and Berkenkotter and Huckin point out, Miller thus extends the concept of genre beyond the much-studied Aristotelian rhetorical forms such as the eulogy or apologia, to incorporate many other types of everyday discourse, such as the letter of recommendation and the progress report. Berkenkotter and Huckin comment that 'Miller's insistence that considerations of genre encompass the typifications of the agora as well as those of the senate has been important to studies in technical and organizational communication' (1995: 6), and the examples they give to illustrate this include Devitt's (1991) study of the genres used by tax accountants and Yates and Orlikowski's (1992) concept of the genres of organisational communication.

9. Bazerman suggests that 'a rhetorical situation consists of all the contextual factors shaping a moment in which a person feels called upon to make a symbolic statement' (1988: 8); and further that the novice member of a community must learn to recognise and reproduce an appropriate symbolic response. The consequences of failing to recognise a rhetorical situation and respond appropriately may be serious, or even tragic, as outlined by Driskill (1989) in her discussion of the miscommunication between opposing groups of engineers and managers in several meetings immediately before the Space Shuttle Challenger exploded in 1987.

10. In addition, a distinction may be made between the exigence in a situation and the individual's intention in response to that exigence, since the response may be viewed as *conventionally* inappropriate by

the members of the social community concerned if it is not included within what Bazerman refers to as 'the range of social intentions toward which one may orient one's energies' (1994: 82). Miller uses an example taken from Bitzer (1980), to illustrate the socially constructed nature of the concept of exigence as an *objectified social need*, which 'provides the rhetor with a socially recognizable way to make his or her intentions known' (1984: 158), and the difference between exigence and intention. Bitzer maintains that in pardoning Nixon, the Ford administration was in fact responding to the exigence that there was a 'need to establish a relationship with the previous administration' (Miller 1984: 158), while at the same time allowing Ford to express his intention of protecting the national interest. In other words, despite his opinion or the opinion of any other member of the US citizenry, Ford could not have acted without the socially constructed recurrent situation – i.e. the change over from one administration to another, and the exigence which that presented.

11. Although Miller does not distinguish between simple and complex genres, there are similarities between her description of the evolution of a potential genre from existing typifications within a social group and Bakhtin's construct of intertextuality leading to the formation of secondary genres.

12. Devitt's (1993) survey of the (written) texts used by tax accountants in six large accountancy firms to carry out their activities identifies thirteen common genres serving three distinct purposes: (1) communication between tax accountants (e.g. memoranda for the files); (2) communication with clients (e.g. response letters to clients); and (3) reference to or comment on existing tax law (e.g. letters to taxing authorities and research memoranda, respectively).

13. Yates and Orlikowski illustrate the conventional nature of the genres of organisational communication and the recursive nature of the relationship between a genre and the social goup which uses it, in the historical development of the office memo from the business letter of the mid-19th century through to electronic mail. For example, business correspondence was conventionally a pen and paper communication in the form of a letter, with no distinction between internal and external correspondence. This was, however, until changes in the external environment, such as the introduction of the typewriter and vertical filing systems, the growth in the manufacturing industry and the increasing need to document business transactions, made the internal memo, as a typed document with a heading rather than a salutation and complimentary close, both necessary and possible. In structurational terms, changes in the social systems of organisations, such as the increase in management levels through expansion at the turn of the century, lead to changes in the structures necessary to sustain the social system, such as in the need to record, store and

retrieve large numbers of internal documents allowing access to several layers of management. This in turn leads to changes in the social action necessary in the production and reproduction of these structures, such as in the emergence of the typed and vertically filed internal memo made easily retrievable through the inclusion of a heading, and the social system is therefore reproduced; e.g. several layers of management gain access to internal communication and the patterning of social relations is sustained. The technological medium and the language used, as in the typed memo with a heading, both contribute to the social action which shapes and is recognised as legitimate by the social system which shapes it.

REFERENCES

Agar, Michael (1985) Institutional discourse. *Text* 5: 147–68.

Akar, Didar (1998) Patterns and variations in contemporary written business communication in Turkey: a genre study of four companies. Unpublished doctoral dissertation, University of Michigan.

Bakhtin, Mikhail (1981) *The Dialogic Imagination* (C. Emerson and M. Holquist, trans). Austin, TX: University of Texas Press.

Bakhtin, Mikhail (1986) The problem of speech genres. In M. Bakhtin, *The Problem of Speech Genres and Other Late Essays*. Austin: University of Texas Press, pp. 60–102.

Barabas, Christine (1990) *Technical Writing in a Corporate Culture: A Study of the Nature of Information*. Norwood, NJ: Ablex.

Bargiela-Chiappini, Francesca and Harris, Sandra (eds) (1997) *The Languages of Business: An International Perspective*. Edinburgh: Edinburgh University Press.

Bazerman, Charles (1988) *Shaping Written Knowledge: The Genre and Activity of the Experimental Article in Science*. Madison, WI: University of Wisconsin Press.

Bazerman, Charles (1994) *Constructing Experience*. Carbondale and Edwardsville: Southern Illinois University Press.

Bazerman, Charles (1995) Systems of genres and the enactment of social intentions. In Aviva Freedman and Peter Medway (eds), *Genre and the New Rhetoric*. London: Taylor & Francis.

Berkenkotter, Carol and Huckin, Thomas (1995) Rethinking genre from a sociocognitive perspective. *Written Communication* 10: 475–509.

Bhatia, Vijay K. (1993) *Analysing Genre: Language Use in Professional Settings*. London: Longman.

Bitzer, Lloyd F. (1980) Functional Communication: A Situational Perspective. In Eugene White (ed.) *Rhetoric in Transition*. University Park, PA: Pennsylvania State University Press.

Boden, Deirdre (1994) *The Business of Talk: Organizations in Action.* Cambridge: Polity Press.

Brown, John S. and Duguid, Paul (1991) Organizational learning and communities of practice: towards a unified view of working, learning and innovation. *Organization Science* 2: 40–57.

Bruffee, Kenneth (1986) Social construction, language, and the authority of knowledge: A bibliographic essay. *College English* 48: 773–90.

Burr, Vivien (1995) *An Introduction to Social Constructionism.* London and New York: Routledge.

Charles, Mirjaliisa (1996) Business negotiations: interdependence between discourse and the business relationship. *English for Specific Purposes.* 15 (1): 19–36.

Contractor, Noshia S. and Eisenberg, Eric M. (1990) Communication networks and new media in organizations. In Janet Fulk and Charles W. Steinfield (eds), *Organizations and Communication Technology.* Newbury Park, CA:Sage, pp. 143–72.

Devitt, Amy J. (1991) Intertextuality in tax accounting: generic, referential and functional. In Charles Bazerman and James Paradis (eds), *Textual Dynamics of the Professions: Historical and Contemporary Studies of Writing in Professional Communities.* Madison, WI: University of Wisconsin Press, pp. 336–57.

Devitt, Amy J. (1993) Generalizing about genre: new conceptions of an old concept. *College Composition and Communication* 44 (4): 573–86.

Drew, Paul and Sorjonen, Marja-Leena (1997) Institutional dialogue. In T. van Dijk (ed.), *Discourse as Social Interaction* v (2): 92–118.

Driskill, Linda P. (1989) Understanding the writing context in organisations. In Myra Kogen (ed.), *Writing in the Business Professions.* Urbana, IL: National Council of Teachers of English/The Association for Business Communication, pp. 125–45.

Faigley, Lester (1985) Nonacademic writing: the social perspective. In Lee Odell and Dixie Goswami (eds), *Writing in Nonacademic Settings.* New York and London: The Guilford Press.

Fairclough, Norman (1989) *Language and Power.* London: Longman.

Fairclough, Norman (1992a) Discourse and text: linguistic and intertextual analysis within discourse analysis. *Discourse & Society* 3 (2): 193–217.

Fairclough, Norman (1992b) Intertextuality in critical discourse analysis. *Linguistics and Education* 4: 269–93.

Fairclough, Norman (1992c) *Critical Language Awareness.* London: Longman.

Fairclough, Norman (1995) *Media Discourse.* London and New York: Edward Arnold.

Firth, Alan (1991) Discourse at work: negotiating by telex, fax and 'phone. Unpublished PhD dissertation. Aalborg: Aalborg University, Faculty of Humanities, Department of Intercultural Studies.

Giddens, Anthony (1979) *Central Problems in Social Theory: Action, Structure and Contradiction in Social Analysis.* Berkeley: University of California Press.

Giddens, Anthony (1984) *The Constitution of Society: Outline of the Theory of Structuration.* Cambridge: Polity Press.

Giddens, Anthony (1987) Time and social organization. In A. Giddens (ed.), *Social Theory and Modern Sociology.* Cambridge: Polity Press.

Grabe, William and Robert B. Kaplan (1996) *Theory and Practice of Writing.* London: Longman.

Gumperz, John J. (1978) The conversational analysis of interethnic communication. In E. L. Ross (ed.), *Interethnic Communication.* Athens, GA: Georgia University Press, pp. 14–31.

Gunnarsson, Britt-Louise (1997) The writing process from a sociolinguistic viewpoint. *Written Communication* 14 (2): 139–88.

Gunnarsson, Britt-Louise, Linell, Per and Nordberg, Bengt (eds) (1997) *The Construction of Professional Discourse.* London: Longman.

Hirsch, Paul M. and Andrews, John A. Y. (1983) Ambushes, shootouts, and knights of the roundtable: the language of corporate takeovers. In Louis R. Pondy, Peter J. Frost, Gareth Morgan and Thomas C. Dandrige (eds), *Organizational Symbolism.* Greenwich, CT:JAI Press.

Hoey, Michael (1986) The discourse colony: a preliminary study of a neglected discourse type. In Malcolm Coulthard (ed.), *Talking about Text,* Discourse Analysis Monographs, 13. Birmingham: English Language Research.

Jenkins, Susan and Hinds, John (1987) Business letter writing: English, French and Japanese. *TESOL Quarterly* 121 (2): 327–54.

Kristeva, Julia (1986) Word, dialogue and novel. In T. Moi (ed.), *The Kristeva Reader.* Oxford: Blackwell.

Lave, Jean and Wenger, Etienne (1991) *Situated Learning: Legitimate Peripheral Participation.* Cambridge: Cambridge University Press.

Lengel, Robert H. and Daft, Richard L. (1988) The selection of communication media as an executive skill. *The Academy of Management Executive* 2 (3): 225–32.

Loos, Eugène F. (1997) Internationale bedrijfscommunicatie: een reconstructief onderzoek naar het intertekstuele netwerk van Nederlandse en Duitse actoren in een bungalowpark. PhD dissertation, Utrecht: Utrecht University.

Manekeller, Wolfang (1980) *So schreibt man Geschaeftsbriefe,* 3rd edn. Munich: Taschenbuchverlag Jacobi KG.

Markus, M. Lynne (1994) Electronic mail as the medium of managerial choice. *Organization Science* 5 (4): 502–27.

Mauranen, Anna (1993) *Cultural Differences in Academic Rhetoric: A Textlinguistic Study.* Frankfurt am Main: Peter Lang.

Miller, Carolyn R. (1984) Genre as social action. *Quarterly Journal of Speech* 70: 151–67.

Mumby, Dennis K. and Clare, Robin P. (1997) Organizational discourse. In Teun van Dijk (ed.), *Discourse as Social Interaction,* vol. 2. London: Sage, pp. 181–205.

Nickerson, Catherine (1994) Business letter writing in English by non-native (Dutch) speakers. In David Marsh and Liisa Salo Lee (eds), *Europe on the Move: Fusion or Fission?* Proceedings of the 1994 SIETAR Conference at the University of Jyväskylä, Finland, pp. 221–6.

Odell, Lee and Goswami, Dixie (1985) *Writing in Nonacademic Settings.* New York: Guilford.

Orlikowski, Wanda J. and Yates, JoAnne (1994) Genre repertoire: the structuring of communicative practices in organizations. *Administrative Science Quarterly* 39: 541–74.

Poole, Marshall S. and DeSanctis, Gerardine (1990) Understanding the use of group decision support systems: the theory of adaptive structuration. In Janet Fulk and Charles W. Steinfield (eds), *Organizations and Communication Technology.* Newbury Park, CA: Sage, pp. 173–93.

Potter, Jonathan (1996) *Representing Reality: Discourse, Rhetoric and Social Construction.* Thousand Oaks: Sage Publications Ltd.

Rafoth, Bennett A. and Rubin, Donald L. (1988) *The Social Construction of Written Communication.* Norwood, NJ: Ablex Publishing.

Rogers, Priscilla and Swales, John (1990) We the people? An analysis of the Dana Corporation Policies document. *The Journal of Business Communication* 23 (3): 293–313.

Rubin, Donald L. (1988) Introduction: Four dimensions of social construction in written communication. In Bennett A. Rafoth and Donald L. Rubin (eds), *The Social Construction of Written Communication.* Norwood, NJ: Ablex Publishing, pp. 1–37.

Schutz, Alfred and Luckmann, Thomas (1973) *The Structures of the Life-World.* Evanston, IL: Northwestern University Press.

Spilka, Rachel (ed.) (1993) *Writing in the Workplace: New Research Perspectives.* Carbondale and Edwardsville, IL: Southern Illinois University Press.

Swales, John (1990) *Genre Analysis: English in Academic and Research Settings.* Cambridge: Cambridge University Press.

Van Leeuwen, Theo (1993) Genre and field in critical discourse analysis: a synopsis. *Discourse and Society* 4 (2): 193–223.

Van Maanen, John and Barley, Stephen R. (1984) Occupational communities: culture and control in organizations. In B. M. Staw and L. L. Cummings (eds), *Research in Organizational Behavior*, vol. 6, Greenwich, CT: JAI Press, pp. 287–365.

Varner, Iris (1987) Internationalizing business communication courses. *Bulletin of the Association of Business Communication* 50: 7–11.

Yates, JoAnne and Orlikowski, Wanda J. (1992) Genres of organizational communication: a structurational approach to studying communication and media. *Academy of Management Review* 17 (2): 299–326.

Yli-Jokipii, Hilkka (1994) *Requests in Professional Discourse: A Cross-cultural Study of British, American and Finnish Business Writing.* Annales Academiae Scientiarum Fennicae Dissertationes Humanarum Litterarum 71. Helsinki: Suomalainen tiedeakatemia.

PART I:

ELECTRONIC MEDIA AND WRITING IN ORGANISATIONS

TWO

The use of English in electronic mail in a multinational corporation

Catherine Nickerson

1. INTRODUCTION

Herring's (1996) seminal collection confirms the role of computer-mediated communication as a distinctive form of communication with increasing numbers of users, and one which provides a rich source of information on the dynamics of group interaction. Although the volume represents a range of electronic genres in a variety of academic and recreational settings, it does not include research on the use of electronic communication in (non-academic) organisational and business settings, such as that presented in earlier studies by Sproull and Kiesler (1986), Sherblom (1988) and Orlikowski and Yates (1994). In addition, although previous studies indicate that English is widely used in international business settings where the majority of users are non-native speakers of English – Robinson (1991), Louhiala-Salminen (1996), Barbara *et al.* (1996) (see also Van Hest and Oud-de Glas (1991) for an overview) – there has been little or no previous research on the nature of authentic electronic communication produced by non-native corporate users of English, or of the reasons why English should be selected rather than the local language as the appropriate *code* in electronic business communication in multinational, multilingual settings.

This chapter reports on the findings of a case-study investigating the use of English in the in-coming and out-going e-mail communication of one Dutch manager working in a large multinational corporation, with particular reference to the interplay between Dutch and English and the reasons why English is used rather than Dutch in that communication. The framework of genres of organisational communication proposed by Yates and Orlikowski (1992) is used to identify the recurrent situations within the corporate context where

English is invoked in e-mail communication, together with the substantive and formal characteristics of that communication. The two working hypotheses are: (1) that the selection of English as the appropriate code in certain e-mail transmissions may not only be a result of the nationality of the message recipient; and (2) that the use of English is embedded in the organisational practices of the multinational concerned.

The first part of this chapter selectively reviews previous research on the use of electronic media in corporations. This is followed by a discussion of Yates and Orlikowski's framework and its application to electronic communication and non-native business discourse. In the second part, the findings of a detailed analysis are discussed, of the use of English in 100 corporate e-mail messages.

2.   THE USE OF MEDIA BY CORPORATIONS

The use of media by a corporation has been discussed by a number of researchers, particularly those writing for a managerial audience. Koeleman (1995), for example, provides details of how a corporation may first assess its internal communication needs and then structure its internal communication accordingly through the use of appropriate media. Written media, such as a monthly newsletter, may therefore be the most appropriate way to communicate corporate policy in general terms, whereas audio-visual media, such as an instructional video, may be more appropriate to bring about changes in working procedures for large groups of employees. Although Koeleman acknowledges that written forms of communication may have advantages over spoken forms, such as the fact that they are asynchronous and may also be used to send the same information to a large number of employees, he warns against too much dependence on written media, since their effectiveness in successfully transmitting a message may often be over-estimated and cannot be easily assessed by the originator of the communication. For Koeleman, the growing use of electronic communication in corporate settings increases the possibility that miscommunication will occur, as a result of the fact that it is often used in situations where face-to-face communication was previously the preferred medium and, moreover, that novice users of the medium are frequently unable to express the same types of messages effectively in a written form that they would otherwise have expressed face-to-face.

Lengel and Daft (1988) investigate the selection of communication media by senior managers. They report an empirical link between the ability to select an appropriate *richness* of media and managerial effectiveness and claim that media-sensitive managers are more likely to receive a higher job performance rating than their less media-sensitive colleagues (see also Davies *et al.*, this volume, for further discussion on this point). Media such as face-to-face communication, for example, are highest in media richness, as opposed to lean media such as electronic bulletin boards, and Lengel and Daft suggest that the more successful managers in their study were better at matching media richness with the routineness of the message; i.e. the less routine the message the richer the medium that was selected and vice versa. Like Koeleman, Lengel and Daft do not consider electronic mail as a substitute for face-to-face communication in all situations, especially when the message is non-routine. They comment, 'Despite their usefulness for some tasks, electronic media should not be seen as suited to the entire range of executive communications' (1988: 231).

For Lengel and Daft, media selection is an individual choice, made on the basis of message content, which may therefore vary from employee to employee. Other researchers have challenged this view, however, on the grounds that the decisions an employee takes in their selection of a medium are more likely to be collective and therefore socially constructed, than they are to be individually perceived. Sproull and Kiesler comment that, 'however sophisticated the communication system, information in organizations does not flow in a vacuum. Senders and receivers are situated within the social context that regulates or influences communication contact (who exchanges information with whom) and communication content (what information is communicated)' (1986: 1494). And Yates and Orlikowski add, 'both decision makers and media are socially embedded within organisational settings' (1992: 309). In other words, successful communicators or not, employees can only use what is available to them and what is socially acceptable, within a specific organisational context.

More recently, Markus (1994) reports specifically on a study of how and why a group of managers within a large corporation used e-mail, in order to investigate the predictions made by the information richness theory; i.e. face-to-face communication will be preferred in non-routine messages. Contrary to the predictions made in earlier research (Lengel and Daft 1988), the managers in Markus's study made extensive use of e-mail for all types of communication, regardless of how routine or non-routine the message content was, since it was viewed by them as 'the primary medium of internal work-related communication' (1994: 519). E-mail was considered appropriate for almost all work-related communication, and was only rejected in favour of face-to-face communication in relationship-orientated messages such as personnel matters. Markus suggests that the selection of e-mail as an appropriate medium for all non-relationship communication was not a matter of individual perception, but was, in fact, socially constructed by the members of the organisation (see also Davies *et al.*, this volume, for a discussion of managerial changes in written documentation as a social construct within an organisation). Markus concludes her study with the observation that one year after the completion of her project, a series of changes in the composition of the management at the corporation that she investigated had apparently brought about a decline in the use of e-mail; i.e. the corporation's socially-constructed definition of the medium's appropriateness had changed.

A social approach to analysing organisational communication in general and electronic communication in particular is also taken by Yates and Orlikowski in their research into genres of organisational communication (Yates and Orlikowski 1992; Orlikowski and Yates 1994). This concept proposes the existence of 'communicative actions' or genres which typically occur in an organisational setting, and it suggests a number of factors which play a role in determining the use and characteristics of those actions. These include the 'recurrent situations' which invoke a particular genre, its 'communicative purpose', its substance and the 'form' it takes, where form is a combination of structure, medium and language. Yates and Orlikowski's framework is intended to provide an analytical approach to investigating an organisation's communicative practices as a reflection of the way it organises its activities and the work it carries out, and they demonstrate its application in an investigation of the electronic communication used during an interorganisational project.[1] The concept of genres of organisational communication and its potential usefulness in investigating the use of English in electronic communication in multinational settings is discussed in more detail in section 3 below.

3.   E-MAIL AS A GENRE OF ORGANISATIONAL COMMUNICATION

According to Yates and Orlikowski (1992), a certain number of recurrent situations will occur in an organisational setting which provide an exigence for documented communication to be invoked, such as the confirmation of an order with a customer or the job appraisal used to plan an employee's career and so on. In addition, previous studies indicate that a certain amount of the documented communication which occurs in a networked organisational setting is transmitted in an electronic form (e.g. Sproull and Kiesler 1986; Sherblom 1988; Markus 1994), and also that a variety of different documents and media are in use in English in corporations with a predominantly non-native speaker workforce (Yli-Jokipii 1994; Louhiala-Salminen 1996; Barbara *et al.* 1996; see also Akar and Louhiala-Salminen, Barbara and Scott, and Vandermeeren, this volume). It therefore seems plausible that some of the recurrent situations which invoke documented communication in a multinational setting may also provide an exigence for that documented communication to be in English and to be transmitted electronically. For example, documents such as the job appraisal form used for international career planning may be written in English and filed electronically, as a result of a recurrent situation in which Personnel is required to disseminate information about employees quickly throughout the corporation in response to the demand for an increasingly mobile workforce.

For Yates and Orlikowski, genres are 'characterised by similar substance and form' (1992: 301), which they define as follows:

> Substance refers to the social motives, themes and topics being expressed in the communication (e.g., the positive or negative recommendation and the supporting characteristics of the recommendee; the proposing of the project including its rationale and design). Form refers to the observable physical and linguistic features of the communication (e.g., inside address and salutation of a letter; standard sections of a proposal).
>
> (1992: 302)

Substance is, in effect, the semantic value of the discourse (i.e. the content appropriate for the context in which it is used), and form is the realisation of its meaning (i.e. how the text means). An organisational genre, such as an internal e-mail transmission in English, can therefore acquire its meaning from the corporate context and the situation within which it is invoked, as long as its substantive features are appropriate and it is realised in an appropriate form.

A number of researchers have provided classifications for business discourse on the basis of substance or 'socially recognised communicative purpose' (Orlikowski and Yates 1994: 543), often as the result of the analysis of specific forms of business communication. For example, Akar and Louhiala-Salminen (this volume) show that communicative purposes such as 'giving specific information', 'making a request' and 'establishing first contact', are common to both Turkish and Finnish fax communication in English; Sherblom (1988) identifies a number of communication functions in a content analysis of 157 electronic mail files, including 'influence attempts', 'providers of information' and 'requests for information'; and Ziv (1996) provides a taxonomy of 28 different communicative purposes for the media used within the (academic) organisation he studied, including 'requesting information', 'forwarding information', and 'reporting information' as three of the communicative purposes often associated with e-mail. The evidence provided by Ziv (1996) and Sherblom (1988), and by Markus (1994) as described above, would seem to suggest that e-mail is primarily used to exchange information in organisational settings, and furthermore, that it may be rejected in favour of other media in messages with a different communicative purpose – e.g. the preference reported by Markus for face-to-face communication in personnel matters in the corporation she investigated. If communicative purpose affects the choice of medium, it may also be the case that it will influence whether or not English is used in electronic mail in multinational settings in situations which would otherwise use the local language; e.g. messages communicating information about corporate policy may be written in English regardless of their originators or recipients. In addition to recurrent situations which invoke the use of English, it may therefore also be possible to link the use of English in multinational settings with certain communicative purposes.

According to Yates and Orlikowski (1992), the formal features of a genre must also be appropriate for the recurrent situation in which it is invoked. Therefore, they divide form into 'structure', 'media' and 'language', each referring to a different feature of the realisation of the substance of the text. The first of these, 'structure', is used by them to refer to formatting devices such as lists in written texts and structuring devices such as an agenda in meetings. In applying this in a useful way to written communication in multi-national settings, 'structure' may best be defined in terms of (text) conventions – i.e. those aspects of form which conventionally contribute to the physical layout of the genre, such as the conventional inclusion of a salutation at the beginning of a business letter. A number of factors may contribute to a conventionally appropriate physical layout for electronic communication. For example, mail transmissions may contain a boilerplate determined by an unchanging electronic template, similar to that reported by Winsor (1993) in press releases where the same piece of text was routinely included at the end of each release, and layout may also be influenced by the direction of the message within the hierarchy of the organisation, as reported by Sherblom (1988) in the corporation he studied where signatures were omitted in downwards communication.

'Medium' refers to 'the physical means by which communication is created, transmitted, or stored' (Yates and Orlikowski 1992: 319) – e.g. fax, e-mail, hard copy and so on – and is theoretically distinct from the genre which is being transmitted, such as a letter, job appraisal form, technical report and so on. Yates and Orlikowski acknowledge, however, that there may be some interaction between medium and genre in that certain genres may be conventionally associated with certain media, as is the case with the letter as a hard copy communication, and also that certain recurrent situations may invoke the use of a specific medium; e.g. an e-mail message responding to an e-mail message. If, therefore, there are recurrent situations in which the choice of medium is reciprocal in nature, it may also be useful to investigate whether this extends to the use of English within that medium; i.e. whether an e-mail transmission in English invokes an e-mail transmission in English, which would otherwise be in the local language. In the case of the corporation that is studied in this chapter, this could be where an e-mail message in English is forwarded from one employee to another, invoking a reply message in English.

The final aspect of 'form' in Yates and Orlikowski's framework is 'language', which they describe as 'linguistic characteristics such as formality and the specialized vocabulary of technical or legal jargon' (1992: 302). However, they give little further suggestion as to what might constitute formality or jargon and so forth, and in addition, their definition of language does not account for the fact that a formal characteristic of any genre of organisational communication in multinational settings may also be the decision to use

English, the local language or an additional non-local language. When researching multinational organisations, a more complex notion of language is needed; one that is comprised of code and discourse. Code is then the choice of an appropriate language for the genre (e.g. English, Dutch, German and so on), and discourse is its linguistic realisation. Bhatia (1993) has suggested that the linguistic realisation of a genre is comprised of three discourse features – characteristic lexico-grammatical features, text-patterns or textualisations, i.e. 'the way members of a particular speech community assign restricted values to various aspects of language use when operating in a particular genre' (1993: 26) – and the structural organisation of the text, such as the similarities in rhetorical moves he identifies in application letters and sales promotion letters. According to such a framework, a combination of all three discourse features will determine the final formal realisation of a multinational organisational genre within a choice of code.

This adaptation of Yates and Orlikowski's framework for use in multinational settings, suggests that the decision to use English in e-mail transmissions may be a result of the recurrent situation in which it is invoked and/or the communicative purpose associated with the message. Its use may also be reciprocal in nature and be invoked in response to an incoming message in English. Once the decision to use English has been taken, it will affect the form of the message in terms of layout and discourse. In order to investigate the use of English in e-mail messages written and received by non-native employees in a multinational corporation and the possibility that its use reflects the organising process and work of the corporation, it is necessary to identify those situations and communicative purposes for which English is invoked, together with a description of the subsequent use of English in the formal realisation of those messages. The findings of such an investigation are discussed in section 5 below.

4.   DATA[2] AND DATA COLLECTION

E-mail transmissions were collected over a period of two months, in February and March 1997, from six managers who comprised the management team of a technological department in one of the Dutch divisions of a large multinational corporation. The management team consisted of one senior departmental manager and five group managers, each with responsibility for between four and seventeen employees. The majority of the transmissions were sent or received within the department, the Dutch division or to other corporate divisions both inside and outside the Netherlands. A few additional messages were sent to recipients outside the corporation via an external e-mail connection. A parallel study of the use of communication channels and media within the same department (Bots 1997) indicates that not only was e-mail the most frequently used written medium for communication both inside and outside the department, but it was also used as an alternative to telephone and/or face-to-face communication if the recipient was either unavailable or located at a physical distance, e.g. two floors away in the same building. Bots reports that e-mail was one of three types of communication within the corporation which used an electronic medium. The other two were an electronic bulletin board and a corporate web site, both of which were used to communicate information internally to all employees.

Two of the six participating managers were native speakers of Dutch and four of English, although all six were able to speak and write both Dutch and English at a level of proficiency that was sufficient to hold departmental meetings in either language. Both Dutch speakers had spent periods of time abroad in parts of the company based in English-speaking countries and all four English speakers had spent a minimum of five years working for the company in the Netherlands. All six managers agreed to save their electronic notelog files, with both in-coming and out-going electronic communication. These were then converted into a readable form and downloaded onto diskette, providing a total of thirty-nine computer files varying from approximately 5 to 500 electronic messages in length. An initial analysis of the files indicated that all six of the managers received e-mail in both languages and all but one of the English speakers, who wrote exclusively in English, also sent e-mail in both Dutch and English. There was no evidence of any other languages being used. Within the confines of the corporate context, the management team therefore constituted a bilingual group to a greater or lesser degree.

The notelogs collected from one of the Dutch-speaking managers were then selected for further investigation, since he had provided large amounts of data and a random sample of 100 messages could be taken. These were analysed for the following information: the recurrent situations where English was required (i.e. the corporate unit involved in the communication, such as the Dutch manager's group, the department, the Dutch division and so on); the communicative purpose of the messages sent and received in English; the use of English in the structure of the e-mail transmissions (i.e. their layout); and one discourse feature, the use of corporate-bound lexis. An example of one of the e-mail messages, slightly adapted for reasons of confidentiality, is reproduced in the Appendix.

5. FINDINGS AND DISCUSSION

Table 2.1 shows the results for code selection for 100 notelog messages divided into In-coming mail, Out-going mail and Forwarded mail. In-coming and Out-going mail referred to single original messages either sent or received by the Dutch manager who provided the notelog file, and Forwarded mail referred to transmissions where one or more messages were sent on to another employee, usually with an original cover note. As indicated, just under one-quarter of the 100 transmissions used English. In addition to the corporate communication patterns discussed in the next section, it was possible to identify two additional aspects of the corporate communication structure in the three message types. The first of these related to the circulation of e-mail transmissions within the corporation. In the sixteen (English) transmissions included in In-coming and Out-going messages, for example, all but four involved multiple recipients. The majority of messages were sent to groups of employees varying in size between one and fifty, with additional groups of employees being copied in to more than half of those transmissions.

Table 2.1: Code selection

Code used per message type		Incoming messages	Outgoing messages	Forwarded messages
English	Total = 23	10	6	7
Dutch	Total = 77	13	44	20

Not surprisingly, Bots (1997) reports that the employees she interviewed within the department considered that the e-mail system was over-used. The fact that as few as sixteen English transmissions could involve a total of more than 200 recipients and, in addition, that the circulation lists often represented formal corporate groupings, such as all department managers or all senior management within the Dutch division, suggests that not only was e-mail (over-) used as a major source of information exchange within the corporation, but also that a considerable amount of that information was exchanged in English.

The second aspect of the communication structure related to the interplay of Dutch and English in many of the Forwarded transmissions. These contained chains of transmissions varying from two to four transmissions in length, and of the seven Forwarded transmissions containing English, five contained both Dutch and English transmissions within the chain. For example, one typical chain of four messages began with a message in English by an English-speaking employee at another Dutch division sent to a Dutch employee in the same division. This was then forwarded by that Dutch employee to another Dutch employee in a different department at the original Dutch manager's division with a cover note in English (!). This Dutch employee then forwarded both English messages on to the original Dutch manager, with a cover note in Dutch, and he completed the chain of transmissions by forwarding all three messages on to a member of his group with a cover note in Dutch. In one other example of four messages, the original message, written by a Dutch speaker, began in Dutch and ended in English. This was followed by another English message, written by a non-Dutch speaker, a Dutch message, written by a second non-Dutch speaker, and a final Dutch message sent from the original Dutch manager to the first writer, the initiator of the chain of messages. In all four messages, all four writers were either sent the message directly or received a copy. Examples such as this suggest that there is considerable reference to written (electronic) sources of information within the corporation as part of the organising process (see also Davies *et al.* and Loos this volume, for further discussion on the importance of referring to written sources of information in organisational settings). It also suggests that at least within the department under investigation, those electronic sources are both in English and in Dutch.

Table 2.2: Recurrent situations for English transmissions as indicated by corporate communication patterns

Message type	*Corporate unit represented in transmission*
Incoming (message originators)	Own department (senior manager) – E **Own group – NL** Own (Dutch) division – E UK division – E Own department (group managers) – E
Outgoing (message recipients)	Own department (group managers) – E/NL **Own group – NL** External contact – non-corporate – E **Other (Dutch) division – NL** **Own (Dutch) division – NL**
Forwarded (message recipients or original message originators)	**Other Dutch division – NL** + other Dutch division – E Non-Dutch division – E + **Own group – NL** Own department (senior manager) – E Own department (other group) – E + **own group – NL** **Own (Dutch) division – NL** **UK division – NL** UK division – E + **own group – NL**

5.1. Corporate communication patterns

Table 2.2 details the recurrent situations in which English was invoked, for each of the three message types. The recurrent situations for In-coming mail were identified on the basis of the originator of the message and their corporate relationship with the Dutch manager, and those for Out-going mail on the basis of his corporate relationship with the recipient, i.e. the corporate communication patterns which had provided an exigence for the e-mail transmission to occur. The recurrent situations for Forwarded messages were more complex as they often involved a chain of transmissions in both English and Dutch. The recurrent situations were therefore identified on the basis of the corporate relationship between the Dutch manager and message recipients where he wrote in English and/or his corporate relationship with the original writers of messages in

English sent, copied or forwarded on to him. For the sake of clarity, details are not given of the Dutch messages in the chain.

Table 2.2 also indicates whether or not the originator of the message in each case was a Dutch speaker; NL indicates a Dutch speaker and E a non-Dutch speaker, in all cases but one an English native speaker. Communication patterns in English where both originator and recipient(s) were Dutch speakers are highlighted in bold-face type.

As indicated in Table 2.2, the following corporate units were involved in In-coming e-mail transmissions in English: the manager's own group, various members of his own department and his own division, as well as the UK division. The group, department and his own (Dutch) division were also involved in Outgoing transmissions, as was a second Dutch division. Finally, all these corporate units were represented in the Forwarded messages with the addition of a second non-Dutch division, a second UK division and a third Dutch division. Since one of the UK divisions within the data set also functioned as a head office for the corporate group, it was possible to conclude that e-mail transmissions in English occurred at all levels within the corporation; i.e. own group, other groups in the department, own department, other departments in the division, own division, other divisions both in the Netherlands and abroad, and head office.

Several of the transmissions in the data set were written in English simply as a result of an English- or non-Dutch-speaking originator, as was the case, for example, in an In-coming message from the UK division written by a British employee and an In-coming message from the manager's own division also written by an English speaker. As indicated in the table, however, there were also several transmissions where both originator and recipient(s) were Dutch. These were of two types. Firstly, for example, a number of messages were written in English in order to give access to non-Dutch speakers either receiving the message directly or copied into it. This accounted for several communications within the manager's own group where the message was sent on to non-Dutch employees within the group or to one of the UK divisions. Where messages were not sent on, the same employees communicated electronically with each other only in Dutch. A second set of English transmissions between two Dutch employees which the transmissions indicated did not involve giving access to non-Dutch-speaking employees directly, occurred in communication with Dutch employees working in other divisions both in the Netherlands and abroad. This was a result of the fact that these divisions apparently required all In-coming and Out-going communication to be written in English regardless of the originators and/or recipients of the messages, and this was also supported by a check of the Dutch transmissions contained within the data taken from the Dutch manager's notelog file which showed that there were no transmissions in Dutch with any of the divisions other than within the manager's own division.

The two sets of examples described in the paragraph above suggest that the decision to use English as the *code* in electronic transmissions was determined by at least two situational factors. Firstly, Dutch employees communicated electronically with other Dutch employees in Dutch within the division, unless a non-Dutch-speaking employee within the division also required access to the communication. Secondly, all corporate electronic communication outside the division was always written in English regardless of the originator or recipient, as a matter of corporate policy. Two types of recurrent situation which invoked documented communication in English could therefore be distinguished: situations in which English was always invoked, e.g. communication outside the division; and situations where the communication was usually in Dutch, e.g. communication within the division, but where English could be invoked for additional reasons, such as where an employee who was unable to understand Dutch required access to the information. These two situations did not, however, account for all the English electronic transmissions in the data set. A third factor, the communicative purpose of the transmission, also provided an exigence for documented communication in English.

5.2.   Communicative purpose

Five additional transmissions in English were sent within the division – three within the Dutch manager's own group, one from the Dutch manager to the other departmental managers and one to another department, with no evidence of non-Dutch speakers included in the circulation list. Of the five transmissions, one involved a single original text and the other four involved two transmissions of the same two texts, separated by a period of several days, where the intention was for the recipients to comment on the version of the text they received. One of these texts was sent twice to the manager's group, and the other first to the other departmental managers and then to another department. Although the majority of the other departmental managers were English speakers, it was unlikely that the message sent to them had been written in English for their benefit, however, not only because the Dutch manager's notelog file indicated that he communicated frequently with them in Dutch, but also because the same English text was sent to a Dutch speaker outside the department one day later.

The communicative purpose of the three texts contained within the five transmissions was similar, in that it concerned the way in which the department formally organised its activities. One text related to career planning for an employee, the second was a reply to a questionnaire concerning the possible replacement of an existing divisional procedure and the third was a document outlining the implementation of an ISO-9000 Quality Management procedure within the department. Although the number of texts was very small, their contents seemed to indicate that there was also an exigence for an e-mail transmission to be written in English in communication between Dutch speakers within the division, if the communicative purpose of that transmission was to report officially on the organisational process. Support for this possibility was also found in the divisional (Dutch) newsletter published in January 1997, which reported on senior management's decision at the end of 1996 that English should become the official language within the division, despite a majority of Dutch employees in the workforce.

5.3. Layout

The layout of the transmissions was pre-determined by the use of a standardised electronic template which provided the meta-text in all the messages in the notelog files of all six managers. This also resulted in the use of English in the layout of messages which were otherwise written in Dutch. For example, all transmissions contained a standard memo header in English with 'To:', 'From:', 'Subject:' and 'cc:' if applicable; some messages carried additional information for the recipient such as 'Reply to note of' and 'Forwarding note from', and some messages from outside the division often contained the following boilerplate text: 'Warning . . . This is

XYZ mail, which might have originated outside your organisation.
. . . Keep this in mind if you answer this message.' In addition to
these unchanging elements in the layout of the mail transmissions,
a number of other items could be determined by the sender for
each message, such as the decision to include a salutation, or the
use of English or Dutch in the subject line. These are discussed in
more detail below.

The salutation was an optional element in the e-mail messages
and was only included if the message was sent to a single (primary)
receiver. If it was included, it always took the form of the first name
of the recipient, e.g. Henk, both across divisions and regardless of
the relative hierarchical distance between the sender and recipient,
suggesting that this was an appropriate *formal* realisation throughout the corporation. Where messages were intended for a multiple
readership, no salutation was included. Almost all the messages
included some form of complimentary close, together with the name
and corporate address of the sender. The complimentary close could
be pre-programmed by each employee, and a variety of forms were
used as follows:

[1]   With kind regards/Met vriendelijke groeten
      Regards/Groeten
      Regards
      With kind regards
      Groet
      M.vr.gr./Regards
      Vriendelijke groeten/Regards
      Kind Regards

Once programmed, the complimentary close remained unchanged,
resulting in English messages with English, and English and Dutch
used in the complimentary close, and Dutch messages with Dutch,
English and Dutch, and English only used in the close. One text
in English written by an English-speaking employee in a UK division even used the following, 'Best wishes and nog veel succes!'
together with 'Met vriendelijke groeten', presumably as a result of
time spent working with the corporation in the Netherlands. It
seemed clear that the *code* used in the text of the message had little
effect on the code used in the complimentary close, as might be
expected in other forms of written business communication such as
a business letter, and the use of either or both languages was viewed

as an appropriate *formal* realisation by those members of the corporation represented in the data set.

As with the complimentary close, the subject lines included in the e-mail messages also used both Dutch and English. English subject lines were used in the majority of In-coming and Out-going English messages and English subject lines were also copied over from English to Dutch messages in the chains of Forwarded messages. This was the only evidence for English invoking English in the data set. There were, however, three English messages, all written by Dutch writers to Dutch writers, where the subject line was given in Dutch; i.e. 'Advies over X, reactie and Project zonder budget, later wel?' (Recommendation about X, reaction and Project without funding, will it be forthcoming later?). One of these messages was written in English, as stated by the departmental writer in Dutch at the beginning, in order to copy in a non-Dutch-speaking employee and therefore give her access to the information contained within the transmission. The other two messages involved communication with Dutch employees working in different divisions where English was used as an official language. 'Advies over X' was the subject of a text written to formalise an agreement between divisions, and 'reactie' was used in a text acknowledging feedback (given in Dutch) on the implementation of new corporate policy. In all three cases it seemed as if the situational constraint which invoked documented communication in English did not extend to the subject line.

5.4. Lexis

A considerable amount of technical and corporate-bound lexis was present in the e-mail messages. The technical lexis referred to what the corporation did (e.g. the technical processes involved and the goods produced), and the corporate-bound lexis referred to the way in which these activities were organised (e.g. acronyms and other lexical items used for procedures, corporate units and positions within the corporate hierarchy). The lexis used within the transmissions therefore reflected both the work activities and organising process of the corporation.

There were three Dutch lexical items in the English transmissions, all of which referred to the organising process. These were, 'monsteroverleg' (sample discussion group), 'X opdracht incl. account nummer' (X contractual agreement together with the chargeable account details) and 'Afdelingchef' (Departmental manager), a position which, in fact, no longer existed within the corporation. What was interesting was the fact that these items of Dutch lexis all occurred in messages with a readership either potentially or actually including non-Dutch speakers; i.e. non-Dutch speakers were included in the circulation list, or the message contained procedural information likely to be referred to outside the Dutch division. This suggests that certain items of Dutch lexis were widely referred to within several corporate units regardless of the code invoked in the text of the message and whether or not its recipients were able to understand Dutch. These items had apparently been assigned a restricted value by the user community and were therefore an example of lexical textualisation (Bhatia 1993).

6.   CONCLUSION

The findings of the study indicate that the use of English in electronic communication is embedded in the organisational practices of the corporation. Electronic mail is a major source of information exchange within the corporation, there is widespread reference to electronic communication in the organising process, and, in both cases, a considerable amount of the information exchanged and referred to is in English. Furthermore, English occurs in electronic transmissions at all levels in the corporation, it is always used in communication outside the division under investigation and in any documentation reporting officially on the organisational process inside the division, and it is also used in communication within the division which involves non-Dutch speakers. Finally, in addition to the situational and substantive factors which determine whether English is used in a transmission, the appropriate formal realisation of the message, such as its layout and lexis, is also embedded within the communication practices of the corporation.

Giddens's theory of structuration considers social activities as recursive in that they both shape and are shaped by the structure of the organisation within which they occur (Giddens 1979, 1984; see also Yates and Orlikowski 1992). Within the Dutch division, the communicative practices in English are shaped by the organisation in terms of the situations which invoke electronic communication in English, the communicative purpose of electronic communication in English, and in the layout and lexis used in those transmissions. In addition, the widespread circulation of and reference to English electronic communication and, in particular, the fact that electronic messages containing official information relating to the organisational process are always written in English, would seem to indicate that the structuring of the organisation, or what Boden has referred to as 'structure-in-action' (Boden 1994: 58), is achieved, at least in part, through the production and distribution of e-mail transmissions in English.

Although the communication practices described above are based on the findings of a single case-study, and therefore are particular to one organisation, they do provide useful information on several aspects of corporate electronic communication, including its role in the structuring of organisations, that would merit further investigation. One practical outcome of future research is expected to be insights on the nature of the writing tasks which many non-native corporate users of English are required to complete in order to be effective members of the growing multinational and multilingual business community.

APPENDIX

MSG FROM: RABCM2–RSXYZM01 TO: NLIFGAM4–APSTOP
10-09-96 10:00:55
To: NLIFGAP4–APSTOP J. Janssen
cc: RP889–RSXYZMO NL/9 Secretariaat
RAJKL9–RSXYZMO–B. v.d.Velde
RPOMK8–RSXYZMO–D. A. Bakker

From: P. de Klein ICS-AMP/1 'Nano-tech'
Nedco Centre, Molendorp
Internal address: ND 32–14 tel.6161
Subject: ICS advies over Tracers Bennekom

Jan
As discussed at our meeting of last friday we have to open a Project.

Can you please send me an official NED opdracht incl. accountnummer for a project 'ICS advice on Tracers for Bennekom' We wil deliver:
– advice on tracers (stable and radioactive)
– advice on analytical techniques to measure these tracers
– participate in meetings/discussions

For this initial stage I think that 80 hours of our time is sufficient.

With kind regards/Met vriendelijke groeten, Paul de Klein
Nedco Centre, Molendorp
Berhardlaan 5,8099 BB MOLENDORP/PO Box 29999, 8000 AA MOLENDORP
tel. +31 20 999 9999, fax. 8888; e-mail: KLEIN5@ics.nedco.nl
22
ICSNEDCO advies over Tracers Bennekom

NOTES

1. The framework enables them to distinguish three genres – memo, dialogue and proposal, and one genre system – ballot – which are distinct in terms of communicative purposes and formal characteristics, and also to show how these genres and genre system became established and were then invoked to varying degrees in response to the (changing) communicative demands inherent in the project.
2. I am grateful to Christine, Gary, Geoff, Robin, Chris, André, Frans, Annemiek and Henk at 'Nedco' for providing me with the data for this study.

REFERENCES

Barbara, Leila, Celani, M., Antonieta A., Collins, Heloisa and Scott, Mike (1996) A survey of communication patterns in the Brazilian business context. *English for Specific Purposes* 15 (1): 57–71.
Bhatia, Vijay K. (1993) *Analysing Genre: Language Use in Professional Settings*. London: Longman.
Boden, Deidre (1994) *The Business of Talk: Organizations in Action*. Cambridge: Polity Press.

Bots, Annemiek (1997) Internal and external communication: a study of the communication structure within the analytical technology group. Unpublished Master's thesis. Business Communication Department, Nijmegen University, Nijmegen.

Giddens, Anthony (1979) *Central Problems in Social Theory: Action, Structure and Contradiction in Social Analysis*. Berkeley: University of California Press.

Giddens, Anthony (1984) *The Constitution of Society: Outline of the Theory of Structuration*. Cambridge: Polity Press.

Herring, Susan (ed.) (1996) *Computer-Mediated Communication: Linguistic, Social and Cross-cultural Perspectives*. Amsterdam/Philadelphia: John Benjamins Publishing Co.

Koeleman, Huib (1995) *Interne Communicatie als Managementinstrument: Strategieën, Middelen en Achtergronden*. Houten: Bohn Stafleu Van Loghum.

Lengel, Robert H. and Daft, Richard L. (1988) The selection of communication media as an executive skill. *The Academy of Management Executive* 2 (3): 225–32.

Louhiala-Salminen, Leena (1996) The business communication classroom vs reality: what should we teach today? *English for Specific Purposes* 15 (1): 37–51.

Markus, M. Lynne (1994) Electronic mail as the medium of managerial choice. *Organization Science* 5 (4): 502–27.

Miller, Carolyn R. (1984) Genre as social action. *Quarterly Journal of Speech* 70: 151–67.

Orlikowski, Wanda J. and Yates, JoAnne (1994) Genre repertoire: the structuring of communicative practices in organizations. *Administrative Science Quarterly* 39: 541–74.

Robinson, Pauline (1991) *ESP Today: A Practitioner's Guide*. London: Prentice-Hall.

Sherblom, John (1988) Direction, function and signature in electronic mail. *Journal of Business Communication* 25 (4): 39–54.

Sproull, Lee and Kiesler, Sara (1986) Reducing social context cues: electronic mail in organizational communication. *Management Science* 32, 1492–512.

Van Hest, Erna and Oud-de Glas, Maria (1991) *Een Onderzoek naar de Technieken die worden Gebruikt bij Diagnose en Analyse van Vreemde-Talenbehoeften in het Bedrijfsleven*. Luxembourg: Bureau voor Officiële Publikaties der Europese Gemeenschappen.

Winsor, Dorothy A. (1993) Owning corporate texts. *Journal of Business and Technical Communication* 7 (2): 179–95.

Yates, JoAnne and Orlikowski, Wanda J. (1992) Genres of organizational communication: a structurational approach to studying communication and media. *Academy of Management Review* 17 (2): 299–326.

Yli-Jokipii, Hilkka (1994) *Requests in Professional Discourse: A Cross-cultural Study of British, American and Finnish Business Writing*. Annales Academiae

Scientiarum Fennicae Dissertationes Humanarum Litterarum 71. Helsinki: Suomalainen tiedeakatemia.

Ziv, Oren (1996) Writing to work: How using e-mail can reflect technological and organizational change. In Susan Herring (ed.), *Computer-mediated Communication: Linguistic, Social and Cross-cultural Perspectives.* Amsterdam/Philadelphia: John Benjamins Publishing Co., pp. 243–64.

THREE

E-mail: uses, issues and problems in an institutional setting

Joan Mulholland

1. INTRODUCTION

Most researchers in discourse analysis currently understand that language study cannot be undertaken without due recognition of the role language texts play within social life. Bakhtin declared that genres were 'the drive belts from the history of society to the history of language' (1986: 65), and in recognition of this, researchers in the social sciences are also coming to accept that the complex interrelations (or intertextuality) between the channels, genres and languages of discourse play a major part in enabling an understanding of the world of human interaction. As Bakhtin's metaphor indicates, not only does the one connect the other, but the two are dynamically powerful in their effect on one another. The present study examines one such channel, and genre, that of e-mail, which has come to prominence in the modern workplace as a major element in business information retrieval and use.

There have been two kinds of academic research on e-mail, linguistic-social and scientific-technological, but until recently little research has been combinatory (but see Herring (1996a) and Murray (1995) on the linguistic and social perspectives of computer-mediated communication). E-mail has been examined as part of the networked organisation: Ku (1996) looks at the impact of some task characteristics, and organisational roles on e-mail usage; Sproull and Kiesler (1991) study the tasks for which e-mail is used – scheduling, task assignment, reporting accomplishments and general awareness; and Volkema and Niederman (1996) focus on e-mail processes in each of the elements of pre-meeting activity. In all cases e-mail appears as a useful bit player rather than a main actor in the management of information exchange. Such research provides much useful material on the electronic and organisational context in which e-mail occurs, while its generic nature and the qualities of its language have received attention in a number of other studies (Korenman and Wyatt 1996; Rice and Shook 1990; Sproull and Kiesler 1986; Walther *et al.* 1994; and Yates and Orlikowski 1992).

E-mail has also been the object of non-academic research, in the educational guides which accompany the purchase of the Internet software, or are published for users by the trade. Although many of these latter publications downplay the generic significance of e-mail, because it is perceived as easy to use and therefore needing little instruction, there are several which focus entirely on it – e.g. Ackermann 1995; Lamb and Peek 1995; and Leblanc and Leblanc 1995. However, users of e-mail often learn to use it by trial and error, or by seeking help from friends. Only *in extremis* will they purchase one of the few published guides. The significance of this situation for a study of the generic properties of e-mail is that e-mailers appear to derive their modes of use, and also their style and language, from their knowledge and experience of related, pre-existing genres, which could be called 'companion genres', such as letters and memorandums. From this, it follows that the e-mail genre uses features from a number of these generic sources rather than being *sui generis*.

2.   GENRE

One book-length study, Murray (1991b), directly attends to the generic aspects of electronic communication, and although her focus is on a variant mode, Emessages, her findings have validity for the analysis of e-mail.[1] Yates and Orlikowski's (1992) article on genres of organisational communication, and Erickson's (1996) study of the Net as participatory genre also provide insights relevant to the study of electronic mail. Specifically on the language of e-mail there are several studies of value, including Collot and Belmore (1993), Ferrara *et al.* (1991), Murray (1991a and 1995), and Sproull and Kiesler (1986). The research interests of the present writer have been focused for some time on the historical emergence of new genres, the discursive situation in which they arise, and on the rhetorical and intertextual aspects of their usage (Mulholland 1992 and 1994). A specific focus on e-mail arose from the increasing role it plays in university life.

This study is based on the assumptions about genre contained in Bakhtin (1986), Miller (1994), and Goffman (1975, 1981). These assumptions are:

1. that genre study allows a consideration of the interplay of the social, institutional and technological factors which influence the discursive practices and outcomes of communication;
2. that people participate in genre usage rather than control it;
3. that one genre exists alongside others and is influenced by them;
4. that regularities of form and substance within a genre arise, become established conventions, and influence all aspects of the communication. However, genres are dynamic entities and they can be adapted to changing circumstances.

The study also assumes that texts exchanged via e-mail are socially important verbal actions and that their language has a major role to play in ensuring that the acts are performed well (Sacks 1992 and Searle 1969).

3. CONTEXT FOR THE E-MAIL GENRE

The first element needed for an understanding of genre use, and of a new genre's place in the communications generated in a workplace, is the contextual one of the historical rise of the genre both in general social terms and in its use within a particular organisation.

E-mail arose as one facility of the Internet, the world-wide network of computers, which itself began in 1969, when the US Defense Advanced Research Projects Agency (DARPA) developed a network to study methods of communicating experimental data that would transcend specific computer software types. By 1975 the network was being used by DARPA to exchange non-experimental data and had become fully developed. By the early 1980s the network had extended its reach beyond the defence establishment, and with the setting up of a separate MILNET (unclassified materials), it took on the role of exchanging more general information among computer users in a range of occupations and settings. By 1995 the number of computers linked to the Internet was well over 3 million and the number of users estimated at c. 20 million (Leblanc and Leblanc 1995).[2]

As this history indicates, e-mail's original application was speedy data information exchange. The system therefore was designed to be formal and precise, and it adopted a set of appropriate systemic features and usages (see Ziv 1996). Moreover, the fast rate of its growth over a short period has meant that its users have had no standardised education in the best practice methods. Most current users of e-mail have learnt to use it by attending short training courses, by trial and error, or through a guide or manual.

Both its primary purposes and the lack of education of its users have impacted on current e-mail practices. For example, when e-mailers have to send large quantities of information and sending these by e-mail might be problematic, they often use the systemic-ally easier process of directing receivers to another part of the system – for example, the Web. If they must use the e-mail medium, again they prefer the easy option, appending the information as the system invites them to do, and this means that they send informa-tion in unprocessed blocks, rather than creating a summary or digest of it. So e-mail users rarely change the form in which the appended material already exists, whether or not this fits the specific needs of their receiver. In their e-mail messages accompanying such informa-tion and in explanation of it they often produce very short messages, as the instruction manuals suggest, minimalising their language; for example, by using acronyms (see section 7 for other forms of brevity) and/or limiting themselves to one screen of text. The com-bination of short explanation and large amounts of information leaves the reader with a good deal of processing and digesting to do in the communication procedure (see also section 6.1.3).

Because e-mail was designed primarily for information exchange there are no systemic means of conveying the important affective and interpersonal aspects of communication, so users have had to find their own methods, and to develop these within an unsympath-etic frame. These methods have not always been good, as witnessed by the sections in many instructional guides on the evils of excessive emotion, defamation, and rudeness or 'flaming'. But some guides do recognise the value of including affect, and recommend the use of 'emoticons' – a set of standardised keyboard symbols which pic-torially represent emotion, e.g. ':)', which shows a happy face on its side (Leblanc and Leblanc 1995). Many users, however, find these inappropriate in more formal e-mail communications.

All the situational factors concerned with the systemic aspects mentioned above have an impact on the generic use of electronic communication. The following section deals with some of the specific discursive consequences of the historical and technological dimension to the e-mail genre, as seen in a set of administrative e-mail messages circulated at the University of Queensland.

4.   THE CASE-STUDY

This chapter reports on an investigation of a number of e-mail messages which were circulated as part of the preparation for formal meetings which took place within the administrative section of a university workforce. The project is an extended and focused application of Rice and Case's (1983) study of a very similar setting.[3] Fourteen years after their study some similarities in e-mail usage remain but there have also been some interesting developments.

4.1.   The e-mail database

The database consists of printout copies of the e-mail correspondence which was sent out and received by administrative and academic staff during the setting up of a number of formal meetings within the university. This particular kind of e-mail activity was selected because it could be predicted to contain a high degree of formality while none the less attempting to incorporate some collegial qualities, and thus to differ from the majority of the research data on electronic communication published so far which has concentrated on informality of use and affect – for example, Erickson (1996) and Murray (1991b). It was also (correctly) predicted that the communications would include a high degree of intertextuality with other genres, including printed agendas and agenda papers, a face-to-face event (the meeting itself), and the printed meeting minutes, and so would be revealing of communicative and generic interplay as this occurs within a real-life workplace setting.

Specifically, the data consist of five sample sets of e-mail messages, totalling seventy-six e-mails, which were collected over a three-month period from members of the secretarial and administrative staff at University of Queensland (UQ).[4] As well as the e-mails, each set contains all the other communications generated both electronically and in hard copy form in order to set up a particular

formal meeting (and in some cases to handle post-meeting matters.)
The meetings in question were three of the monthly meetings of the
main academic and administrative board, and two meetings of different academic and administrative committees. It could not include
phone calls made as part of the process. The sets were supple-
mented by forty other e-mails (total 116) which played some part in
making arrangements for other formal meetings but where whole
sets were not available. The data also include oral comments on the
use of e-mail which were recorded during focused interviews with
the secretarial and administrative informants involved in the sample
sets. Other, directed, comments were obtained via phone calls, and
were registered in fieldnotes during and immediately after the event.
In addition, the present writer is a member of several formal committees at UQ, and hence has access to materials presented to the
membership of the committees which were used in the project.

4.2.   Methodology

The study reported here was an empirical, qualitative examination
of the selected group of e-mails. The study had two parts: the first
was an examination of the technological situational influences on
e-mail practices at UQ; and the second was a detailed analysis of the
rhetorical and linguistic features of e-mail texts as they were sent
and received. The present writer adopted a participant observer
position in the study, being both a sender and receiver of committee e-mails.

A major problem in the research study of e-mails is that there can
be no expectation of homogeneity in usage practices and text language. A first reading of the data showed plainly that, for UQ users,
the committee e-mailing processes are new and evolving (but note
that Ferrara *et al.* 1991: 9 found the language conventions in their
data had stabilised). The lack of homogeneity confirmed that a qualitative study might be more useful than a quantitative one, but this
presented difficulties for the establishment of good coding practices
with respect to both parts of the study. Therefore the study began
with a focus on *perceptions* of the way the e-mail processes might
influence their usage. Perceptions, and data-based facts, were drawn
from the research literature, and these were augmented by focus-
group discussions with the UQ administrators whose task it was to

manage the committee preparations. It was felt to be important not to constrain the investigation too narrowly, since this might miss the features which, while not obviously significant at the moment in e-mails, might come to be significant in their future evolution. There was a high measure of agreement among the (fifteen) informants that there were two major problems with the use of e-mail alongside other channels of communication. One was the matter of ensuring that committee members understood how the e-mails were to be read and responded to, and to have this happen in a very brief timeframe; and the other concern was the question of how to manage successful intertextual relations between the e-mails and other relevant communications. These two concerns could be characterised as a concern for communication efficiency. A related issue raised by many of the administrators was the difficulty of combining in e-mails the need for haste with the maintenance of good relations between the committee members and the administrators.

It was decided that the study should address the first issue by examining each e-mail for manifestations of efficiency (or lack of it), and should consider in each instance whether the technological features of the channel were a help or hindrance. The second issue, of affect or interpersonal relationship, was addressed by noting all politeness markers in the language of the texts, based on the positive and negative forms in Brown and Levinson's seminal study (1987).

After the two kinds of data were gathered, an account of them was presented to the informants and their responses were sought. The data were later re-assessed in the light of their comments.

5.   THE INFLUENCE OF CONTEXT ON E-MAIL USE

UQ can be taken as an example of an established organisation which is conservative in its work practices, and which retains the more traditional genres of communication as well as incorporating the new computer-mediated genres in its administrative discourse. Its workforce, both administrative and academic, have not all taken kindly to the new electronic genres: a good proportion have resisted them, others allow them only a minor place in their work activity, and still others are at present trying to opt out of them wherever possible. One reason for the resistance is that the UQ workforce operates through a vast array of often incompatible computer systems and platforms and hence has difficulty in achieving simple or swift access to others via electronic channels. To illustrate, a recent e-mail message used these words to members of a committee who needed to make submissions to the next meeting:

[1]   Depending on the browser in use, users will be able to key in the details on the browser screen and print it off for signature, or if their browser version does not support this, they may print from the browser screen and complete the form by hand. [SS12.2]

(In addition, hard copies of the 'details' were sent to those members without computers.)

In another example, a channel difficulty gave rise to the following e-mail comments:

[2]   This is the third time I have posted this [. . .] Thank you for your patience and understanding. [P39.1]

and

[3]   it would appear that the error is at Geometry. From the headers the mail is directed to BROWN@geometry.uq.ed.au. The address is missing a 'u'. [SS2.1]

and

[4]   Last chance for non computer buffs. the agenda deadline is extended till first thing Thurs. [JM21.1]

The varied and incompatible systems at UQ make this study markedly different from that undertaken by Murray (1991b), which took its data from a very technologically sophisticated workforce, with well-established and stable computational work practices. Her material, therefore, acts as an interesting contrast to that used in the present study. One major difference is revealed in Example [4]. At UQ the introduction of e-mail for committee work at once reduced the individuality of members by classifying them as, e.g., 'non-computer buffs' or 'Mac users' or 'members who have WWW access'. Members are formed into newly differentiated groupings, based entirely on computer use, and these groupings are represented frequently in messages such as [1] to [4] above. In addition, value judgements are made about the groups, expert users are praised and unskilled users are shown their failings. This new labelling for members is bound to have some interpersonal impact on those who receive it, both on their sense of self and on their attitude to those who do the labelling.

The wide range of attitudes to computer-mediated communication at UQ may be typical of those found in medium-sized private and public sector organizations. While managers may see advantages in computer-mediated communications for some of their work, other levels of the workforce may not (Rice and Shook 1990), and this should be taken into account. If, in addition, many different types of staff, from accountants to personnel officers, and staff at different ranks must all manage inter-communications, management may well feel tentative about shifting to new modes of communication since these may not be perceived in the same way from person to person, and may be seen as more or less appropriate across the workforce, and hence fail to achieve the desired efficiencies.

Another significant contextual factor is that, in common with many other workplaces in Australia and round the world, UQ is at present in a transitional state as it adapts to the changes in employment patterns taking place in the nineties. While it is true that, as Sproull and Kiesler (1991: 131) state, all organisations need to establish clear routines for their information procedures 'to ensure efficiency and co-ordination [of information retrieval and exchange]', where organisations are in transition this may prove impossible. The workplace scene at present is dominated by cost-reduction exercises in administration and other areas, through restructuring, downsizing and multiskilling. This is perceived by the members of the UQ community, for example, as a threat to several important aspects of the workplace such as collegial interactivity and individuality of work habits, as well as to democratic participation in any decision-making that affects members' working lives (Fowler 1995). New operating systems and work practices, like those involved in e-mailing, are therefore viewed with suspicion while workers assess their threatening aspects. And this resistance can cause delays in both the adoption of new systems, and adjustments to them, in order to take demands and fears into account. In the data sets, for example, because of the 'democracy' principles held by university staff, there are instances of 'over-communication', where committee document drafts are sent out one at a time, as emendations trickle in from members, rather than preventing readers from having access to them until emendation has been finalised. The result may be less efficiency in the short term as staff have to note carefully new emendations and distinguish them from early ones, and perhaps even in the long term, as these practices then become set conventions in the eyes of staff, and hence cannot easily be discontinued.

Another social situational factor which appears to have influenced the e-mail messages in the present database is that the committees which were being arranged via e-mail have a diverse membership – some are *ex officio*, others are appointed or elected. This is relevant to an analysis of their e-mail discourse in that members vary according to what materials for the meeting they wish to see, and when the material should be communicated to them. For example, elected members could feel that they have an obligation to discuss the agenda items with their constituents before the meeting (and might set up a personal distribution list for giving and receiving information), while the appointed members might want only to see the agenda in time to do some thinking about it before the meeting. Therefore some staff insist on early drafting of agenda papers, while others do not mind late or even tabled papers. Because e-mail has the facilities of easy text-transfer from word-processing to broadcast mail, the secretarial staff can quickly produce papers early, and circulate them without a great deal of extra work, so that the elected members get what they want. However, the other members get more than they want and earlier than they want and complain of communication overload and wastage. Systemically, there is an easy answer to this: secretaries could set up two lists of member types, one for early receipt of papers, and one for later receipt, so that each type of member could be satisfied. But this decision would have personal and democratic implications for members' freedom of choice, which they may find unacceptable, since it would require them to categorise themselves as one type or the other, and to accept that they will only be communicated with according to the type chosen. In other words, making use of the technological potential of the e-mail system could have a limiting effect on members' knowledge of the committee papers. This instance of the mix of systemic ease and personal values of receivers shows the complex effects that can arise from even the simplest possibilities in computer-mediated communication.

At UQ, as in the workplaces used in Ferrara *et al.*'s, Ku's and in Rice and Case's data, although e-mail is used in a number of ways it is always as an ancillary to other genres, as evidenced by the fact that it is rarely if ever used for formal notices of appointment or promotion, policy statements and so on, which are examples of major institutional communications (on this point, see also Nickerson, this volume). In committee meeting preparation, these include printed documents, phone calls, the Web, and face-to-face discussions, while the formal agenda and agenda papers are always finalised into hard copy. Within e-mail itself at UQ, a variety of methods are adopted to circulate the agenda papers; for example, via the Web, e.g. as a Committee Home Page, or as attachments, each with a different pragmatic effect. Which channel is chosen affects receivers differently; for example, informants have indicated that they feel that papers received via the Web are to be treated as virtually fixed in form, and that emendation, even though it may be explicitly requested, is neither wanted nor expected. They contrast this with attachments sent via e-mail to the receiver's word-processor where the request is seen as more genuine because of the ease with which these documents can be emended and returned.

However, it is obvious from the UQ database that as yet many members, because of their own lack of expertise, are unable to emend the agenda papers, regardless of which electronic channel is used. Many instances in the data sets show that meeting organisers go to a lot of trouble to choose a process which would permit committee members to contribute but they do not always succeed, through no fault of their own, as Examples [5] and [6] illustrate:

[5]   Some of you found yesterday's Web-use bulletin to be overly technical and were confused as to how it related to you. I hope that this message will help to clarify matters. [PM1.1]

[6]   In order to remove the current confusion as to who should receive comments – please ring Ann on 12345. [PM18.1]

There are also many examples of advice on handling the process:

[7]   the problem some of you are experiencing when attempting to access APComm via WWW is overcome by (. . .). Good luck!! [PM34.1]

Although participation at this stage of committee work has become available to many, only those with computational expertise can take advantage of it. To offset this situation, the agenda papers are still distributed in both hard and soft copy, letters are sent, and phone calls made to stakeholders and interested parties.

The choice of e-mail as the channel for committee members' emendation and comment affects the document's rhetoric in another intertextual way. Users can easily isolate and extract a single section, or even a line, from the agenda papers, and broadcast it. While, as we have seen, one effect of this is to indicate that the sender is serious about wanting consultation, another and very important effect of such particularisation is to distort the receiver's understanding of the information, in that the co-text, which may be of significance for an interpretation of the information, is omitted.

Since it costs money for an institution or business to take advantage of computer-mediated communication, the financial costs and benefits must be carefully assessed before any decision is made, particularly in the present depressed economic climate. Senior UQ managers hope that the lack of e-mail expertise among staff, and hence the need to operate with several communication systems, is merely a transitional phase, but they acknowledge that it may last for some years yet and prove costly to the organisation. But there is also another type of cost that might prove troubling to management: e-mail allows (though it does not necessarily produce) a shift in power from the previously recognised authority figures within an organisation. For example, because UQ committee members now have access to the draft stages of agenda papers and some of them know how to manage e-mail in order to emend them, they may soon develop conventionalised expectations that their emendations will be accepted. This could result in a new way of viewing the authority of agenda papers, since no longer would they be perceived as imbued with the chair's authority and fixed in form and content, but rather as variable texts, which could be altered if members see fit. So, although a hard-copy printout of the agenda might be thought of as a waste of time and money in a time of computer-mediated communication, it might be worth maintaining because of the high social and authoritative status of the written form relative to the electronic form. In a wholly electronic form its social value and its power might change in ways that have not been thought through. An institution may, of course, be prepared to accept this democratisation as a possible consequence of computer-mediated communication. In another possible shift in power caused by e-mail, committee members might forward agenda papers to any readers they choose, once they discover that this is extremely easy via the e-mail process. This could be done at the committee member's will, and without the chair's knowledge, and on occasion could bring previously restricted information into the open.

From a rhetorical perspective, the broadcasting of committee texts could mean that they are read in close proximity with other texts, as the member desires. E-mail allows texts to be forwarded in combination with a receiver's comments upon them, so they will be read as a 'double' text, one that the committee member has designed for their own purposes, which may differ markedly from those of the committee chair. In this way, the representation of the matters contained in the original text would be altered, and this could have a rhetorical effect on readers, as in Examples [8] and [9]:

[8]   <The University seeks prioritisation of staff flexibility> [comment added] I detect John's fine Machiavellian hand here . . . [JMP7.2]

and

[9]   <it seems appropriate in this economic climate to do . . . > [comment added] typical managerial tactic [JMP15.1]

Anyone receiving these texts would hear two voices in juxtaposition, one a very cynical one, and may find it hard to separate them, with consequences for their interpretation of the original material.

6. THE E-MAIL MESSAGE TEXT AND SYSTEM ELEMENTS

At the intra-textual level of a single e-mail message, if its information is to be efficiently retrieved and used, the document in which it is presented must be clearly labelled, its source indicated, and its place in the stream of related communications made clear; i.e. its *document definition* must be well designed, as too must any action required of the receiver. This must be followed by a competent presentation of subject matter, i.e. its *content representation*. Section 6 deals with issues of precision in document definition, and then, in section 7, an account is given of a selection of e-mail practices of language usage which occur within the main body of the message.

6.1. Document definition

E-mail correspondence is received with document definition automatically set by the electronic system, with only certain details to be supplied by the sender. The system components of the definition therefore dominate this part of the text, and can, paradoxically, give rise to informational problems by being too precise and too detailed, or, as Murray (1995: 72–4) writes, by being random sets of numbers and letters which are hard to identify and recall.

6.1.1. The 'From:' lines

Staff at UQ state that even after several years of e-mail use they still have problems isolating the identity of the sender of the message from the many details of the typical e-mail heading, as in:

[10]   Date: Thu 16 january 1997 17:41:48 + 1000 (GMT + 1000)
       X-Sender: aasmith@dingo.uq.edu.au
       To: jbrown@mailbox.uq.edu.au
       From: asmith@mailbox.uq.edu.au [sic]
       Subject: next meeting SHC
       Sender: owner-shccom-group@mailbox.uq.edu.au

In such a conglomeration of sender information it can be hard to differentiate the relevant from the irrelevant. E-mail is a genre, like its companions, letters and memos, which passes through a number of channel intermediaries before reaching its receivers, but whereas the postal service only franks the envelope of a letter, and the sorting room passes a memo to its intended receiver without any sign that it has done so, the system servers of e-mail leave their mark on each text. It is unclear what kind of rhetorical influence the explicit mention of the channel-processing has on the ways in which the text's contents are read, but it is unlikely that it has no influence at all, since every element of a text has potential to affect the meaning of the whole. The mass of detail given in the example does not, of course, hinder the receiver from replying to sender, since clicking on the 'reply' option should automatically select the sender's address. However UQ staff have noted that it is relatively easy to make mistakes in replying to e-mails; e.g. instead of replying just to the sender, sending the reply to all those listed on the 'To-line' if it contains a distribution list, as committee messages frequently do.

A related manifestation of confusing intertextuality is generated when a sender, whose name and e-mail address occurs on the 'From-line', is acting only as conduit for another sender's message. If the message included requires a reply, the routine of clicking on Reply will automatically send it to the conduit sender, and not the intended one. Wise senders learn to begin the body of their message with a warning line like 'DO NOT SEND REPLY TO ME; SEE MEET-ING ORGANIZER.'

The 'From-line' can cause another type of textual problem, since in a large institution of around 1000 staff, an e-mail receiver may not recognise the sender's name, and hence his or her status, institutional position, and power. This can happen particularly where the sender acts as another's agent. Whereas in the formal letters genre, the notepaper headings and a 'ps' below the writer's signature would quickly indicate this, the e-mail system does not allow for the inclusion of similar information on the 'From-line', where it would be most useful. E-mail messages are most frequently marked as coming from an individual, who is named in the 'From-line', rather than a department or section. So where a boss and a secretary each have access to e-mail they will have separate names, and accounts. Depending on which account is used, and this may vary from day to day with the exigencies of work, that name will appear first in a receiver's In Mail Index, and if the name belongs to an unknown secretary, it may insufficiently contextualise the message such that it is ignored, even before the information is retrieved. When it is retrieved, the absence of this contextual information may affect the perceived authority of the text, its urgency and hence the very nature of the response. Part of the problem is that all e-mails look alike in format and font, and do not always contain information at the start of documents which would inscribe the authoritative source of the message. Though e-mailers can include such information, the system invites them to leave it to the end, to the technologised 'signature' of the text, so that a first reading of the screen-text can occur without this aid to interpretation. To add to the confusion, it is not useful nowadays to assume that a boss's intentions are always being channelled through a secretary; in a time of multiskilling, secretarial staff have taken on a great number of communicational originating roles in their own right.

6.1.2.   The 'Subject' lines and 'In Mail Index'

The words typed as the 'Subject' lines in an e-mail message will also appear in the 'In Mail Index'. This dual occurrence can have important consequences. An example appeared in the present writer's In Mail Index:

[11]   dbrown [time] salary negotiations st [JM47.3 +ph]

It was selected to be read because it sounded relevant to my (academic) salary, but after selecting the (large, 10-page) message it was found to be about general staff and their salaries, and hence of little interest. This problem, like several others, appears to arise because of the generic connection with letters. In printed letters there is no byte limit on a heading to a document, and no compositional pressure to put the most identifying words first. However, in e-mail communications senders need to plan their headings differently, with the In Mail Index in mind; in this case 'general staff salaries' would have saved the reader's time.

Example [11] illustrates another information problem in e-mail usage: there is a need to separate those who need to know from those who do not, so that staff do not receive so many communications that important and relevant ones get lost among the crowd. All e-mail etiquette guides recommend targeting only people who need to know, but in real life this is not always simple to achieve. When I queried the fact that the general staff information had been circulated to me, the sender stated that it was thought to be of value to academics as a parallel to their own salary negotiations (taking place at the same time), the budgeting implications of the general staff salaries would affect departments which contained both academic and general staff, and that 'anyway, academics are always complaining that they are not told what goes on in the University so I told them'.

A second message appeared in my In Mail Index as:

[12]   crobinson [time] information on computer [DP 14.4.97 +ph]

This was ignored until I received a phone call asking when I was going to supply information about my computer configuration. If the index line had read 'comp info please' Robinson would not have wasted his time. There is a specific language aspect to this example worth mentioning. The suggestion that 'comp info please' would be a better Subject line was made by many of the project informants. Some were in favour of the polite passive form as in 'X is needed' or 'Needed: meeting times'. But they all rejected the use of a directly expressed grammatical imperative in a subject line, as in 'Send computer inform' because it was too brusque, and they preferred the politeness marker 'please' to mark the existence of a command. (For a discussion of politeness markers, see Brown and Levinson (1987); section 7.1 in this chapter discusses e-mail politeness in relation to minimalism.)

6.1.3.   Appended messages

Another technological feature of e-mail communication that appeared to give rise to problems in the case-study is the frequent practice of appending the responder's messages to the original one. This being the default form, the users who wish to vary from it must take the trouble to delete any part of the original they think it is unnecessary to include. The result is that few people bother to delete, and so it is possible to receive in a single e-mail message a long string of copied originals and replies in sequence with full document definitions for each. Even a simple string of this kind can be difficult to interpret, because of the number of differently sourced contributions that might occur in it. The basic linearity of the string offers little in the way of 'framing markers' like 'first', 'next', 'most recently' (Goffman 1975; Tannen 1979) to help in the cognitive assessment of each text's relation to the others. The situation is also complicated by the fact that different e-mail servers order the strings differently, either from first to last or from last to first (one instance in the data came in the order last, first, second [SS35 1.2]). The difference in order has a major impact on the rhetorical power of the texts in the string, since, as classical rhetoric has shown, both primary and last position in a textual reading are given particular attention by readers. In e-mails, however, these highlighted positions are not given by the sender intentionally to important matters in a rhetorically designed message; rather they occur as the technology dictates, and in most cases it is quite fortuitous that the string takes the form it does, and emphasises the matters that it represents.

It was also found in the data that senders of strings rarely supplied intertextual commentary to frame the reader's understanding of the texts (but see Examples [8] and [9]). No particular items or texts were highlighted for attention; in most cases there was only an accompanying note, for example: 'These came Mon and Tues – needs attention. Bill' [MP31.1]. The significance of such absences is that a good deal of interpretative skill is asked of the receiver even to sort the 'Mon' and 'Tues' matters into chronological order; it is much easier with a file of dated letters in a manila folder. If the receiver has this skill, then the communication could be an efficient one, but if he or she cannot interpret the message order it could generate further exchanges and may delay dealing with the matter that originally needed attention. However, there is a democratic virtue to such unordered strings, precisely because no authoritative sender has digested and summarised the information in the string of texts for the reader; there is therefore less prior control of that information. Apart from its string ordering, it arrives as raw and unrestricted information, as it were, for individual interpretation. It is less rhetorically managed by the senders, who have simply copied it and sent it out. This clearly contrasts with the texts of a different genre, like agenda papers, committee reports and journalistic comment, where senders put others' messages into their own words, omit matters, and use selective quotation to suit their own purposes.

7.   THE E-MAIL MESSAGE TEXT AND PERSONAL LANGUAGE STYLE

Rice and Case (1983) show that users of computer-mediated communication have individual 'media styles'; i.e. they have individual preferences for letters, phone calls, face-to-face contact and computer communications. This present study takes this individuality a stage further and suggests that just as users have an individual style of language within their letters, phone calls and so on, they also do the same within their e-mails. The individuality of e-mail texts is, of course, enhanced by the lack of training in best practices (in contrast with the training most people receive at school about essays, letters and so forth). However, the present project suggests that there is a set of informal language practices current at UQ which are rapidly becoming conventionalised. One of these is a preference for minimalism, though it may take different, individualised, forms.

Minimalism or brevity in language use (Mulholland 1994: 189–90; Murray 1995: 79–82) is becoming the preferred style for e-mail messages, probably because of the historical foundations of computer-mediated communications, which lie in the efficient and speedy exchange of information. It may also have arisen because of e-mail's generic and (to a degree) physical resemblance to memos, and its difference from letters. Minimalism can either be a disadvantage or an advantage in terms of information exchange, depending on the needs of the receiver. Some minimalism is just omission of some kind, such as of the specifics of subject matter, or qualifications of opinion or act. If this correctly predicts the knowledge of the reader, it 'makes sense', and the fit between the sender's message and the reader's understanding of it means that the omission is hardly noticed as a feature and is unproblematic. However, any omission or brevity which receivers come to recognise, particularly if they can attribute it to an interpersonal cause, will have a rhetorical impact, as is discussed in the following sections.

7.1. Politeness markers

One might assume that minimalism in e-mail messages would take the form of the reduction or absence of politeness markers, the language forms which normally occur as additions to the basic message, and are included in order to protect the interrelationship aspects of the communicative act being performed. Murray (1995: 88) notes that several studies have found an increase in politeness markers, which she attributes to the transactional forms of many computer-mediated communications. The absence of politeness could leave receivers uncertain about the illocutionary force of the request (see Searle 1969) or annoyed at the impoliteness and perhaps the inappropriate assumption of authority. It would nevertheless be likely to make them respond immediately, since a blunt command looks urgent. In the present data, however, it is clear that whatever else is absent, signs of politeness are not, as the following examples show (italics added to indicate the politeness markers):

[13] *It would be appreciated if* I could have your responses by Friday [MP1.1]

[14] you *might* email these to all of us for consideration at the meeting [MP2.1]

[15] Request that you *please* reschedule this date for our weekly meeting [MP3.1]

[16] I want to see this issue progress smoothly and expeditiously. (. . .) I *should be grateful* for your comments on these matters [MP6.1]

[17] 1. SL/L in Geometry (half time) When *do think* we can expect an interview date [MP10.1] (= fix a date)

In Example [17] the subject pronoun is missing, but not the politeness of the phrase 'do [you] think'.

These examples notwithstanding, the most frequent markers of politeness found in the data are placed in final rather than initial or medial position. One consequence is that the polite element can be read as an afterthought rather than an integral part of the message. How significant this reading will be could depend on whether the reader sees e-mail as similar to memos – where the afterthought has become standardised – or as letters where, if politeness is to be understood as 'true' or 'sincere', it should be readable as an inherent part of the communication design, and therefore seen as 'meant' by the sender from the start of the message. Since a reader may take final politeness in differing ways, any sender who wishes to be understood as polite should either make special efforts to integrate signs of politeness throughout the text, or increase the politeness in final position.

What interpersonal effects arise from minimalist politeness may vary, as with all politeness forms, depending on the kind of relationship which exists between sender and receiver, their relative power, and the demands of the speech act that they accompany. Even though the politeness is present and clearly signalled, readers may not know who is intending the politeness – that is, who is committed to having it expressed – and who is demonstrating the relationship that occurs in the text. Is it the person who asked that the e-mail message be sent, or the agent who sent it? One can contrast this uncertainty with the reader's certainty about politeness in the letter genre, because it is understood that the originator usually sees the text before it is sent, and it can be assumed that they either inserted the politeness or at least gave tacit approval to it by signing the letter. Informants in the present project thought it very rare to submit an e-mail in draft form for approval, and if this practice is understood by readers, the politeness is not easily attributable. The reader may find this a serious obstacle to the interpretation of the text. When both politeness and agency (see section 6.1.1 above) are uncertain, this can create doubt and personal distance in the communicational activity which could have implications for future collegiality.

Many workplace communication genres have standardised ways of showing reciprocal politeness, but surprisingly in the e-mail data it was found that degrees and kinds of politeness could vary significantly between an initial message and its reply, so a polite request was met with a blunt answer, and vice versa, whether the answer was a refusal or an acceptance. Although it has been impossible to test whether e-mail differs in this respect from its companion genres, the informants in this project speculated that it does. And if it does, then one reason might be the instability of politeness conventions in the newer genre. The comments of informants also show that while they are conscious of uncertainty in politeness usage, they are not clear whether this is technologically driven or is personally designed. If they think it is the latter they have a negative response to it, but they are aware that they might be misjudging the sender.

Some longer sentence or phrase examples from the range of politeness markers appear to be avoided in e-mail messages, possibly for reasons of brevity. The most frequent politeness marker found in the data is the very brief form 'OK?' as in 'We need the paper by Friday OK?' [JM23.2], and there are many examples of a bare 'please', as in 'where are the supplementary papers, by 15th please' [MP38.1]. In letter form this request might, for instance, have been written as 'where are the supplementary papers, I need them, I really do, and by the 15th' with a repetition, and an explanatory clause sentence. So e-mail appears to be conventionalising only certain politeness forms and avoiding others; what rhetorical significance this will have for interrelationship is as yet unclear, but one could postulate for example, that the avoidance of qualifying hedges like 'sort of', 'perhaps', and 'a bit of' and so on, might lead to an impression of the absoluteness of the text's authority.

One e-mail in the data read:

[18]   Professor Smith is withdrawing the proposal [for new
       courses]. He was sending a letter which you wouldn't
       get till Tuesday. Regards [SS19.1]

The receiver commented that she felt an apology was due to her, and that it might have taken the form of an explanation, since this 'withdrawal' had caused her a good deal of work as she had already typed up the proposal for the agenda papers, and now had to delete it. She noted that an apology was offered, and in explanatory form, but not in this e-mail; rather, it came in the Tuesday letter. This absence of politeness from the message, an extreme form of minimalism, and re-location of politeness to the letter form might suggest that Professor Smith felt that the standard letter form with its well-known conventions was more appropriate to an apology than an e-mail message. When asked about this, he stated that the extra work that it took for him to write, print and send a letter would act to indicate the measure of his regret. Several informants agreed with this view, and felt that to apologise via e-mail was 'too easy' and that if this channel had to be used for some reason, the apology needed to be emphasised with more politeness than it would in letter or memo form to be sure of indicating the sender's intent.

7.2. Reduced subject-matter representations

Because of the generic link with memos, e-mail messages are often produced with their subject matter unadorned, briefly stated, and even in abbreviated vocabulary form. They can also be shortened grammatically; for example, articles like 'a' and 'the', subject pronouns like 'I' and 'we' and the copula 'and' are all often omitted (Ferrara *et al.* 1991: 23), as well, capitalisation is omitted and dashes are substituted for commas and so forth. Grammatical errors abound; for example, in subject–verb agreement, and sequence of tenses (Murray 1995: 80–2). Informants stated that because of their sense that e-mails had to be handled at speed, they rarely reviewed their e-mail style (though they checked significant content words). Whether appropriate or not, the rhetorical effect is to suggest that the subject matter is simple in itself, and that its objects and actions are labelled straightforwardly, with no qualification, in the hope of their recognition and hence their unquestioning acceptance by readers. It also suggests that the style of representation of the subject matter has not been given considered attention but dashed off in a hurry, or that the channel is a more important factor in language choice than the substantive content. And this can be reinforced if e-mail messages include few of the elaborating devices of formal writing; for example, complex noun groups, adverbial clauses or relative clauses (and there were very few in the present data). This too will have a rhetorical impact. The message can thereby appear 'spontaneous', and for some readers this can mean 'sincere' or 'genuine', and they will respond appropriately.

In another example of brevity, which appears to support the perception that there is a lack of planning in e-mail text design, intra-textual references (like 'that', 'this', 'these', 'those') are used in a confusing way, as in:

[19] *This* looks good. [referring to a following, appended text of 14 sentences] [MP17.1]

In Example [19], the complexity of the text referred to, and the fact that the referring word came before the referent (a cataphor, or forward reference) makes the word 'This' difficult to interpret: which element of the following text is being approved, or is all of it approved? If textual references are omitted, and there are many examples in the data of this kind, then the subject matter can appear to be unlinked to its surroundings, as something 'a-contextual' and isolated, and in these cases too its meaning can be affected. There are other textual features of minimalism which have less significance; for example, the preferred (read: the easiest) mode of emphasising a part of the subject matter is by the use of block capitals rather than by word choice and clause arrangement, but this remains an unsubtle and unenriching mode of presentation.

Even experienced e-mail users can be uncertain whether the minimalism of the text they are reading is just brevity in response to the channel's needs, or whether it plays a part in delineating the ideational meaning, or the interactional bluntness, of the text. They might read it as a rhetorical power-play;[5] for example, as a withholding of information so that they are hindered from playing their part in any ensuing communication, or are forced to petition the speaker for fuller information. Staff at UQ know themselves to have rights to information, have strong attitudes about participation in university affairs, and so could find both scenarios unacceptable.

7.3. Absence of metalanguage

Instances of metalanguage – i.e. reflexive references to the act of communication as it is occurring (Mulholland 1994: 309–10) – are rare in the UQ e-mail data. There are only two examples in the database (metalanguage is italicised):

[20] *Can I ask* where are non-starred items from last meeting recorded. [SS10.2]

and

[21] *I need info on course proposals,* can I submit them at next meeting or am I too late. [SS13.1]

The value of metalanguage is that it adds extra information to enable a reader to interpret the acts, of 'asking' (Example [20]), and 'needing information' (Example [21]) immediately, and hence quickly to think of a response. In both examples the metalanguage also acts as a politeness marker, the first by positively implying that the sender needs permission to ask a question, and in the second, as negative politeness, by putting at the start what the reader is required to do. Brown and Levinson call this latter example 'negative' (1987: 17–21), since it makes the minimum imposition on the receiver's reading time.

Example [21] shows another striking feature of the 'add-on' e-mail style (see section 7.1). Here the e-mailer 'adds on' a second way of presenting their difficulty. They first ask in the form 'can I submit them at the next meeting' then add another version 'or am I too late'. This reads like a lack of editing or revision, and is frequent in e-mail. It has an interestingly complex effect, in that it appears to allow the reader to see something of the processes of the sender's mind as they translate an idea into first one set of words and then, without deleting the first, into a second set of words. This apparent revelation of senders actually making choices, preferring a second to a first version, can have many rhetorical effects. As self-disclosure, it can suggest a close relationship, and so its use could offset many of the distancing effects that the systemic document definition aspects of e-mail can produce. It differs in an interesting way from another frequent e-mail minimal language 'add-on' form, the use of the slash '/'. Here, also, two versions of a subject are represented side by side, but the data examples suggest that this double message, marked by '/', is an apposition, where the two versions are to be understood together as a richer or more detailed representation of a single referent rather than as a first choice rejected for a second. The following are examples from the data:

[22]   the next meeting of the Board/10 March meeting will
       consider . . . [SS8.1]

and

[23]   does the department want a kickback/percentage of my
       fee? [JM43.1]

Although this is a casual form which occurs in memos and informal letters and notes, and is probably derived from the frequent use of '\' in computer directory headings, it is interpreted the same way as the more formal apposition. It is one way in which minimalism can actually increase the detail of the text's subject matter.

8. CONCLUSION

While other qualitative studies of committee preparation which include computer-mediated communication exist (e.g. Volkema and Niederman 1996), and other research studies have considered the impact of the computer technology on the compositional processes (e.g. Murray 1991a and 1995), this study is distinct in analysing the combination of influences of workplace procedures and conventions, and the effect of technology on the genre of e-mail, and in demonstrating how these influences affect not only the distribution processes and language of e-mail activities, but beyond that, how they can impact on the whole workplace situation and set up possibilities for change in the nature of the institution in which they occur.

This study has attempted to describe and account for e-mail as a distinct genre in the evolutionary stage it has reached in one particular institution, and in one set of communications, those which manage the preparation of committee agendas. Using both examples of e-mail texts and perceptions about texts and processes held by their senders and receivers, the project has focused on issues of (1) efficiency and (2) interpersonal relations in e-mail practice. With regard to efficiency, something has been shown of the consequences of the variation in computational expertise between senders and receivers, and within the group of receivers. One consequence has been inefficient over-communication, but the project informants state that some of the systemic possibilities for preventing this could have adverse interpersonal effects among the committee members. The implication of this, and other matters in this study, is that any change in process will have both content and interpersonal results, and these need to be taken into account in the development of e-mail usage. For example, a change of process intended to improve efficiency by matching distribution lists to members' expertise would have the effect of creating a division among the membership, which is already very diverse. Also on efficiency, the study found that the technical aspects of e-mail usage caused the most dominant problems at the intertextual level, in the ways in which combinations of texts are circulated. E-mails present members with, for example, an opportunity to pass on easily the e-mailed texts to non-committee members, with consequences for loss of authority to the chair and perhaps the committees.

In the account of the interpersonal aspects of e-mail the study has demonstrated that, in spite of the influence of minimalism and haste that are usually associated with e-mail processes, some inter-personal elements are retained in the texts. But the study also notes that only a few of the wide range of politeness markers are judged appropriate to e-mail usage, and that these are the most brief of the possibilities, thus suggesting that politeness is only a minor matter. Also, politeness is most frequently found at the end of texts, rather than being incorporated throughout the text (as they might be in letters and other printed documents). This apparently late inclusion of the interpersonal makes them appear to be of lesser importance to the sender, and this too will have an effect on the reader.

In short, both the computational processes of this particular genre and the lack of technical skill in its readers have a social and inter-personal effect which may prove detrimental to the qualities of individuality and collegiality which the UQ staff currently hold dear. If they can take advantage of its opportunities for democracy the future will go one way, but if the management learns how the genre allows workforce manipulation at least within the committee structure of the university, then the future will go another way. The data suggest that either is still possible.

NOTES

1. She notes, for example, that the very severe temporal and spatial con-straints in the context of Emessage practices result in generically distinct cognitive processes in writing style and compositional design.
2. This appears to rise exponentially each year; a recent survey of Aus-tralian usage by the Bureau of Statistics gave the 1996 figures for com-puters as some 2.5 million (excluding games machines) in domestic settings and an additional 1.1 million in business use (Richardson 1997).
3. Rice and Case show that there was staff resistance to the use of elec-tronic communication, but that it varied with the personality of the staff member. Individual staff had a sense of what communicative tasks could be performed via computer and which tasks were inappropri-ately handled in that way. Among the tasks for which they preferred not to use e-mails were decision-making, resolving disagreements, get-ting to know someone and negotiating.
4. Many thanks are due to those members who kindly provided copies and gave permission for their use in this chapter. All names quoted from the database have been changed to preserve confidentiality.
5. See: Ng and Bradac (1993) and *Language and Social Psychology* (1995) 14:5, special issue on Power and Language.

REFERENCES

Ackermann, Ernest (1995) *Learning to Use the Internet*. Wilsonville, OR: Franklin, Beedle.

Bakhtin, Mikhail (1986) The problem of speech genres. In M. Bakhtin, *The Problem of Speech Genres and Other Late Essays*. Austin: University of Texas Press, pp. 60–102.

Brown, Penelope and Levinson, Stephen (1987) *Politeness: Some Universals in Language Use*. Cambridge: Cambridge University Press.

Collot, Milena and Belmore, Nancy (1993) Electronic language: a new variety of English. In Jan Aarts, Pieter de Haan and Nelleke Oostdijk (eds), *English Language Corpora: Design, Analysis and Exploitation*. Amsterdam and Atlanta, GA: Rodolphi, pp. 41–56.

Erickson, Thomas (1996) Social interaction on the net: virtual community as participatory genre. In Robert Sprague (ed.), *Proceedings of the Thirtieth Annual Hawaii International Conference on System Sciences*, vol. 1, Maui, HI: IEEE, pp. 13–21.

Ferrara, Kathleen, Brunner, Hans and Whittemore, Greg (1991) Interactive written discourse as an emergent register. *Written Communication* 8 (1): 8–34.

Fowler, Robert (1995) Community: reflections on definition. In Amitai Etzioni (ed.), *New Communitarian Thinking: Persons, Virtues, Institutions, and Communities*. Charlottesville, VA: University Press of Virginia, pp. 21–35.

Goffman, Erving (1975) *Frame Analysis*. Harmondsworth: Peregrine.

Goffman, Erving (1981) *Forms of Talk*. Oxford: Blackwell.

Herring, Susan (ed.) (1996a) *Computer-mediated Communication: Linguistic, Social and Cross-cultural Perspectives*. Pragmatics and Beyond, New Series 39. Amsterdam/Philadelphia: John Benjamins.

Herring, Susan (1996b) Two variants of an electronic message schema. In Susan Herring (ed.), *Computer-mediated Communication: Linguistic, Social and Cross-cultural Perspectives*. Amsterdam/Philadelphia: John Benjamins, pp. 81–108.

Korenman, Joan and Wyatt, Nancy (1996) Group dynamics in an e-mail forum. In Susan Herring (ed.), *Computer-mediated Communication: Linguistic, Social and Cross-cultural Perspectives*. Amsterdam/Philadelphia: John Benjamins, pp. 225–42.

Ku, Linlin (1996) Social and nonsocial uses of electronic messaging systems in organizations. *The Journal of Business Communication* 33 (3): 297–325.

Lamb, Linda and Peek, Jerry (1995) *What You Need to Know: Using E-mail Effectively*. Sebastopol, CA: O'Reilly & Assocs.

Language and Social Psychology (1995) 14 (5). Special issue on Power in Language.

Leblanc, Dee-Ann and Leblanc, Robert (1995) *Using Eudora: The User-friendly Reference*. Indianapolis, IN: Que Corporation.

Miller, Carolyn (1994) Genre as social action. *Quarterly Journal of Speech* 70: 151–67. Reprinted in Aviva Freedman and Peter Medway (eds), *Genre and the New Rhetoric.* London: Taylor & Francis, pp. 23–42.

Mulholland, Joan (1992) Interpreting events: features of comment journalism, 1640–1710. *Journal of Newspaper and Periodical History* 8 (1): 19–26.

Mulholland, Joan (1994) *Handbook of Persuasive Tactics.* London: Routledge.

Murray, Denise (1991a) The composing process for computer conversation. *Written Communication* 8 (1): 35–55.

Murray, Denise (1991b) *Conversation for Action: The Computer Terminal as Medium of Communication.* Pragmatics and Beyond, New Series 10. Amsterdam and Philadelphia: John Benjamins.

Murray, Denise (1995) *Knowledge Machines: Language and Information in a Technological Society.* London: Longman.

Ng, Sik Hung and Bradac, James (1993) *Power in Language.* Newbury Park, CA: Sage.

Rice, Ronald and Case, Donald (1983) Electronic message systems in the university: a description of use and utility. *Journal of Communication* 33: 131–52.

Rice, Ronald and Shook, David (1990) Relationships of job categories and organizational levels to use of communication channels, including electronic mail: a meta-analysis and extension. *Journal of Management Studies* 27 (2): 195–229.

Richardson, Nancy (1997) Logged into IT. *The Bulletin* (June 10): 46.

Sacks, Harvey (1992) *Lectures on Conversation,* vols. I and II. Ed. Gail Jefferson. Oxford: Blackwell.

Searle, John (1969) *Speech Acts.* Cambridge: Cambridge University Press.

Sproull, Lee and Kiesler, Sara (1986) Reducing social context cues: electronic mail in organizational communication. *Management Science* 32: 1492–512.

Sproull, Lee and Kiesler, Sara (1991) *Connections: New Ways of Working in the Networked Organization.* Cambridge, MA: MIT Press.

Tannen, Deborah (1979) What's in a frame? Surface evidence for underlying expectations. In Roy Freedle (ed.), *New Directions in Discourse Processing II: Advances in Discourse Processes.* Norwood, NJ: Ablex, pp. 137–81.

Volkema, Robert and Niederman, Franz (1996) Planning and managing organizational meetings. *Journal of Business Communication* 33 (3): 275–96.

Walther, Joseph, Anderson, Jeffrey and Park, David (1994) Interpersonal effects in computer-mediated interaction: a meta-analysis of social and antisocial communication. *Communication Research* 21 (4): 460–87.

Yates, Joanne and Orlikowski, Wanda (1992) Genres of organizational communication: a structurational approach to studying communication and media. *Academy of Management Review* 17 (2): 299–326.

Ziv, Oren (1996) Writing to work: how using e-mail can reflect technological and organizational change. In Susan Herring (ed.), *Computer-mediated Communication: Linguistic, Social and Cross-cultural Perspectives.* Amsterdam/Philadelphia: John Benjamins, pp. 243–64.

FOUR

The mass production of unique letters

David Sless

I know that some people feel that marriage as an institution is dying out, but I disagree. And the point was driven home to me rather forcefully not long ago by a letter I received which said:

'Darling, I love you and I cannot live without you. Marry me or I will kill myself!'

Well, I was a little disturbed by this, until I took another look at the envelope and saw that it was addressed to 'Occupant'.

1. INTRODUCTION

As Tom Lehrer's acerbic observation suggests, mass-produced letters sit uneasily at the intersection of public and private domains. One might even regard the term 'letters' as an inappropriate description of this type of printed, yet individualised, communication. This chapter is about these misfitting missives; it is about the types of 'letters' that have emerged out of a research programme undertaken on behalf of large Australian organisations to help them improve their letters, notices and bills for citizens, customers and clients.

2. MASS-PRODUCED LETTERS IN A CONSUMER MARKET

There is nothing new about mass-produced letters and notices. Even before the invention of the printing press, scribes faithfully copied existing letters to deal with routine correspondence. With the advent of printing in Europe in the fifteenth century, the mass production of all types of written material burgeoned. Probably one of the first such 'letters' were Indulgences. They were printed by the Church in large numbers, signed by Church leaders, and sold on the promise of absolution for sins. In this early stage of mass-produced letters, one can clearly discern the uneasy and unequal relationship between, on the one hand, the institution and its false personalisation, and, on the other hand, the individual person regarding the communication as truly personal; an uneasy and unequal relationship that persists to this day.

The development of postal systems and the invention of the typewriter enabled institutions to use this false personalisation in a new, more customised way. Mechanised and industrialised copy typing made possible the large-scale production of individualised letters, written according to pre-constructed formulas. Even though each letter was individually typed, typists were taught to use standardised typewriter layout conventions, and the words, phrases, sentences, paragraphs and, in some cases whole letters, were reproduced from established formulas. Thus, even during a period when letters were individually produced, the discourse that prevailed was highly conventionalised and controlled within the institutions.

More recently, with the introduction of corporate computerised databases, the advent of high-speed line printers, and then the invention of high-speed laser printing, there has been a radical transformation in the way that letters can be produced. Three major changes can be discerned. Firstly, the army of typists in the typing pools, who individually wrote letters, have disappeared. Thus any possibility of personalisation by individuals, small though it was, has also disappeared. Secondly, the computerisation of individual records, and the capacity to store and merge both fixed and variable data electronically, have transformed institutions' capacity to automate business-letter writing. Thirdly, laser printing technology has opened up many more typographical and layout possibilities, extending the range of conventions that can be used in the construction of text.

Thus at the very time when business has become more anonymous, paradoxically it also has a much greater capacity than at any time in the past to customise and personalise communication with individuals. Parallel with the recent technological changes, there have been political and economic shifts that have led to an increasingly powerful consumer lobby. Organised consumer interest groups have had a major impact on business regulation and practice. Issues of comprehensibility, openness, and fairness for consumers have been brought to the fore through consumer protection legislation and regulation; businesses dependent on consumer markets have responded to the rising tide of consumerism by adopting 'customer-focused' policies and practices.

3. AN OPPORTUNITY FOR RESEARCH

Taken together, the technological and political changes have created a climate in which it has been possible to undertake research to rethink and redevelop ideas about business letters, their content, construction and design.

The Communication Research Institute of Australia, established in 1987, with a broad agenda to help industry and government improve communication practices through research, was invited by a number of large corporate bodies in Australia to investigate and suggest ways of improving letters, notices and bills (Sless 1992a). The corporate bodies included government departments, utilities and financial service organisations. While each body was largely concerned with its own communication problems, the Institute was able, through a series of case-studies, to develop an overall approach to these types of problem (Sless 1996). This chapter reports for the first time on the linguistic and typographic features that have emerged from this ongoing research programme.

4. ASSUMPTIONS AND METHODOLOGY

The Institute's research programme on letters is broadly within the applied interdisciplinary context of information design (Sless 1992b). It thus draws on the crafts of writing and typographic design, on the procedures of usability engineering (Nielsen 1993) and design methods (Jones 1980), and in particular on participative design methodologies (e.g. Schuler and Namioka 1993).

The theoretical underpinnings of the Institute's research programme are constructionist (Pearce 1995). Constructionism is concerned with how we mutually construct our social realities through conversation. This paradigm has its intellectual origins in the social philosophy of George Herbert Mead (1934), the aesthetic theory of John Dewey (1934), the moral philosophy of Martin Buber (1961), the linguistic and literary criticism of Bakhtin (Holquist 1981), and the language philosophy of the later Wittgenstein (1958). Contemporary theorists within this broad church include social psychologists such as John Shotter (1993) and Rom Harré (Harré and Gillett 1994), communication researchers such as Kenneth Gergen (1994) and W. Barnett Pearce (Pearce and Cronin 1980), and some designers. Recent interviews with Edwin Schlossberg and John Seely Brown in Mitchell's (1997) book *New Thinking in Design* seem to be converging on a constructionist view of design similar to our own, though the interviews are too brief to provide a full view of their methodology (Mitchell 1997).

The central theoretical assumption of this paradigm, as it has been applied in this study, is that the basic unit of analysis in any communicative activity is the conversation. Thus, in contrast to functional or structural linguistics, which treat text or discourse as legitimate units of analysis in their own right (Halliday and Hasan 1985; Saussure 1916), the research reported here takes the relationship between text and user as irreducible. At the risk of over-simplifying, one can say that while traditional linguistics studies *text*, the methodology used here studies the *texts as they are used*. Thus, instead of using formal linguistic categories to study examples of text, the focus here is on people using text. This leads the research to turn inside out the familiar linguistic domains of semantics, syntactics and pragmatics: meanings are not immanent within texts either semantically or syntactically; rather they arise pragmatically, they are emergent properties of text usage. Semantic and syntactic features of language are treated as constructions, abstractions arising out of particular contexts of human action.

It is important to note that this work is not concerned with creating universal principles or generalisations about human behaviour. The detailed observation of human action is concerned with understanding the highly contextualised social interaction between people and documents. At most, it is possible to claim that this work leads to the creation and articulation of conventions; i.e. mutable rules of social conduct, not immutable laws of human behaviour. No attempt has been made in this research to hypothesise underlying linguistic or cognitive processes. The research focuses on the actions of readers, and the textual features that enable or disable action. The observation of text usage is the primary data used in this type of research.

It is also important to note that the research reported here is interventionist: it is concerned with bringing about desirable change. From a constructionist point of view, all research activities are interventionist; they, no less than the conversations they study, are generative activities giving rise to new possibilities which emerge out of the interaction between researcher and researched. As an aspect of information design, the research reported on here is by definition interventionist and constructive (Sless 1997). Moreover, from the point of view of the organisations commissioning the research, the objective has all along been interventionist, designed to improve an aspect of their communication. Out of this research emerged principles for the construction of standard letters, of which the letter in the Appendix is an example. This chapter argues that this has led to the creation of a hybrid set of conventions which may constitute an emergent new genre of business letters which are, at once, unique and mass-produced.

5.   SOME LIMITATIONS OF THE NEW GENRE

This chapter discusses the manifest output from the research programme undertaken by the Institute: a typical example of a unique letter that is produced for an individual customer by the combination of database and highspeed laser printing technology.

The full research programme on standard business letters encompassed a multitude of organisational and technical issues to do with programming, writing, designing and implementing standard letter systems. The evidence from the successful implementation of such systems suggests that well over 50 per cent of the effort in a project can be dedicated to organisational and technical issues (Fisher and Sless 1990). It would therefore be misleading to suggest that the material presented in this chapter constitutes in itself the 'solution' to the standard letters problem. It is only one manifestation, the output of an intricate and complex process.

6. DATA PRESENTATION

The letter shown in the Appendix has been modified to ensure confidentiality of both the company and the individual, but in all other respects it is the output from an actual system. The letter is the end result of a complex methodology involving many rounds of diagnostic testing and refinement with customers to ensure that all variants of letters in the system are comprehensible and acceptable in tone to the company's customers, as well as adhering to the company's business rules and system constraints (Sless, 1998). Diagnostic testing, as the name implies, is concerned with identifying faults in the document that lead to inappropriate readings by users. Each round of diagnostic testing – usually involving between ten and twenty participants – is followed by refinement or changes to the design to remove any faults and enhance the design so that it performs optimally with users. The testing and refinement cycle is repeated until the letter is performing optimally. As with the letter, the exact results from the testing are confidential to the company. However, the principles applied and the results as manifest in the letter do not involve any breach of commercial confidentiality.

This letter replaced a traditional letter and accompanying forms. The letter it replaced, though produced on a high-speed laser printer, followed the normal typewriter conventions for letter design, using a single, non-proportional font and multiple pages. The new letter uses the same customer data and business rules as the original. However, this letter differs in three ways from its predecessors: in its production, performance and content.

Firstly, no single person actually wrote this letter. It was produced by 'assembling' a variety of prefabricated components according to a set of algorithms. Indeed, if a letter in this system needs to be modified in production, then it is the algorithms and components that are changed, not the letter itself. Secondly, the letter's performance – the extent to which it is accessible and usable by customers – is not only better than its predecessor, its usability is largely known ahead of its implementation. Typically, a letter of this type results in far fewer transaction errors or queries than the traditional business letter. Thirdly, as this chapter discusses, this letter does not look like a conventional business letter, nor does it follow the normal conventions of business-letter writing.

7.   CHARACTERISTICS DEFINING THE CONVENTIONS USED IN MASS-PRODUCED LETTERS

7.1.   Three structures in one

The most noticeable initial characteristic of this letter is its division into three zones, made visually distinct by the background preprint stationery and the arrangement of elements on the page: the top left is the nearest to a traditional letter, the top right is a summary of the customer's policy information, and the bottom section is a payment slip. Each zone is designed to be used differently by readers: the letters zone is to be read, the right-hand column is to be used for reference only, and the bottom slip is to be completed for payment. These correspond to the three main groups of tasks that readers need to perform in their dealings with the insurance company involved.

These structures were, like all aspects of the letter, derived by a combination of design decisions and subsequent refinement about the structure and content of the letter, as a result of diagnostic testing of the letters with users. This mixed-genre letter, reference list and payment slip is a good example of what can be achieved with contemporary technology. The fact that the genre makes sense to users is indicative of a widespread ability to deal with such mixed genres on a single document.

7.2.   Typography

The second characteristic is that the document uses a range of fonts and spacing to guide the reader, unlike traditional business letters which follow the conventions of typewritten text, using a single mono-spaced font for all text. In traditional business letters, the burden of providing readers with visual queues to the structure and content of the text depended almost entirely on the vertical spacing of elements: addressee, date, reference, salutation, paragraph breaks, closing salutation, signature space and name of sender. White space, in the form of blank lines, differentiated between different parts of the letter.

Contemporary high-speed laser printers give an extensive choice of fonts and spacing that did not exist in a typewriter, giving a much wider range of visual queues for guiding readers. However, it is important to realise that this enhanced choice falls short of the choices available in today's word-processing software, and a long way short of what is possible using high-end desk-top publishing software. This means that the range of ways in which typography and spacing can be used is restricted, even though it is a significant enhancement on the typewriter. In the example shown, the software used to create the letters imposed a number of limitations. These included: the number of fonts that could be used, the font family they could be chosen from, the interline spacing within each zone, and the letter spacings both between and within words.

7.3. Unity of form and function

Most linguistic analyses of text ignore typographic considerations. Moreover, texts on business writing tend to give typographic issues a low priority, and mention it only briefly (e.g. Murphy 1989; Petelin and Durham 1992; Putnis and Petelin 1996). However, as Waller persuasively argues, typographic features are an integral part of the way in which we construct meaning out of text (Waller 1987).

In the letter shown in the Appendix, the typographical variety available through the new technology is used as an integral part of the letter; there is a direct correspondence between form and function; the appearance and position of the text matches the function of the text for the reader. As part of the research and development of these letters, the Communication Research Institute created and tested a set of rules governing the functions of the text from the users' point of view and the use of the typographical and spatial specifications to match those functions. Particular functional features of the text always appear in the same font and in the same positions relative to other elements, and the whole document follows a consistent typographic hierarchy.

The illustration in the Appendix clearly shows how function and form come together in a strict hierarchy. Within the letter zone, there are always topic headings followed by statements or instructions, which are sometimes followed by an explanation or elaboration. Each of these three functional elements – topic headings, instructions and explanations – have their own distinctive typographical manifestation; section headings are in bold and preceded by a space, the instructions or statements are in roman, and the explanations or elaborations are in italics.

The diagnostic testing used in this project showed, as in many others, that a consistently applied set of rules that are visually distinct to readers help those readers use the documents appropriately (Mackenzie 1992).

7.4. Temporal sequencing

The letter follows the temporal order of events from the reader's point of view, with the headings making this temporal order visibly part of the structure by using the following section headings:

- What has happened
- What we would like you to do
- What will happen if you do not do this

This type of temporal structuring is a routine part of such letter systems and is also used in other types of documents (Penman 1993). Its use is derived from widely used narrative structures in which the telling of a story follows the temporal sequence of events. Thus, it is a widely understood cultural convention. It has also been found to be highly effective in other types of documents. For example, in consumer medicines information, a similar structure has been used to great effect, taking consumers through the sequence of actions which begin with 'before you take the medicine' and ending with 'how to store and dispose of the medicine' (Sless and Wiseman 1997).

From the user's point of view, such a structure has two functions: firstly, it provides a coherent way of understanding the document as a continuous, interconnected series of actions; secondly, it provides a highly usable reference structure, so that the reader can easily find the particular section they are interested in, at any time in the future. For example, it would not be unusual for a customer to read the letter when it arrives and put it to one side to deal with later. When the customer returns to the letter at a later date, their primary question is: 'What do I have to do and when?' At that moment their reading is quite different from their first reading. They are more likely to scan the letter, looking specifically for the answer to their question, rather than reading the whole letter, starting from the beginning. The letter is structured to help them also with this second type of reading activity.

7.5. Absence of false personalisation

One of the most enduring features of the business letter, enduring long after the demise of personalised correspondence, is the use of the opening salutation, 'Dear X', and the closing salutation, 'Yours faithfully, etc.'

In discussions with many businesses and government agencies, it is clear that many managers feel extremely uneasy about abandoning this formal convention. The reasons are complex: resistance to change; concern over losing the 'authority' of authorship either personally or legally; and a concern that customers will not read the letter because it does not have the appropriate letter conventions.

There are, however, a number of practical considerations that make the retention of the convention difficult. The person 'signing' the letter is not necessarily the person who will deal with the customer if they ring up or write, particularly with contemporary business call centres. In an attempt to maintain a level of personalisation, some organisations do direct customers to specific individuals who know about their 'case'. Unfortunately, because of the rapid turnover of call centre staff, this too becomes impractical. Further, even in situations where it is practical to give customers a specific person to contact, adding a facsimile of their signature to the electronic laser printing system increases the memory requirements of the system, which can slow down the mass production of the letters.

In the event, the testing of these letters with customers revealed no problems with the absence of these formalities. Indeed, most customers did not even notice the abandoned convention and did not see anything odd about it when it was drawn to their attention. Whether this would be the case in cultures outside Australia is not clear, but the fact that these letters work effectively within their own context and milieu suggests that, at least in Australia, we have seen the emergence of a new genre, a new set of workable conventions for business letters.

8. CONCLUSION

The emergence of a new genre in business-letter writing is the result of a combination of changes in technological, social and methodological factors. In the future we may expect to see this genre evolve as these factors themselves change. Indeed, the work reported here has already evolved, from the large-scale production environment of a mainframe computer and high-speed printers accessible only to large organisations, into the more modest and generally accessible desk-top system that can be used by medium to small organisations.

While there is some reason for celebration in the development of a genre that makes the mass-produced business letter easily accessible to customers, there are also good reasons for expressing caution about this development. There is evidence from studies in plain English that customers can be lulled into a false sense of confidence about their capacity to understand a business document because it is in a 'plain English' style (Sless 1996). It is only repeated testing and retesting, applying the most rigorous standards of good conduct, that ensures the letters are intelligible rather than just seeming to be so.

Even though this genre eliminates the false personal relationship of earlier letters, it does not alter the basic uneasy power relationship between large corporate bodies and individuals – a relationship that is always open to abuse. It would take more than a letter to change that relationship.

APPENDIX

See overleaf.

The Safe Insurance Company Australia Limited ACN 123 456 789
Private Bag 21 West Melbourne Vic 3200

Cancellation warning

Your Life Insurance Policy

25 April 1995

Mr Joy
Citizens Road
HAPPY TOWN NSW 1234

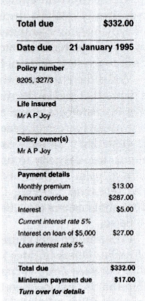

Total due	$332.00
Date due	**21 January 1995**

Policy number
8205, 327/3

Life insured
Mr A P Joy

Policy owner(s)
Mr A P Joy

Payment details

Monthly premium	$13.00
Amount overdue	$287.00
Interest	$5.00
Current interest rate 5%	
Interest on loan of $5,000	$27.00
Loan interest rate 5%	

Total due	**$332.00**
Minimum payment due	**$17.00**
Turn over for details	

Your overdue premium and loan interest
Unfortunately, we have not received your premium and loan interest payment which were due on 21 January 1995.
See the next page for loan information.

What we would like you to do
Please pay $332.00 before 14 May 1995.
See the payment slip for how to pay.
If you have paid in the past few days, please ignore this notice.

What will happen if you do not do this
If we do not receive any further premiums by 14 May 1995, we regret your policy will be cancelled and all entitlements discontinued.

The Safe Insurance Company Australia Limited ACN 123 456 789
Private Bag 21 West Melbourne Vic 3200

Payment slip

- You may pay by cheque, money order, credit card or at your post office.
- Please make cheques and money orders payable to Safe Insurance, or complete credit card details on this payment slip.
- If you are paying by mail, please return this payment slip with your payment, in the envelope enclosed.

Total due	$332.00
Minimum payment due	$17.00

Date due	14 May 1995

000000021 00026643 00000000 00025190 00000847391840 1301001331

Paying by credit card
Please deduct the amount from my:
❏ Visa ❏ Mastercard ❏ Bankcard

card number

expiry date
/

cardholder's signature

REFERENCES

Buber, Martin (1961) Dialogue. In *Between Man and Man*, Ronald Gregor Smith, trans. (first published in 1929 as *Zwiesprache*). London: Fontana Library edition, pp. 17–59.

Dewey, John (1934) *Art as Experience*. New York: Milton, Balch.

Fisher, Phil and Sless, David (1990) Information design methods and productivity in the insurance industry. *Information Design Journal* 6 (2): 103–29.

Gergen, Kenneth J. (1994) *Realities and Relationships: Soundings in Social Construction*. Cambridge, MA: Harvard University Press.

Halliday, M. A. K. and Hasan, Ruqaiya (1985) *Language, Context, and Text: Aspects of Language in a Social-Semiotic Perspective*. Victoria, Australia: Deakin University Press.

Harré, Rom and Gillett, Grant (1994) *The Discursive Mind*. Thousand Oaks, CA: Sage.

Holquist, Michael (ed.) (1981) *The Dialogic Imagination: Four Essays by M. M. Bakhtin*, Caryl Emerson and Michael Holquist, trans. Austin, TX: Austin University Press.

Jones, Christopher J. (1980) *Design Methods: Seeds of Human Futures*. London: Wiley.

Mackenzie, Maureen (1992) New Standards for ABS publications; a case study. In Documents in Context. *Australian Journal of Communication* 19 (3): 43–70.

Mead, George H. (1934) Mind, self and society. In Anselm Strauss (ed.) (1964), *George Herbert Mead on Social Psychology: Selected Papers*. Chicago: University Press, pp. 115–282.

Mitchell, Thomas (1997) *New Thinking in Design: Conversations on Theory and Practice*. New York: John Wiley & Sons.

Murphy, Elizabeth M. (1989) *Effective Writing: Plain English at Work*. Melbourne: Pitman Publishing.

Nielsen, Jakob (1993) *Usability Engineering*. Cambridge, MA: AP Professional.

Pearce, William. B. (1995) A sailing guide for social constructionists. In Wendy Leeds-Hurwitz (ed.), *Social Approaches to Communication*. New York: Guilford Press, pp. 88–113.

Pearce, William B. and Cronin, Vernon E. (1980) *Communication, Action, and Meaning: The Creation of Social Realities*. New York: Praeger.

Penman, Robyn (1993) Conversation is the common theme: understanding talk and text. *Australian Journal of Communication* 20 (3): 30–43.

Petelin, Roslyn and Durham, Marsha (1992) *The Professional Writing Guide: Writing Well and Knowing Why*. Melbourne: Longman Professional.

Putnis, Peter and Petelin, Roslyn (1996) *Professional Communication: Principles and Applications*. Sydney: Prentice-Hall.

Saussure, Frédéric de (1916) *Course in General Linguistics*. Edited by Charles Bally and Albert Sechehaye (1966). Translated from the French by Wade Baskin. New York: McGraw-Hill.

Schuler, D. and Namioka, A. (eds) (1993) *Participatory Design: Principles and Practices*. London: Laurence Erlbaum.

Shotter, John (1993) *Cultural Politics of Everyday Life: Social Constructionism, Rhetoric and Knowing of the Third Kind*. Buckingham: Open University Press.

Sless, David (1992a) Designing documents that work. *Xploration* III (1): 14–16.

Sless, David (1992b) What is information design? In D. Sless and R. Penman (eds), *Designing Information for People*. Canberra: Communication Research Press, pp. 1–16.

Sless, David (1996) Better information presentation: satisfying consumers? *Visible Language* 30 (3): 246–67.

Sless, David (1997) Theory for practice. *Communication News* 10 (4): 1–5.

Sless, David (1998) Building the bridge across the years and disciplines. *Information Design Journal* 9 (1): 3–10.

Sless, David and Wiseman, Rob (1997) *Writing about Medicines for People: Usability Guidelines and Glossary for Consumer Product Information*. Canberra: Australian Government Publishing Service.

Waller, Robert (1987) 'The Typographic Contribution to Language.' Unpublished PhD thesis, Reading University: Department of Typography and Graphic Communication.

Wittgenstein, Ludwig (1958) *Philosophical Investigations*. Translated from the German by G. E. M. Anscombe, 2nd edition (revised). Oxford: Blackwell.

PART II:

IDENTITIES, DISCOURSE COMMUNITIES AND RHETORICAL STYLES

Discourse community, culture and interaction: on writing by consulting engineers

Karl-Heinz Pogner

1. INTRODUCTION

The origins and establishment of 'composition studies' as an area of research are inseparably linked to the cognitive approach which interprets writing mainly as a rhetorical problem-solving process and deals with individual writing processes (Nystrand *et al.* 1993). In research into 'nonacademic writing' (Odell and Goswami 1985; Spilka 1993; Duin and Hansen 1996), the cognitive paradigm has been complemented by a social perspective (Thralls and Blyler 1993; Van Gemert and Woudstra 1996). This social approach is premised on the fact that language is never independent of the social context and therefore it concentrates on the process 'whereby language learning and thinking capacities are shaped and used in particular communities' (Bizzell 1982: 215).

This chapter takes a social approach in analysing the written communication by consulting engineers. It focuses on the elaboration of an Energy Concept document written by a group of Danish engineers for the town of Wendenburg[1] in the eastern part of Germany. By concentrating on the original text and further revised versions of the introduction to this document, the chapter examines how the German reader (= client) commented upon the drafts of the Danish writer (= consulting engineer) and how the writer in turn reacted to these comments. The study is based on the assumption that writing is a form of social interaction (Nystrand 1986) which, in the case of the Energy Concept document, is partly carried out as a negotiation activity.

In the course of text production, contrasting expectations and interpretations of the function and the audience of the Energy Concept emerged, despite the fact that the writer/consultant and the reader/client followed the same conventions as members of the engineering discourse community. Although the reasons for these discrepancies could be explained by national culture, professional sub-culture or corporate culture, in accordance with the social-interactive approach, they will be identified and analysed primarily with reference to the narrower interactional context.

The following sections introduce a central concept of the social perspective on writing, that of the discourse community (section 2) and discuss it with reference to the field of engineering (section 3). This is followed by the contextualisation of the Energy Concept document (section 4) and the reconstruction of the genesis of its Introductory Section (section 5). Using this reconstruction, the chapter discusses the question as to what role discourse community, culture and social interaction play in the context of technical writing in a foreign language (sections 6 and 7).

2.   ON THE CONCEPT OF 'DISCOURSE COMMUNITY'

The concept of 'discourse community' (e.g. Swales 1990, Olsen 1993) is based on the mutual dependence of language use and membership within a group. Bizzell, for instance, comments:

> *Discourse* emphasizes that the group shares more than a particular native tongue or symbol manipulating skill. It connotes a complex set of conventions for assembling lengthy stretches of written or oral text, conventions shaped by cultural as well as current circumstances. *Community* emphasizes that the people feel connected by virtue of their shared discourse and work that the discourse enables them to do.
>
> (Bizzell 1994: 395)

In order to be noticed and accepted as (new) members of a discourse community, writers must write their texts in the same way as other members of the community do, but, in order to be able to do so, they must adopt the cognitive patterns of the community members. This creates an ambiguity that 'echoes the paradoxical situation of discourse community membership in which one must talk [or write] like an insider in order to belong but must more or less belong in order to have learned appropriate language use' (Winsor 1996: 96). Ethnographic case-studies show that enculturation, or socialisation, in professional discourse communities often takes place as a process full of tension in which novices repeatedly mediate between their individual view and the norms of writing and thinking considered 'normal' by the discourse community (Berkenkotter *et al.* 1989; MacKinnon 1993; and Winsor 1996). This process unfolds in everyday interaction with experienced members of the discourse community such as supervisors and other colleagues in the workplace, and with typical texts written by them.

3. THE ENGINEERING DISCOURSE COMMUNITY

The work of the discourse community of engineers mainly serves to produce technical knowledge. As Winsor argues,

> [e]ngineering is knowledge work. That is, although the goal of engineering may be to produce useful objects, engineers do not construct such objects themselves. Rather they aim to generate knowledge that allows such objects to be built. . . . knowledge is formed in interpersonal negotiation over interpretations of evidence rather than simply in the close individual examination over interpretations of an unambiguous reality.
>
> (Winsor 1996: 5)

The typical way of generating technical knowledge within larger companies is to break down a broadly defined technical problem into precisely defined partial problems whose solution is then delegated to individual engineers or teams of engineers in the company. Or, as one Danish engineer characterised this division of labour in an interview:

> Well, to say it in a general way, I'd think the thing is to – how shall I say – turn some larger goals into some concrete projects or partial goals – how shall I say – individual goals, which can then be processed so that the whole thing hangs together in the end.
>
> (Electrical Engineer Danielsen)[2]

The knowledge produced in this way is then often conveyed further inside or outside the company by means of written texts.

Writing by engineers is thus a form of technical writing. The main function of technical writing can be described as the transfering of information which serves to promote the progress of science and technology. Another important function is the dissemination of technical knowledge and available technology (Göpferich 1996). Hence,

> [t]echnical writing moves outward: from designer to millwright, from engineer to manager, from distributor to customer. At each point, the reader is a user. (People do not read technical writing for fun but because they need to do a task.) . . . Technical writing is writing that accommodates technology to the user.
>
> (Dobrin 1983: 230 and 242)

The production and use of technical data invest engineers and the texts they write with authority and status, just as belonging to a certain company does (Winsor 1993). Writing engineers – the professional group which is the focus of this study – adhere to their specialist values such as 'scientific objectivity' and 'professional judgement', as well as to the values of the company for which they work (Couture 1992). The professional ideology of engineering mainly stresses the 'arhetorical, "objective" nature of writing work: technical data should speak for themselves' (Winsor 1990: 67). In contrast, however, professional practice shows that (especially consulting) engineers do write strategically and 'construct' reality not only according to the norms of the community, but also according to the situation at hand; i.e. engineers *produce* technical data and *select* them in relation to specific situations. These apparently contradictory attitudes to rhetorical practice – i.e. using a rhetorical style and denying that it is being used – seem to be able to co-exist, since 'in many disciplines, particularly in science and technology, effective rhetoric involves the denial that one is using rhetoric' (Winsor 1996: 7).

In writing research, the concept of discourse community in the sense of a 'Specific Interest Group' (Swales 1990: 24) has mainly been used in the context of academic writing. For academic writers, the other members of the community are usually a group of 'ideal readers', or, at least, a somewhat anonymous one, for communication is often via articles, lectures and so on, and not through face-to-face-conversation – even if some actual colleagues also play an important role in the conceptualisation of the 'ideal' audience. What then is the role of a discourse community in real-life interaction with specific readers partly known to the writers, such as those for whom consulting engineers write their texts? In order to throw some light on this issue, the production and revision of the Introductory Section of the Energy Concept document will be analysed in section 4.

This Introductory Section in question has a pronounced 'programmatic' character in that it constructs a common reference frame, or expectation horizon, for the whole of the Energy Concept text.

4. WRITING AND CONSULTANCY: CONTEXTUALISING THE ENERGY CONCEPT DOCUMENT

This section describes the background to the work of the Danish engineers involved in the production and revision of the Introductory Section of the Energy Concept document. In 1992 the Danish company Power Advice was asked to advise the former East German town of Wendenburg on the re-organisation of its energy supply. The task of drawing up an Energy Concept document was assigned to Power Advice by a (West) German investors' pool for municipal projects, Cominvest, which wanted to finance the construction of new power and heating stations in Wendenburg. The Energy Concept document was to be developed for the newly founded department of works (Municipal Services) in Wendenburg, who were to take over the energy supply and part of the energy production.[3]

In the course of six months, the members of the project group wrote five versions of the Energy Concept, each based on the one preceding it (one preliminary draft, three other complete drafts and one final version). The final version comprised approximately 150 pages and numerous appendices. Text production was divided among the group; i.e. under the co-ordination of the project manager Hendriksen the individual members of the group wrote the sections and sub-sections relating to their own technical specialisation. Power Advice's consultancy task was purposefully defined very vaguely in the original consultancy contract: a considerable part of the technical advisory work in Wendenburg therefore consisted first of defining the main technical problem, later of subdividing it into partial problems, and finally of working towards technical and organisational solutions. In the course of the specification of the task, contrasting perceptions as to the status and function of the Energy Concept document led to conflict with the client. The differences became particularly visible in the discussion between the Danish Power Advice's project manager and his German client over the Introduction to the Concept document, as described in section 5 below.

5.   WRITING AS NEGOTIATION:
PHASES OF TEXT PRODUCTION AND REVISION

The first part of this section (5.1.) concentrates on a discussion of the contents of the preliminary version of the introduction to the Energy Concept document, followed by a detailed examination of the reader's comments (5.2.) and the reactions of the writer to these comments (5.3.).

Shortly after taking on the project, the Danish project manager, Hendriksen, prepared a table of contents for the whole Energy Concept which served as a plan for the structuring of the work of the project group, as well as a framework for the Energy Concept document. The individual contributions of the various engineers (= writers) were then inserted into this framework. In the contents table, three sub-sections (General Description of the Town, Purpose of the Report and Methodology used in the Preparation of the Energy Concept) were planned as an introduction to the document. These headings seemed to fulfil the expectations of the discourse community and the conventions of the genre, because the subdivision was never criticised by the German (technical and non-technical) readers, and therefore remained unchanged in all later versions of the text.

As project manager, Electrical Engineer Hendriksen was in charge of the Introduction. Two months after the contract was signed, he wrote a first preliminary draft (see Appendix).[4] In addition to the three sub-sections mentioned above, the preliminary draft included a preface indicating the distribution of responsibilities for energy planning in what were referred to as the new states of Germany. In this chapter Hendriksen stresses the general importance of Energy Concepts in the conversion of the power supply in these new states. He outlines the consequences of the legal battle between the ex-East German towns and West German energy suppliers, which want to take over the whole power supply in the eastern part of Germany. He states that as a result of the unclear legal situation, especially with regard to the question of ownership, the present regional suppliers have carried out only limited repairs, and kept maintenance and investments to a minimum, and consequently there is much to be done in Wendenburg and other towns in former East Germany. The section closes with a list of the tasks to be completed by Power Advice, taken from the original consultancy contract. In the sub-sections that follow, the town of Wendenburg is described in brief and the 'Purpose of the Report' is determined, using information quoted almost exclusively from the preliminary consulting contract. Using a state of the art of the current energy production and distribution, and a forecast as starting points, the Energy Concept proper is to be elaborated.

In the section entitled 'Methodology used in the preparation of the Energy Concept', the different steps in preparing the document are reported in chronological order and Hendriksen thanks Mr Schulze from Wendenburg Municipal Services for his help. Then Hendriksen indicates that part of the material, consisting of data, plans and drawings, has still not arrived. This is followed by more acknowledgements and thanks, this time to the Wendenburg Heat Supply Company for making information and drawings available. Hendriksen also emphasises that the rapid pace in the commissioning of the new power and heating stations has influenced the structure of Power Advice's studies, accelerating the second half of the Energy Concept preparation process.[5] Finally, the last paragraph of the sub-section sums up the stages once again: interviews with individuals familiar with the places and subjects under discussion, evaluation of the drawings, plans and measurement results obtained, evaluation of preceding Concepts and inclusion of the know-how of the Power Advice engineering office and of the knowledge of Danish energy suppliers.

5.1. The reader's perspective: a German reading of the introduction

As the introduction was of essential importance for further planning and text production, it was negotiated at managerial level. Shortly *after* the rushed order of new combined power and heating stations, the executive manager of Wendenburg Municipal Services, Schmidt, crossed out or underlined parts of the text, adding comments in the margin (see Appendix).

To begin with, Schmidt describes the statements made by Power Advice on the responsibilities for energy planning and the accusation that the regional suppliers have neglected maintenance, as wrong in a note in the margin. Furthermore, he characterises the statements on the special problems prevailing in the new German states and on the necessity for action on the part of the municipalities as 'diffuse'. He also comments on Power Advice's description of the

task, in which a feasibility study, in his opinion an essential element for an application to the Municipal Services for permission to
take over energy supply, is missing.[6] In another note in the margin,
Schmidt expands on the requirements of the Municipal Services
with a demand for information on the future energy requirements,
'taking into account the potentials for saving and the development
of the municipal infrastructure'.[7] Finally, he adds a 'Record of Success over 20 Years' item to the list of planned contents of the Energy
Concept.

His strongest objections are to '1.3 Methodology used in the Preparation of the Energy Concept' section. The thanks given to the
Municipal Services are crossed out and the remark is added that
this co-operation goes without saying. The other points of criticism
show clearly that Schmidt does not agree with Power Advice's view
of the purpose and organisation of the Energy Concept – neither
with regard to (1) the audience of the text, nor with regard to (2) the
methodology for the preparation of the concept, as is detailed below.

(1) The paragraph on the impact of the purchase of the
combined power and heating stations on the structure of the
concept and on the accelerated treatment of the final part of
the Energy Concept is crossed out. In the margin, Schmidt
indicates that this paragraph could lead the reader to conclude
that many data and documents were only given estimated
values [due to lack of time]. In his opinion, the energy
supervision authority is sure to pick up on this, thus enabling
them to cast doubt on many of the results. Schmidt's remarks
indicate that he is concerned with secondary readers of the
document, as, in his opinion, the concept should become part
of an approval application according to Section 5 of the
German Energy Economy Law. (The readers here are the
approval and supervision authorities.) In contrast, Hendriksen
is primarily concerned with the primary readers in the West
German investors' pool Cominvest and in Wendenburg's
Municipal Services, to whom he demonstrates the difficulties
experienced in obtaining the necessary data [recall his note on
missing data].
(2) Schmidt also objects to the description of the
methodology used in the preparation of the Concept. He
crosses out Power Advice's summary of the sources of the Energy
Concept (interviews, interpretation of drawings, plans and

measurements, reworking of the preceding study and inclusion of own know-how) and replaces it with the following structure:

(a) Inventory
(b) State of the art
(c) Development of the demand for energy
(d) Representation of the results through projections based on success record (including different variants).

Schmidt appears to value an abstract representation of the calculation of the energy demand and, last but not least, an economic examination of the proposed measures and concepts. He expects a description of a methodical procedure for the purpose of verifying the analyses and forecasts carried out both on a technical and economic basis, and one which could be checked at any time by third parties. In contrast, Hendriksen had described how Power Advice learned about the situation in Wendenburg, and he had outlined the way in which the Danish project group – in conjunction with the Municipal Services – had reached an agreement on how to define the planning task and on recommending the chosen technical solutions.

5.2. Negotiating text:
the subsequent versions of the introduction

The comments added by Schmidt to the preliminary, incomplete draft of the Introduction led to numerous corrections and alterations to the content of the second complete draft. Thus, the paragraph on the responsibility in energy planning marked as 'wrong', was deleted, and the paragraph on the special problems in the eastern part of Germany, which was considered too 'diffuse', was re-worded. The explanation given for the current need for repair and maintenance, also criticised by the manager, was omitted. Hendriksen still felt that his assessment of the situation was correct, but as Schmidt did not wish the argument relating to the neglect of maintenance to be included, Hendriksen agreed to delete it. In this negotiation, omission functioned as a kind of gentlemen's agreement to suspend, and thus to tolerate, differences (local 'misalignment') under certain conditions, even if, or perhaps because, the general goal of the negotiation is the mutual agreement (general 'alignment') of the partners involved (Wagner 1995). And, of course, both Hendriksen and Schmidt agreed that there was a great need for repairs and new equipment in Wendenburg.

In a newly added paragraph, a different reason for the urgently needed investment in new and more efficient equipment is given: i.e. to comply with the demands of the German large-scale heating regulations:

> In the towns in the Eastern part of Germany, action is absolutely necessary in the field of the municipal energy supply. The existing systems have considerable emission problems and are also partly worn out. There is a great need for exchange and maintenance as well as investments in new plants that are more efficient with regard to energy in order to do justice to the demands of the regulations for large-scale heating systems.

This new argument is not based on accusations but, rather, on 'objective' (i.e. legal and technical) requirements, and it is thus closer to the 'rational' ideology of the engineering discourse community, which demands facts and not assumptions. In the end, the introduction did not undergo any further changes in the two last versions of the Energy Concept document, because commentary on and revision of the Energy Concept had shifted from general considerations to the technical details of gas supply, and power and district heating generation/supply due to progress both in the decision-making and technical planning processes. The rest of the planning and designing processes were then negotiated by the individual Danish experts with their technical counterparts at the Municipal Services. Hendriksen himself said that he considered the drafts for the introduction as 'suggestions' for further negotiation towards a more precise definition of the planning task and the identification of the way forward which would eventually lead to the problem's solution. The extracts taken from the original consulting contract opened this process, in the course of which the task would emerge more precisely and the conditions accepted by both Power Advice *and* the Municipal Services could be 'inscribed' (Winsor 1990: 68) into the planning discourse.

Whereas reference to the original contract is quite customary in Energy Concepts and other technical reports, this does, however, not apply to the numerous 'acknowledgements' included by Power Advice. They are a clear indication of Power Advice's interactive view of the planning task, as also emerged during the follow-up interviews with members of the project group. As the introduction establishes the initial 'reciprocity between writers and readers' (Nystrand 1986), the criticism of it made by Schmidt is especially significant, since through that criticism, contrasting views of the function of the Energy Concept text become clear.

On the one hand then, the Municipal Services consider that the document, as a source of technical information, should be the final product of the consultancy work, which could then be used independently, without any further interaction with the consultants. On the other hand, Power Advice views the document as a means of facilitating consultancy activity, in the course of which interactants reach agreement on a mutual understanding of, and a solution to, the problem. This process could be recorded constantly in a kind of working report, such as that represented in the Energy Concept document.

6. TEXT EXPECTATIONS AND INTERPRETATIONS:
THE 'CULTURAL' AND THE 'INTERACTIVE' PERSPECTIVES

The discussion that follows attempts to provide different explanations for the contrasting expectations and interpretations of the same text. After looking at the expectations of the engineering discourse community, it moves on to consider the differences between the cultures involved (the 'cultural' explanation), and concludes with an analysis of the central role played by social interaction in creating and negotiating meaning (the 'social interactionist' explanation).

6.1. Discourse community and culture

Both Schmidt, the German executive manager of the Wendenburg Municipal Services, and Hendriksen, the Danish project manager of the consulting agency Power Advice, adhere to the ideology of the arhetorical representation of facts. Both consider it the task of the project group to generate and organise 'objective' technical data which legitimate the recommended, or already adopted or implemented, solutions. Due to the demand for (quasi) scientific objectivity and for professional judgement, the laws of thermodynamics and other laws of physics are the starting point of argumentation. Even the *differences of opinion* with regard to the passage on rushed subcontracting and its effects on the Energy Concept can be interpreted with reference to the expectations of the discourse community. As mentioned earlier in this chapter, the generation and organisation of exact technical data are some of the main tasks required of engineers. Against this background, Schmidt makes an appeal to the conventions of the discourse community when he deletes the criticised passage from the introduction, as it could otherwise cause the readers to doubt the project's compliance with professional (engineering) conventions. In contrast, Hendriksen perceived the criticised passage as an explanation for missing data. He wished to indicate that Power Advice was only partly able to fulfil the demand for exact data. In both cases, however, conventions are recognised: in one case, they serve to argue the case for omission, and in the second they support the inclusion of the criticised passage. Contrasting interpretations are thus not caused by a differing understanding of the conventions but by the (different) anticipated audiences of the Energy Concept.

One expression of professional competence is the use of a specific language such as 'Power Station German' (a name coined by the Danish project group), which stands for precision and the absence of ambiguity and serves the purpose of communication among technical experts in 'classical technical texts' (this is also a phrase coined by the Danish engineers). However, technical insiders are not the only readers/users of the Energy Concept. These also include political, economic and administrative authorities. The remarks made by Schmidt clearly show that the Energy Concept document is expected not only to reflect reality as closely as possible, but also to be adapted to the intended audience in its selection and presentation of the facts. Therefore, when he requests that criticism of the regional suppliers' investment behaviour should be omitted, he has a specific audience in mind, the current regional suppliers, with whom he wishes to co-operate in future. And Schmidt also considers the authorities, who could possibly refuse permission from being granted, and the competitors, who could obstruct and prevent permission, when he wishes to omit the mention of the significance of rushed subcontracting in the Energy Concept. His reference to the arhetorical ideology of the discourse community is thus not only easy for him to combine with tactical and political considerations, but is even ultimately motivated by them.

This assessment by the German Municipal Services is matched by the Danish consultants' classification of the Energy Concept as a strategic text or 'political instrument'. Therefore, both groups seem to observe the same conventions of the discourse community. Why then, in spite of the fundamental agreement in the expectations, do the manager of the Municipal Services and the leader of the Power Advice project group differ in their opinions as to the purpose of the document?

Firstly, it is important to note that Power Advice did have problems in obtaining the necessary data from the current suppliers and could therefore not always guarantee the Energy Concept's 'durability', as required by the Municipal Services. Also, Power Advice only considered the Energy Concept to be a political instrument *after* the Wendenburg project had been completed. This re-classification was, in part, simply due to the experience they had gained in interacting with the Municipal Services. Characteristically, at the end of the Wendenburg project one Power Advice engineer called the Wendenburg project 'a lesson' (Electrical Engineer Danielsen). However, this only explains some of the differences of opinion which occurred. Deeper divisions could be attributed to factors such as

1. differences between the national cultures;
2. differences between the professional (sub-)cultures;
3. Power Advice's corporate culture.

These three possibilities are examined in detail below.

Firstly, in interviews and discussions on the progress of the Wendenburg project, Power Advice's employees themselves voiced two closely linked hypotheses as to why, in their opinion, the German readers criticised their work and the document so strongly. They assumed that, in Germany, a higher degree of official permission is customary and necessary than in Denmark. This explanation goes hand in hand with the stereotypical *topos* on over-formal and over-bureaucratic Germany mentioned repeatedly in the follow-up interviews, and it is closely linked to a further attempt at an explanation which suggests that the (in)famous 'German thoroughness' is also responsible. Accordingly, in a German Energy Concept, all possibilities and variants should be examined and documented with equal thoroughness – an approach which the Danish respondents felt did not find a parallel in their own country.

These tentative explanations attribute a certain German mentality not only to the actual communication partners, but also to their colleagues and opponents. From the point of view of the Danish project group, 'German thoroughness' has the positive effect that, in Germany, more emphasis is placed on written documents than it is in Denmark. However, it also causes 'irrational' and 'narrow-minded' solutions to problems which, in the opinion of the Danish project group, are solved more easily and without unnecessary complications in Denmark (that is, by negotiation and consensus).[8]

In a comparison of this kind, Denmark appears to be a country in which, in contrast to Germany, problems could often be solved by uncomplicated agreements and in which reaching an agreement seems to be an essential goal of work (another stereotype perhaps). It would be tempting to attribute Power Advice's difficulties to national differences in managerial and negotiating culture (cf. Schramm-Nielsen 1992; Fant 1989; and Villemoes 1995) according to which the 'egalitarian Scandinavian consensus culture would clash with the hierarchical German culture'. However, this is not absolutely certain, since Power Advice's problems could just as easily be explained in terms of differences between the Wendenburg assignment and the tasks which Power Advice normally undertakes in Denmark (see below). They could also be attributed to the legal and political situation existing in the ex-East German towns after reunification and the struggle between the (ex-)East German municipalities and the West German energy trusts. Moreover, the actual significance of cultural differences in intercultural communication is far from clear.[9]

Secondly, in addition to national differences, there are also *subcultural differences* within the engineering discourse community which must be taken into account. After all, power station engineers do not only meet up with colleagues working within the same field, but also with energy managers and executive managers with a business background. As a result of the changing preconditions in the course of the project, Schmidt places increasing emphasis on the question of economic feasibility. Most of the fundamental technical decisions were made shortly after the contract to build the new power and heating stations had been awarded to a German corporation. The next important task for Schmidt is to convince the approving authorities that it is both technically feasible and that it makes good economic sense to allow the Municipal Services to take over the energy generation and supply.

The expectations of the discourse community of engineers and technicians are thus joined by the conventions of the discourse communities of energy managers and the business community. The differing expectations of the executive manager from the Municipal Services and of the project manager from Power Advice can therefore also be explained in terms of the differences between the discourse communities of power station engineers (technical community), energy managers (technical and commercial community) and/or that of corporation directors and executive managers (business community).[10]

Thirdly, in the interviews, the members of the project group refer again and again to the specific *corporate culture* prevalent at Power Advice. For some of them, this is closely related to the tasks which Power Advice usually carries out. Power Advice developed from the planning department of a large Danish energy supplier (DanPower), and within Denmark, it would normally carry out projects according to the principle of individual allocation.[11]

The Power Advice engineers are 'arrangers' (Mechanical Engineer Ulriksen) who represent the interests of the client with respect to the subcontractors (suppliers). Metaphorically speaking, they are 'the arms and legs of the client in question' (Electrical Engineer Danielsen). The Danish clients are often energy supply companies or municipal works departments which themselves have a high degree of technical know-how. They could actually carry out many of those tasks themselves, but they do not have a sufficient workforce. As a result, they ask Power Advice to intervene, usually only after the basic data have been determined and the prior examinations and economic studies have been completed. Due to their own technical expertise, Power Advice's Danish customers are happy with short reports containing hard facts, from which all superfluous information has been omitted.

This is, of course, in sharp contrast to the expectations of the manager of Wendenburg's Municipal Services, who wants to use the Energy Concept in later communication with third parties. Due to their own technical competence, Power Advice's Danish clients play a strong role in negotiation with the consultants. In the Wendenburg case, the project group reported afterwards that the task was not so much to come to a mutually acceptable solution with a strong partner, but that the expectation was that Power Advice would supply an independent recommendation for which Power Advice would then be held solely responsible. Therefore, in the Wendenburg task, Power Advice was entering new territory with regard to the energy planning task at hand, the text genre 'Energy Concept' and the client. The task deviated considerably from the planning and designing tasks that Power Advice had carried out up to that point. This poses the question as to what degree the structure of the company and its organisation, as well as the composition of its staff, were a hindrance rather than a help in finding a solution. At the time of the Wendenburg project, for example, there were no financial experts in the project groups, because the consultancy had mostly been of a technical nature.

6.2. The role of interaction

The three attempts at an explanation discussed above take the view that context is *static* and that the actual interactions are affected, or even determined, by norms, attitudes and values of a discourse community, or of a national or corporate sub-culture. In contrast, a social interactionist approach provides an explanation for the different perceptions of Power Advice and the Municipal Services, at an interactional level.

In the course of the interaction, the context for writing the Energy Concept is dynamic. Due to the constant acquisition of information and the unfolding of the decision-making and planning processes to which the document and the accompanying interactions contribute, the situation is subject to constant change. The document itself constantly creates a new reality (or at least a new construction of it) which, in turn, affects the text and often leads to further revisions. The political and economic context of the eastern German municipalities changed in the course of the project, and the 'Electricity Struggle' was ended (at least temporarily) when an 'Electricity Compromise' was agreed upon. This also considerably affected the position of the town of Wendenburg and its Municipal Services. It was no longer simply a case of organising the energy supply of the town, but also of obtaining permission to produce energy and/or (significantly) sell it to third parties. This resulted in the need for a technical *and* economic feasibility study which was now expected to be discussed within the 'Energy Concept'. In addition, because of the investment bonus opportunity, the contract to build new energy-generating units was awarded to a contractor as quickly as possible. This order was placed *before* the Energy Concept was completed. One of the Energy Concept's central concerns was, in fact, to make recommendations on the central energy-generating units. As the general design and the technical conception of those central units were determined with the contractor in the course of inviting tenders and awarding the contract, Power Advice's task changed dramatically. In short, it was necessary to put the cart before the horse: Power Advice was now to plan what was originally intended to be the result of the preparation of the Energy Concept. The key to solving the task was provided by a number of decisions which had in fact already been taken. Therefore, the Energy Concept was now given a retrospective, legitimating function instead of its original prospective planning aim.

7. CONCLUSION

The analysis of the revisions made to the introduction to the Energy Concept document has demonstrated that its composition was indeed a social activity. This can clearly be shown by looking at the reasons for the ongoing revision of the document. On the one hand, the revisions served the purpose of correcting and/or making the text more precise in order to demonstrate the writers' membership of the discourse community, their compliance with its conventions and their willingness to meet the expectations of the client in terms of 'objectivity' and 'professional judgement'. On the other hand, however, the revisions reflected the state of the decision-making process in Wendenburg and thus, simultaneously, contributed to and represented the continuing advances in the process of finding and determining solutions: processes in which both Power Advice and Municipal Services were engaged. This is especially significant in view of the fact that several planned meetings, as opportunities for the exchange of opinions between the Municipal Services and Power Advice, hardly ever materialised.

The discussion contained in this chapter and further analyses of the revised versions of other parts of the Energy Concept (Pogner 1995; Pogner forthcoming) also show that due to the constantly changing context, expectations towards the document and the technical planning task are constructed *in situ*. The expectations are continuously negotiated, specified and revised. These expectations, which partly follow the conventions of the discourse communities and of the participating culture(s), are not simply given, but are rather *constructed* in interaction. Determining which aspects of the norms, values and conventions (including genre conventions) of the discourse community must be complied with within the actual social and rhetorical situation involved, is carried out interactively.

APPENDIX: FIRST VERSION OF THE INTRODUCTORY SECTION ('PRELIMINARY DRAFT')[12]

Summary and recommendation

1. *Introduction*[13]

In the Federal Republic of Germany, the responsibility for basic decisions with regard to energy policy lies with Bonn and the federal states. [Note: *wrong!*] Towns and municipalities can have a considerable influence on the local realization of the energy supply. [Note: *wrong!*] This now also applies to the municipalities of the 'new federal states' [in the Eastern part of Germany; khp.], who will thus experience a considerable expansion of their responsibilities.

In addition to many other problems, the municipalities of the 'new states' will also be forced to act in the field of the municipal energy supply. [Note: *?*] There are emission problems because of a bad degree of efficiency with regard to the primary energy consumption and partial use of coal without environmental protection measures. [Note on entire paragraph: *diffuse.*]

In addition, the current situation due to the municipal constitutional complaint has led to a situation in which there is a relatively large need for replacement and maintenance [Note: *wrong*], because the current regional suppliers have limited investments for this to a minimum.

~~In October~~ [crossed out] 1992 [overwritten: *September 1991?*], the town council of Wendenburg decided to transfer the municipal tasks in the field of the energy supply to the newly founded Wendenburg Municipal Services Ltd.

Wendenburg Municipal Services has set up the following strategic objective for the energy supply:

- a profitably and environmentally justifiable energy supply.
- a concept for an integrated solution that is an overall solution for a large Municipal Services company.

- the construction of the supply unit must be designed in a future-oriented fashion and must therefore take into account the development of the consumption rates.
- the energy supply must be designed for reliability and safety of operation.
- the technical design of the energy supply must be based on modern and recognized technologies in order to guarantee an optimal supply for the citizens of the town of Wendenburg.

[Note on the last three sections: *What has happened to reductions? What has happened to the use of local resources?*]

An important instrument of a municipal energy policy is the Energy Concept, which is to allow a <u>directed</u> [Note: ?] harmonization of municipal development, energy supply and energy use while taking into account the reciprocal relationship between heat supply systems and the existing building and residential structures.

[Note on last section: *!*]

The town of Wendenburg commissioned Energy Consult Heimstadt Ltd. (ECH) to develop an Energy and Environmental Concept for the town of Wendenburg. A draft of this Energy Concept exists. In its present form, the concept makes no clear-cut statements on the <u>future energy supply of the town of Wendenburg</u>.

[Note: *the municipal assignment was 1) calculation of heat required 2) savings 3) ecolog. optimization.*]

With the approval of the town council, in Autumn 1992 Municipal Services initiated the co-operation with the ComInvest, a financial counselling company for municipal projects,[14] in order to set up an overall solution for the future energy supply of the town of Wendenburg. For this reason, ComInvest founded a company: ComInvest Investor's Pool for Municipal Projects Ltd. & Co. Energy Supply Wendenburg Ltd. (CIPMP). In this context Power Advice Ltd. was asked to carry out the following tasks in co-operation with CIPMP:

- Revision and, if required, completion of the existing basic data described in the ECH report in order to confirm the circumstances for the expansion and modernization of the municipal energy supply.
- Development of an Energy Concept that takes the superior objectives into account as far as possible. In addition to the technical solutions, the concept will also deal with investment calculations, execution plans and consumer prices.

[Note in the margin on last section: *Where is the feasibility study, an important component for a § 5?*]

- Preparation of a technical design plan that describes the projects to be carried out.
  [note in the margin: ø]
- Co-operation as part of an application for a § 5 permit.
  [note in the margin: ?]
- Evaluation of the bottlenecks and the temporal risks in conjunction with execution of the project.

1.1. General description of the town

[...]
[This section was omitted for reasons of anonymity, khp.]

1.2. Purpose of the report

In order to solve the problem of the [addition: *development of the energy requirements*] municipal electricity, heat and gas supply, Municipal Services require an overview of the present state of the generating units and of the transmission network and a description of the current structure of consumption.

[Addition: *and of the future energy requirements while taking into consideration potential for savings and the development of the municipal infrastructure*]

Commencing from this starting point and from a calculation of the requirement forecast, an Energy Concept is to be prepared for the town of Wendenburg. The Energy Concept includes:

- Determination of the priority areas for the supply of gas and district heating. [Ticked off]
- Decision on future energy generating units and mode of operation. [Ticked off]
- Determination of back-up capacity. [Ticked off]
- Determination of the necessary investments in order to be able to guarantee the necessary security and stability of the overall energy supply. [Ticked off]
- Separation of the electricity supply systems with simultaneous compilation of a concept for the distribution between the regional electricity supplier and Wendenburg Municipal Services Ltd. [Ticked off]

- Estimation of the personnel requirements for operation and maintenance of the electricity, gas and district heat departments of Municipal Services.

[Addition: *Record of success over 20 years*]

1.3. Methodology used in the preparation of the Energy Concept

The starting point for the preparation of this report by Power Advice Ltd. is the draft for the final report on the comprehensive Energy and Environmental Concept for the town of Wendenburg that was prepared in XX 1992 in Neustadt by Energy Consult Heimstadt.

This study covers the topic of district heating very well, but gas and especially electricity are hardly or insufficiently dealt with.

[Note in the margin: *was not the object of the assignment to the ECH*]

After going through the report of Energy Consult Heimstadt, Power Advice Ltd. prepared a catalogue of questions and went through it with Wendenburg Municipal Services Ltd. Power Advice Ltd. has prepared a schedule for the activities to be carried out (Appendix 1.3) and gone through these with Professor Dr. Maier and the client.

When going through the catalogue of questions with Mr. Schulze, it soon became obvious that it was necessary to talk to the regional supplier REVAG[15]. Mr. Schulze from Wendenburg Municipal Services Ltd. has been very helpful during the execution of our studies: he contributed a lot to our knowledge of the future development of the town as, as far as we know, there is no accepted plan.

[Note in the margin on the last section: *superfluous! Co-operation should be taken for granted*]

On XX.XX.1992 there was an initial discussion with REVAG in which REVAG agreed to supply data for the studies. Power Advice Ltd. presented REVAG with a limited catalogue of subjects and REVAG invited the experts to examine the generating equipment, selected substations, selected switching stations as well as old and more recent 20/0,4 kV stations. REVAG also presented Power Advice Ltd. with a District Heating Study prepared for REVAG by NEW[16] as well as drawings and measurements.

The examination of the equipment took place on XX.XX.1992 in the presence of several REVAG experts. On X. and on X.XX.1992, Power Advice received important information on the power generation units and the supply system, but it was also realized that the measurements required for assessment and evaluation are not available due to a lack of installed measuring instruments. REVAG is still (calendar week X, 1993) compiling drawings and plans for Power Advice Ltd. Thus, in the short time available, it was not possible to obtain all necessary drawings and plans. However, the data included in the report suffice as a basis for assessment.

The WHS (the Wendenburg Heat Supply Company) also helped Power Advice Ltd. The secondary system was worked through with Mr. Lehmann and some of his colleagues, and WHS gave out drawings that were important for assessment.

During the studies, a resolution of the German federal government decided, against all expectations, not to extend the investment bonus law for companies of the energy industry in the Eastern part of Germany. ComInvest, Wendenburg Municipal Services Ltd. and Power Advice Ltd. then agreed at short notice that they should try to commission the construction of combined heating and power stations to a manufacturer as general contractor by the end of 1992. Of course, this decision, which was made on XX.XX.1992, interfered with the planned structure of the studies, and this accelerated the last half.

[Whole section is deleted and commented upon as follows: *This section allows the conclusion that many data and documents were given estimated values. The energy supervision will surely draw attention to this and will be able to cast doubt on many results!*]

The Energy Concept thus developed on the basis of

- interviews with experts in the field and with people who know their way around (REVAG, WHS, Municipal Services)
- studies of received drawings, plans and results of measurements
- revising the report of Energy Consult Heimstadt
- inclusion of experience and knowledge of Power Advice Ltd. and the DanPower supply companies.

[The whole section is deleted and given a very big question mark. The following note is to be found above the section:

1. *Inventory*
2. *State of affairs*
3. *Development of demand for energy*
4. *Presentation of results through projections based on success record (including different variants).*]

NOTES

1. All names of persons, companies and places have been changed to protect anonymity. For an analysis of the complete Energy Concept document, see Pogner (1995).
2. All quotations from the interviews have been translated into English from the Danish original. Extracts from the Energy Concept have been translated into English from German.
3. The consultancy work carried out by Power Advice involved co-operation in general designing, planning, inviting tenders and the allocation of orders for the new power and heating stations. It also required a comprehensive report in German (the 'Energy Concept'), intended to examine the current supply situation of the town and to present a concept for the future supply of gas, district heating and power. In order to elaborate the Energy Concept document, Power Advice formed a project group consisting of five engineers and technicians from different departments.
4. The Appendix contains the English translation of the original preliminary draft with the comments added by the German executive manager of the Wendenburg Municipal Services, Mr. Schmidt.
5. The Investment Bonus Law according to which investments in former East Germany were subsidised by the government in Bonn was expected also to be extended beyond the year 1992. However, at the end of 1992 it became clear that this extension would not apply to investments in the field of the power supply. For this reason Power Advice, the investors' pool Cominvest, and Wendenburg Municipal Services hurriedly decided in November 1992 to award the contract to build two new combined power and heating stations (combined circle). Important technical and economic decisions were made in inviting tenders and awarding the contract to a German company.
6. In the course of the conflicts over the power supply in the new German states, the German Federal Constitutional Court made the following compromise suggestion at the end of 1992: the ex-East German municipalities were allowed to take over the power supply if they renounced the capital share from the regional supplier which they had a right to. In return, the local supply equipment would be left to them free of charge. However, supplying power (and gas) was linked to the condition that, in accordance with section 5 of the German Energy Economy Law, the town in question was given permission to take over the energy supply. This permission would be given by the Regional Ministry of Economic Affairs after an examination of the technical and economic feasibility (!).
7. Forecast sections were lacking in the first draft. They were listed in the contents table but they had not yet been written. Power Advice

assumed that the complete draft, which was to include forecasts of the power, gas and district heating requirements, would meet the wishes of Executive Manager Schmidt at this point.

8. From the viewpoint of the project group, this applies, for example, to the separation of the power supply systems whereby the municipal power supply must be taken out of the existing regional grid for political reasons and to comply with Energy Law, as the Municipal Services only have the right to supply power within clear demarcation lines. In contrast, in Denmark it is customary for the suppliers involved to come to mutual agreements on the power supply and possible compensation payments.

9. On the one hand, the original assumption that discourse communities are quite uniform or univocal communities has been questioned in numerous studies orientated towards text linguistics (e.g. Clyne 1991 and Gunnarsson, *et al.* 1995). In these studies, the textual divergences observed are attributed to differing national professional cultures, text traditions, communication styles and/or other culture-specific issues. On the other hand, in contrast to these contrastive rhetorical studies (Connor 1996), which emphasise text linguistics, Firth (1991) concludes that national cultural differences are *not always* as significant as they are made out to be as demonstrated in his own study of international business negotiations via telex, fax and telephone. In sales negotiations, for example, they are superseded by the international trade and negotiation practice. However, Firth only deals with special communication types; i.e. lingua franca communication and highly routinised interactions in which interpretations, norms, goals and expectations are predictable or can be controlled by the interlocutors. In the case of Power Advice and Wendenburg Municipal Services, the activity focused upon is not routine, and, from Power Advice's point of view, communication takes place in a *foreign* language. Accordingly, in spite of the reference point provided by the common discourse community, the safe ground of routine international or supra-national interactions is missing. The negotiation of Power Advice's task in the introduction of the Energy Concept document is therefore very problematic and full of tension.

10. The target interlocutors for Power Advice's work change in the course of the project because the needs of the town of Wendenburg with regard to consultancy change. These changes make Power Advice's work as an engineering consultancy considerably more difficult. In Hendriksen's own words: 'it is really impossible – or it is not easy – to sit down, or rather to find out which chair to sit on when you're writing an Energy Concept. But first you have to be completely sure whose shoes you're in when you are to write it.' Although he and Schmidt both belong to the top management of their organisations – i.e. both are mostly occupied with questions of administration and

leadership and of the definition of problems and the organisation of work tasks – their differing professional backgrounds (technological versus economic) could have affected their perceptions of an Energy Concept. In Hendriksen's opinion, an Energy Concept should mainly solve technical problems. In Schmidt's view, it is primarily to solve economic problems once the basic technical decisions have been made. However, as illustrated above, these two views are not necessarily static but in fact depend on the actual state of the decision-making process and the related and changing needs for information and action.

11. This principle maintains that tenders are invited separately for the functions and components of a power station. Power Advice's main task before construction can begin is therefore to plan in detail the individual parts of a power station (buildings, generators, other machines, electrical equipment and other components) as well as their purchase. Starting from the basic data, the technical staff (engineers and technicians) divide the individual parts of the plant into smaller projects and later monitor their assembly by subcontractors.

12. The names of the towns, persons and companies involved have been changed to protect anonymity. Dates have been changed or omitted for the same reason. Obvious spelling or grammatical mistakes in the original have been corrected.

13. The crossings out and underlinings of the executive manager of Wendenburg Municipal Services are marked in the document, and his comments have been added in brackets.

14. ComInvest is the (West) German investors' pool which finances the construction of new power stations in Wendenburg.

15. REVAG is the regional supplier of electricity and district heat.

16. NEW is a West German supplier.

REFERENCES

Berkenkotter, Carol, Huckin, Thomas and Ackerman, John (1989) Social contexts and socially constructed texts: the initiation of a graduate student into a writing research community (Technical report 33). Berkeley, CA, and Pittsburgh, PA: National Center for the Study of Writing.

Bizzell, Patricia (1982) Cognition, convention, and certainty: what we need to know about writing. PRE/TEXT 3: 213–43.

Bizzell, Patricia (1994) Discourse community. In Alan C. Purves (ed.), Encyclopaedia of English Studies and Language Arts. New York: Scholastic, 395–7.

Clyne, Michael (1991) The sociocultural dimension: the dilemma of the German-speaking scholar. In Hartmut Schröder (ed.), Subject-oriented Texts: Languages for Specific Purposes and Text Theory. Berlin and New York: De Gruyter, pp. 49–67.

Connor, Ulla (1996) *Contrastive Rhetoric: Crosscultural Aspects of Second-language Writing*. Cambridge: Cambridge University Press.

Couture, Barbara (1992) Categorizing professional discourse: engineering, administrative, and technical/professional writing. *Journal of Business and Technical Communication* 6 (1): 5–37.

Dobrin, David N. (1983) What's technical about technical writing? In Paul V. Anderson, R. John Brockmann, and Carolyn R. Miller (eds), *New Essays in Technical and Scientific Communication*. Farmingdale, NY: Baywood, pp. 227–48.

Duin, Ann Hill and Hansen, Craig J. (eds) (1996) *Nonacademic Writing: Social Theory and Technology*. Mahwah, NJ: Lawrence Erlbaum.

Fant, Lars M. (1989) Cultural mismatch in conversation: Spanish and Scandinavian communicative behaviour in negotiation settings. *Hermes* 3: 247–66.

Firth, Alan (1991) Discourse at work: negotiating by telex, fax, and phone. Unpublished dissertation. Aalborg: Aalborg University.

Göpferich, Susanne (1996) Zum Begriff des 'Technical Writing' als Inter-textualität schaffendem Prozess. *Fachsprache. International Journal of LSP* 18 (3/4): 98–117.

Gunnarsson, Britt-Louise, Bäcklund, Ingegerd and Andersson, Bo (1995) Texts in European writing communities. In Britt-Louise Gunnarsson and Ingegerd Bäcklund (eds), *Writing in Academic Contexts* (TeFA 11). Uppsala: Uppsala University, pp. 30–53.

MacKinnon, Jamie (1993) Becoming a rhetor: developing writing ability in a mature, writing intensive organization. In R. Spilka (ed.) (1993) *Writing in the Workplace: New Research Perspectives*. Carbondale and Edwardsville, IL: Southern Illinois University Press, 41–55.

Nystrand, Martin (1986) *The Structure of Written Communication: Studies in Reciprocity between Readers and Writers*. Orlando, FL: Academic Press.

Nystrand, Martin, Greene, Stuart and Wiemelt, Jeffrey (1993) Where did composition studies come from? An intellectual history. *Written Communication* 10 (3): 267–333.

Odell, Lee and Goswami, Dixie (1985) *Writing in Nonacademic Settings*. New York: Guilford.

Olsen, Leslie, A. (1993) Research on discourse communities: an overview. In R. Spilka (ed.), *Writing in the Workplace: New Research Perspectives*. Carbondale and Edwardsville, IL: Southern Illinois University Press, pp. 181–94.

Pogner, Karl-Heinz (1995) Energiekonzept für Wendenburg. Arbeitsteilige Produktion fremdsprachlicher Texte an einem technischen Arbeitsplatz. Unpublished dissertation. Odense: Odense University.

Pogner, Karl-Heinz (forthcoming) Schreiben im Beruf als Handeln im Fach (Forum für Fachsprachenforschung 46). Tübingen: Narr.

Schramm-Nielsen, Jette (1992) Dansk–fransk samarbejde i erhvervsvirksom-heder (Ph.d. series 2.93). Copenhagen: Samfundslitteratur.

Spilka, Rachel (ed.) (1993) *Writing in the Workplace: New Research Perspectives*. Carbondale and Edwardsville, IL: Southern Illinois University Press.

Swales, John M. (1990) *Genre Analysis: English in Academic and Research Settings*. Cambridge: Cambridge University Press.

Thralls, Charlotte and Blyler, Nancy Roundy (1993) The social perspective and professional communication: diversity and directions in research. In Nancy Roundy Blyler and Charlotte Thralls (eds), *Professional Communication: The Social Perspective*. Newbury Park, CA: Sage, pp. 3–34.

Van Gemert, Lisette and Woudstra, Egbert (1996) Changes in writing in the workplace: a literature survey and a case study. Paper presented at the conference Organizational Communication and Change: Challenges for the Next Century, Southwest Texas State University (February).

Villemoes, Annette (1995) Culturally determined facework preferences in Danish and Spanish business negotiation. In Konrad Ehlich and Johannes Wagner (eds), *The Discourse of Business Negotiation*. Berlin, New York: Mouton de Gruyter, pp. 291–312.

Wagner, Johannes (1995) 'Negotiation activity' in technical problem solving. In Alan Firth (ed.), *The Discourse of Negotiation: Studies of Language in the Workplace*. Oxford: Pergamon, pp. 223–45.

Winsor, Dorothy A. (1990): Engineering writing/Writing engineering. *College Composition and Communication* 41 (1): 58–70.

Winsor, Dorothy A. (1993) Owning corporate texts. *Journal of Business and Technical Writing* 7 (2): 179–95.

Winsor, Dorothy A. (1996) *Writing Like an Engineer: A Rhetorical Education*. Mahwah, NJ: Lawrence Erlbaum.

SIX

Meaning creation and genre across cultures: human resource management magazines in Britain and Italy

Francesca Bargiela-Chiappini

1. INTRODUCTION

The aim of this chapter is twofold: (1) to develop an understanding of the categories of 'purposes, participants and themes' (Devitt 1993), as the obligatory elements denoting a genre; and (2) to illustrate this through the comparative analysis of the British and Italian official magazines for human resources and personnel professionals,[1] on the assumption that they share common generic features.

Within a semiotic perspective of genre, human resource management (HRM) magazines are analysed as dynamic and interactionally shaped tokens of management discourse and practice. Given the focus of this volume, the investigation undertaken in this chapter will concentrate on the discursive dimension of the 'magazine' as a semiotic object, where discourse is defined as the textualisation of 'a rhetorical and semiotic situation' in a socio-historic context.

The discourse analytic approach adopted here, based on the principle of 'cooperative interpretation' (Piccardo *et al.* 1992), relies on a framework for rhetorical analysis that focuses on pragmalinguistic features. The reader-researcher is actively encouraged to re-construct images of human resources and personnel professionals as textualised in 1995 in their official magazines in Britain and Italy.

2. GENRE AND CONSTRUCTIONIST SEMIOTICS

Of the various analyses of genre undertaken by linguists (e.g. Halliday, Hasan, Ventola, Kress, Swales, Martin and Bhatia), the approaches of Halliday and Hasan (1985) and Kress and Threadgold

(1988) are well established within the social semiotic tradition. However, neither approach specifically addresses the contribution made to genre by the cognitive dimension, or what Gunnarsson (1995: 113) refers to as 'a certain way of viewing reality, a certain way of highlighting different aspects of the surrounding world'. Swales and Rogers (1995) in their study of corporate mission statements, remark that a deep understanding of the social and institutional role of genres depends on the additional 'sociocognitive input' that corporate history and culture can offer. And while the adoption of the Gumperzian notion of 'contextualization'[2] would greatly benefit a generic approach to the study of communicative practices in organisational settings, it would still fall short of a socio-cognitive input, the workings of which remain under-estimated and under-investigated.

In this chapter, the centrality of the linguistic dimension to the definition of the 'genre' construct is taken for granted. However, it is also contended that a socio-semiotic perspective of genre can and should also accommodate a cognitive dimension, expressed in the discursive (and non-discursive) choices consciously or unconsciously realised by readers and writers. Such a social constructionist epistemology points to the pivotal role of language as the interconnection between cognitive, social, spatial and temporal planes. On this point, Bazerman comments:

> The writer or speaker presents a dynamic universe for the reader or listener to reconstruct actively within the receiver's dynamic universe. The words are what go between and negotiate the intersection of these moments within the worlds of production and reception. Through language deployed at the moment, we assert the connection of past and future as well as the connection among human beings creating a shared universe of action.
>
> (Bazerman 1994: 171)

Consequently, far from being a fossilised specimen of an ideal prototypical text, 'genre not only responds to but also constructs recurring situations' (Devitt 1993: 577).

The semiotic-constructionist understanding of genre that underpins this chapter extends the discussion in Briggs and Bauman (1992), where genre is defined as:

- *interactive*, in that it is 'a discursive realization [accomplished by writer *and* reader] at the historic junction between language and context';

- *relational,* in that it calls 'writers' and 'readers' to take up roles (social, institutional, emotional, etc.) which are necessary for interpretation, and 'verbalises' them in these roles;
- *rhetorical,* because 'structure, form, function and meaning are seen not as immanent features of discourse but as products of an ongoing process of producing and receiving discourse';
- *polysemic,* because it is open to multiple interpretations and, as an object, it is expressed in a multiplicity of forms (text, image, polychromy, choice of materials, etc.);
- *heterogeneous,* because no genre is 'pure' but a mix of generic forms;
- *intertextual,* because discourse structure and meaning is shaped by prior discourses, real or imaginary, which have already taken place and into which writers and speakers 'insert' their current discourses, thus building competing perspectives;
- *historical,* because a genre is firmly placed within a 'semiotic space' of negotiated meanings that social actors constitute at a given point in time.

Table 6.1:   A first analytical matrix for the interpretation of genre

Generic parameter	Textual realisation
interactive	pronouns, direct speech, dialogue, interviews
relational	forms of address and reference, including titles
rhetorical	persuasive language
polysemic	layout, graphics, polychromy, etc.
heterogeneous	various embedded genres (letter, review, feature, report, interview, etc.)
intertextual	dynamic relation with other artefacts (written or oral), cultural trends and fads, etc.
historical	synchronic features of the language (neologisms)
(others)	?

Table 6.1 suggests some of the textual manifestations of the generic parameters listed above, where the notion of 'textual' is extended to include non-linguistic constituents of genres.[3] Against this background, the traditional, positivist concepts of 'writer' and 'reader'[4] become fuzzy, if not irrelevant. The principle of 'relationality' of genre, as adapted from Briggs and Bauman (1992), encompasses 'inter-relationality' in that it can be argued that, for example, the

contributors to a professional magazine with a specialist restricted
circulation are at once potential readers, writers and practitioners;
i.e. the three roles can and often do overlap to a varying extent.
Therefore, readers and writers of this type of professional discourse
often share a cognitive and experiential baggage that informs the
linguistic, and possibly the para-linguistic, dimensions of the genre.
In a semiotic-constructionist understanding of genre this also
means that a cognitive, experiential interpretation of discourse is
enriched and expanded by the readers to include their personal
baggage, and then fed back into the historical context through modified verbal and non-verbal behaviour. This text-to-context process
also happens in reverse through 'intertextuality' (see, e.g., Loos,
Akar and Louhiala-Salminen, this volume). It is interesting to note
how, for example, both *People Management* and *Direzione del Personale*
show traces of 'discursive transfer', most noticeably, but not exclusively, from management literature, as in the following extracts
('transfers' in italics):

> The *change programme*, known as 'Performance Through People',
> addressed four areas where improvements were crucial for the future
> success of the business:
> * physically relocating the manufacturing centre;
> * radical changes in *working practices*;
> * development of a *world-class* process for *managing relationships* with
>   suppliers;
> * organisation changes, creating a *leaner* and more *customer-focused*
>   *business*.
>
> Dee Proctor (1995: 28)

> Aggredite dalla recessione degli anni novanta, le aziende hanno
> tentato di modificare la loro struttura, modellandosi sui *segmenti di
> mercato* e sulla *tipologia del prodotto*; hanno ridisegnato i loro *processi
> interni*; hanno identificato il *'core business'*, hanno deciso cosa
> cancellare e cosa *demandare a partern esterni*. *Flessibilità, snellimento e
> focalizzazione* sono così diventate espressioni tipiche del lessico del
> lavoro; e il loro significato è diventato sinonimo del *recupero dei costi*,
> della ricerca di *più efficienti processi* da introdurre e dei *tagli
> occupazionali*.
>
> Villa (1995: 13)

> Attacked by the recession of the Nineties, companies have attempted
> to modify their structure on the model of *market segments* and *product
> typology*; they have re-designed *internal processes*; they have identified

the *core business*, they have decided what to eliminate and what to contract out. *Flexibility, lean enterprise* and *focusing* have therefore become typical items of the work jargon; they are synonyms of *cost recovery, more efficient processes* and *redundancies*.

3. CONTEXT AND GENRE

The symbiotic and dynamic relationship between text and 'writer–reader' in a constructionist epistemology of genre forces a re-definition of the concept of context. Anthropology, linguistics, pragmatics and sociology have all contributed to the debate on what constitutes the 'context' of a verbal interaction (see review in Bargiela-Chiappini and Harris 1997). If one agrees with Malinowski's provocative contention that context 'must burst the bonds of mere linguistics and be carried over into the analysis of the general conditions under which a language is spoken [or written]' (1923: 306), then, Silverstein's (1992) characterisation of context as 'indeterminate' begins to sound quite apt, if not particularly helpful. 'Capturing infinity' – Cook's (1990) characterisation of the transcriber's task in dealing with oral data – also provides a fitting description of the contextualising effort required by the analysts of written texts, who find themselves operating within the fluid boundaries of reader–writer relationships across temporal and spatial frames. At first sight, this appears to be a predicament that spells analytical paralysis. However, a socio-linguistic concept of 'context' may be of assistance here, where 'context' is characterised as 'reflexive' and 'flexible'. This understanding of 'context' was first suggested by Jenny Cook-Gumperz and John Gumperz in the seventies and is implied in Gumperz's later notion of 'contextualisation' (see note 2). The relationship between context and text is predicated in terms of 'reflexiveness' (i.e. the language contributes to the construction of context) and 'flexibility' (i.e. the context is in constant evolution during the interaction) (Auer 1992: 21).

To what extent do writers and readers of the generic-type 'professional magazine' contribute to the 'context' of an interaction? A helpful assumption is to think that 'each piece of discourse [is] accompanied by a contract that sets forth the definition of social context within which the text ought to be interpreted' (Rafoth and Rubin 1988: 11). However, the tacit contract that engages writer and reader within the arena of the text is not merely the process of decoding interpretative rules that the former almost imposes on the latter, since as Briggs and Bauman make clear:

> [s]ome elements of contextualization creep in, fashioning indexical connections to the ongoing discourse, social interaction, broader social relations, and the particular historical juncture(s) at which the discourse is produced and received. In short, other pragmatic and metapragmatic frameworks must be brought into play in shaping production and reception.
>
> (1992: 149)

These frameworks are not incidental to the process of genre creation jointly enacted by the writer and the reader but are derived from their experiential baggage.

For the purposes of this study, context is defined as a 'cultural snapshot' informed by understandings and meanings jointly contributed by the writer and the reader when they meet in the semiotic arena to textualise and interpret. Therefore, against this contextual backdrop, the magazines in question do not *represent* images of human resource management (HRM) as inscribed by the writers at a socio-historic juncture: they *are* HRM in verbal and pictorial form for the readers to interpret through their own experiential understanding. What the writers choose to foreground discursively and non-discursively, in fact, configures generic texts. Beside sharing distinctive features, these generic texts are 'multiple symbolic systems' which interplay towards 'meaning making' (Witte 1992: 290). Therefore, while rejecting the traditional functional dichotomy of 'context of use' and 'context of writing', an approach to professional discourse based on a social-interactive understanding of writing as developed by Nystrand (1989),[5] owes much to both pragmatics and to Bakhtin's dialogism (Chin 1994).

4.   THE METHODOLOGY

Mary Douglas (1994: 19) remarks that, although objects are commonly seen to 'denote' relationships, they first 'exemplify' them: '[t]o be given a meal does not signify hospitality, it is actually, truly a sample of hospitality'.

In the same fashion, HRM magazines analysed in this chapter are tokens of human resource management rather than its representations. According to Piccardo *et al.* (1992), when employing 'cooperative interpretation', the reader is not a mechanical and passive decoder but a subjective and active interpreter who employs fantasies, associations and intuition to re-construct meanings interactively.

In the sections that follow, an analytical framework based on 'cooperative interpretation' is discussed and modified with a view to employing it as a tool for the interpretation of the discursive constructions of HRM and personnel professionals in their official magazines in Britain and Italy.

4.1. A hermeneutic tool for investigating genre

According to Piccardo et al. (1992), 'cooperative interpretation' consists of three levels of rhetorical analysis which in this chapter will be defined as Rhetorical Framing, Thematic Profiling and Lexical Mapping. In our understanding of genre, Rhetorical Framing has to do with the socio-historical and perceptual character of the magazines as (1) physical and functional objects and (2) relational artefacts. The cognitive dimension of socio-constructionism demands sensitivity to the editorial and publisher's choices displayed in the physical presentation of the magazines as generic objects, as these affect the reader's contribution to meaning construction.

Through Thematic Profiling, (3) the structural levels and contents identified are highlighted, as are (4) the recurring themes and common themes.

The third and last level of analysis is concerned with lexis. Thus, Lexical Mapping looks at (5) concordances and (6) keywords and semantic clusters.[6]

The simple three-dimensionality of this rhetorical analysis framework does not presume to map the complex pragmalinguistics of the 'professional magazine' generic type in their entirety. Instead, it should be seen as a 'window' on the interconnections of meaning creation in action; i.e. a hermeneutic tool for exploration rather than a self-contained explanatory model.

Within its limited scope, this chapter can only provide a selective analysis of a sample of three 1995 issues of the two magazines in question; i.e. *People Management* and *Direzione del Personale*.[7] After a descriptive introduction to the selected magazines under the heading of Rhetorical Framing, the chapter will focus on the second level of analysis, Thematic Profiling, and will apply the principle of co-operative interpretation to one specific lexical cluster: the 'human resource and personnel cluster' (see section 5.2).

5. THE ANALYSIS

5.1. Rhetorical Framing: socio-historic and perceptual features

Table 6.2 provides a descriptive identikit of the two magazines in question. Perceptually, the two magazines are quite different. In

Table 6.2:   Comparative synopsis of *PM* and *DdP*

Descriptive parameters	People Management	Direzione del Personale
No. of pages	110	43
Format	>A4	<A4
Frequency	fortnightly	bi-monthly
Circulation (1995)	58,500 *ca.*	1500
Target readership	72,000 members (+ 6000)	1416 members
Subscription	£62 (free to members)	£32/£20 (free to members)
Job advertisements	yes (40 pp. +)	no
Commercial adverts	yes, interspersed	yes, interspersed
Polychromy	yes, throughout	covers only (ads) blue frames throughout
Thematic front cover	yes	yes
Photographs	yes	rare
Text layout	multi-columns	two columns
Tone	colour magazine	quasi-journal
Paper quality	(light) glossy	(heavier) glossy
Contents break-down	functional title + thematic title + title proper	thematic (or functional) title + title proper
News (general)	yes	no
News (association)	yes	yes
Letters	yes	no
Features	yes	yes
Book reviews	yes	yes
Cartoons	no	yes
Appointments	yes	no
Directory	yes	no

(Italics indicate entries which differ in the two magazines, i.e. are present in one but not in the other.)

contrast to the verbal and pictorial exuberance of its British counterpart, *Direzione del Personale* (DdP) appears to be a rather low-key, under-stated quasi-journal, neatly contained within its (average) 45 pages, and unconcerned with the money-spinner section of job advertisements. There are few concessions to 'personal appearances' in the black and white photographs, and the delicate sky-blue borders that frame the articles give it an unexpected 'soft' touch in a largely male-dominated profession.

People Management (PM) is twice the size of *DdP*. The extra text is mostly devoted to job advertisements and commercials. It employs colour photographs and displays passport-size and full-size human subjects in a portrait gallery that goes a long way to establishing 'interactionality' between the magazine and those who 'read' it.

5.2.   Thematic Profiling: levels and clusters

As Table 6.3 shows, the layout of the contents pages of *People Management* (PM) is more highly structured than those of *DdP*, with three heading levels in full evidence in all issues together with a fourth (sub-title) included in many (see contents pages shown in italics in Table 6.2). A comparative analysis of the layout of the contents pages, which could be treated as the 'identification plate' of a magazine, highlights some important differences in the visual impact that these pages have on the reader.

In *PM*, the news, a very minor feature at the back of *DdP*, always appears as the opening section in the magazine, followed by the letters from the readers (absent in *DdP*) and then the feature articles, which represent the 'core' of both magazines. This layout suggests

Table 6.3:   Quantitative profile by heading type (with number of pages of non-advertising text in brackets)

Type-face	Heading type	People Management			Direzione del Personale		
		Jan. (35)	Mar. (25)	May (26)	Jan. (35)	Mar. (32)	May (35)
18 pts	fixed	7	7	6	6	5	6
14 pts	topic	27	27	25	6	5	6
12 pts	title	23	25	21	7	6	9
10 pts	sub-title	15	28	22	2	0	3

tighter control over the progress of the reader towards the core of the magazine; i.e. the features, dealing with themes that are given prominence by the editorial office. This may be interpreted as indicative of the 'low context' culture that is prevalent in Britain, where rules and procedures are far more in evidence than in a 'high context' culture (such as Italy), where individuals are left to work out for themselves what behaviour is required and acceptable in the circumstances. 'Low context' is also suggested by the detailed and intricate web of 'pointers' (headings) in *PM* that provide the reader with a maximum amount of information on how to 'navigate' the magazine and which are far fewer in *DdP*. In *DdP*[8] the restricted number of 'pointers' affords the magazine's contents page a 'leaner', frill-free design which conveys the impression of a relaxed space in which the readers can exercise their choices without sacrificing efficiency. This may be contrasted with the 'busy' look of the print-packed contents pages of *PM*, where colourful pictorial elements and contrastive typefaces create a dynamic and eye-catching look.

Structurally, minimal divergence between the two magazines is noticeable at the highest hierarchical heading level (fixed headings), with maximal divergence at the level immediately below (topic headings), since these are non-existent in the Italian magazine. However, one could argue that the fixed headings in the Italian magazine are more informative than their equivalent in the British magazine, as illustrated by the top heading levels in the two magazines (first issue of 1995), given in Table 6.4. It therefore appears as if in the Italian magazine, two headings ('fixed' and 'topic') are collapsed into one, a technique which further contributes to the streamlined look of its contents page.

Table 6.4:   Examples of fixed and topic headings in *PM* and *DdP*

	Fixed headings	Topic headings
People Management	News analysis Features Monitor IPD Report	People Management Redundancy Management Profile Business Strategy
Direzione del Personale	The company/Society The company/Management Tools and Methods International Monitor	no equivalent

The mapping of Thematic Clusters – that is, groups of articles containing related discourses – aims to narrow the focus of the analysis from the macro-level of perception and structure (Textual Framing) to an intermediate level identifying topical issues within the contemporary panorama of management writing.[9] In the first three 1995 issues of both magazines, two major Thematic Clusters can be identified in the features, which represent the 'core' of the magazine and which are composed of the items highlighted in Table 6.5. These are the self-perceptions cluster (or, how HRM professionals see themselves now) and the self-projection cluster (or, what HRM professionals think they ought to become). These two discourses clearly interplay with less important ones in the same features, and they are also traceable in some of the features not highlighted in Table 6.5.

Table 6.5:   Topic selection in the first three 1995 issues of PM and DdP

People Management	Direzione del Personale	Cluster (perception = PER) (projection = PRO)
Objectives for the new magazine	For a corporate environmental policy	PRO
Helping survivors to stay on board	*Stages* in Italy: an opinion from the Polytechnic of Milan	PRO
Listening banker	The behavioural effects of outplacement	PER
How HR can help to win the future	Trust and understanding, strategic resources for the company	PRO
Success in the big league	The province of Genoa: an organisational development plan	
A different path to paradise?	Accelerated course for the HR manager USA year 2000: new issues in HRM	PRO
Quelling the storm over top salaries	Tools and methods of environmental policy and management	
Blue thunder	The causes of work-related stress in managers	PER

continued overleaf

Table 6.5:   Cont'd

People Management	Direzione del Personale	Cluster (perception = PER) (projection = PRO)
Getting the most out of your people	You write esternalizzazione, you say spin-off	PRO
Learning that is far from academic	Integrating disabled staff into work	
Clear benefits of multi-skilling	Writing to communicate and persuade	
Charting a course on hi-tech seas		
Prepare to make a moral judgement	Eco-reports and budgets	PRO
Getting teams off the ground	Stress: prevention is better than cure	PER
Fresh mandarin	CENSIS research on female manager at ENEL	
Reducing trauma after the event	HRM: ancient prudence and timid tendencies	PRO/PER
An underground movement	Second level bargaining: risk or opportunity?	
	Telework: no thank you	PER
	No longer jobs but bits of work	PRO
	How to manage employment termination successfully	PER
	Job change: a problem turned into an opportunity with the outplacement	PER

The British titles make frequent use of rhetorical figures, word play and clichés which appear only occasionally in the Italian titles. The writers' ingenuity in the British titles is contrasted with plain 'informativeness' in Italian. The Italian writers are apparently uninterested in gaining the readers' attention through the witty use of the linguistic medium, nor do they use non-linguistic features such as colour and photographs. (Incidentally, this curiously contradicts the fame for 'creative flair' often attributed to Italians.) By contrast, the construction of the managerial persona that matches Italian expectations of 'professionality' is a powerful motive which influences

DdP's choice of language (precise and informative) and physical profile (soberly elegant and serious), and which distinguishes *DdP* from *PM*.

5.2.1. HRM perceptions and projections: negotiating present and future in the profession

As an introduction to the discussion of HRM perceptions and projections, a historical note on Italian personnel managers appearing in the last issue of *DdP* in 1994 may be illuminating. This is the engaging account of the development of the personnel function in Italy according to a human resources manager at Nokia Telecommunications:

> Dal modello normativo degli esordi a funzione 'giudiziaria' e exufficiali dei carabinieri a capo del personale, all'avvento delle Human Relations negli anni '50 e '60, con la scoperta della persona condotta da quei capi del personale cortesi e pedagoghi, laureati e manipolativi. Poi il momento di gloria negli anni settanta, l'esproprio legalizzato della gestione delle risorse umane che viene tolta al management e conferita agli esperti delle relazioni industriali concentrati in team consortili e potenti, mentre i sessantottini delle formazioni manageriali inneggiano al cambiamento e si irradiano nelle imprese e nella consulenza. Nel frattempo siamo arrivati ai metodi e gli strumenti dello sviluppo e della compensation, e il mondo si rappresenta e si precisa nei punti Hay. Con gli anni '80 si compie il riconoscimento della valenza strategica delle risorse umane, e i direttori del personale si aggiudicano una sedia nei comitati ristretti.
>
> (Lolli 1994: 15)

From the normative model of the early days, to the legalistic function with ex-'carabinieri' officers [paramilitary police] as heads of personnel, through the human relations of the fifties and sixties, following the discovery of the individual achieved by those polite and manipulative heads of personnel with degrees and a didactic attitude. Then the heyday of the seventies, the legalised eviction of the human resource function which is removed from the management and assigned to industrial relations experts converging in powerful interest groups, whilst the 'sessantottini' [the revolutionaries of 1968] of the managerial formations sing the praise of change and spread into companies and consultancies. In the meantime, we have reached the period of the tools and methods of development and compensation, and the world is represented and defined in terms of Hay points. In the eighties, the strategic value of human resources is acknowledged and personnel directors allot themselves a chair on senior committees.

Notice the normative and legalistic HRM models founded on the principle of 'control' which preceded the 'discovery of the individual' ('la scoperta della persona') and which, in the fifties and sixties, revealed to personnel managers the 'human' side of their resource, and therefore the 'caring' component of their job.[10] Karen Legge identifies the roots of this contradictory 'control–care' paradigm in the capitalistic ideology which still bedevils the function in Britain (and not only there):

> The fact that personnel specialists oscillate between the 'personnel' and 'management', between 'caring' and 'control' aspects of the function, can be attributed to their role in mediating a major contradiction embedded in capitalist systems: the need to achieve both the control *and* consent of employees.
>
> (Legge 1995: 14; emphasis in the original)

The dualism in the role of the personnel managers, the 'double bind' in which they are caught up, is a consequence of either their claiming a share in the strategic decision-making process, and therefore being seen as power-thirsty, or, alternatively their being labelled as 'passive administrative nobodies'. Either way, they seem confined to a role of 'perpetual marginality' (Watson 1986) engendered by the secondary (= service) role that staff departments such as personnel fulfil with regard to line departments such as production.

In Italy, radical changes are predicted which will affect the current view of Personnel as a staff function; i.e. as a function that does not contribute to core business. 'De-specialisation' ('despecializzazione'), outsourcing and staff cuts are all consequences of the re-engineering, re-structuring and 'lean enterprise' policies now prevalent in the business world, and as a result, beside its service role, Personnel will have to continue to exercise a social control role. As Lolli suggests, because of the importance that behaviour plays in strategic action:

> quello che cambiera' sara' piuttosto la natura del controllo sociale esercitato dalla funzione del personale, che si trasformera' da una logica lineare di controllo esterno ad una logica complessa di controllo sull' autocontrollo del management: insomma, dalla direzione delle persone alla facilitazione dell'empowerment.
>
> (Lolli 1994: 18)

> what will change [in the personnel function] will rather be the nature of social control exercised by the personnel function, which will be

transformed from external control to control over the self-controlling management. Hence, [a shift from] directing of people to facilitating empowerment.

Meanwhile, in Britain, traditional Personnel responsibilities and tasks are being shifted to line managers or contracted out in what the editor of *PM* describes as 'dramatic, sometimes even bewildering changes' (MacLachlan 1995: 25). And all this takes place in the context of widespread frustration among employees who are not always given the opportunity to contribute to their company's success through their own personal development. In the launch article of the Association's new magazine (*PM*) in January 1995,[11] Geoff Armstrong, the director general of the Institute of Personnel Development (IPD), argues that the professionality and credibility of the personnel function is at stake: 'People management' should not be treated as 'a series of bolt-on, flavour-of-the month initiatives'. Instead, it is 'a systematically learnable discipline which needs to be studied and applied by all managers, not just the professional specialists whose primary focus it is' (Armstrong 1995: 24).

Back in Italy, the British *PM* vision of the democratisation of the personnel function, made accessible to, and indeed, expected of all managers whether personnel or not, is a far cry from the picture of Personnel emerging from the pages of *DdP*. The HRM philosophy might have changed in the last three decades in Italy, but the praxis is still anchored in the same traditional tasks associated with the function, such as recruitment. And it is in fact through the sarcastic discourse of a typical recruitment interview that *DdP* effects a powerful and amusing self-chastising routine which is quite unexpected in an otherwise self-controlled and 'factual' magazine.

'interviewee's phrase book'	'interviewer's phrase book'
My company is still holding on despite the recession (the receivers are coming in tomorrow)	I'm sorry for the appointment at this late time of the day (I must be free in less than 20 minutes: at 8.30 I'm going out to dinner with Luisa, at last)
Money is important but isn't everything (I want the salary offered increased by 30 per cent)	It's a position with a great potential for growth (the appointment is at the lowest point of the scale)
My strong point is people management (I want to work	It doesn't matter if the candidate doesn't possess

| off my inferiority complex by playing at being the boss) | all the required technical skills since we believe in people and invest in their development (I know he isn't good enough for the job but he's the MD's nephew) |

(Rossi 1995)

This parody of interviewing discourse deconstructs the surface meanings, and, more importantly, it reassures the reader-practitioner that the writer-professional-reader are all able to take themselves less seriously than the magazine's tone at first suggests.[12] It also deflates the tension that is often built into such an encounter in real life and inflicts a severe blow to the highly ritualised set-up of such an occasion in an Italian context.

Intertwined with this ironic vein, and in sharp contrast to it, the omnipresent discourse of *trust* dominates the first 1995 issue of *DdP*. Trust is 'an essential organisational lubricant' in the complex interrelationship between communication, understanding and 'fidelizzazione' (loosely translatable as 'binding by faith'). For a function such as Personnel, traditionally emerging as untrustworthy in the tales of Italian employees, this is a tall order. It requires nothing less than a change of beliefs and attitudes, away from the old paradigm of the anonymous, impersonal 'direction' ('direzione'), towards an open and transparent relational approach to staff. Trust engenders understanding which enables communication, which, in turn, increases trust. The move towards recognition of 'staff as human beings' is one that requires a willingness on behalf of Personnel to expose their own 'human face' and therefore to take risks. There is no longer room for the secrecy or opportunism of the past if the aim is a long-term relationship between Personnel and the employees (Bordogna 1995).[13]

If Italian HRM sounds markedly influenced by humanism and idealism, at least on paper, its British counterpart in early 1995 is having to contend with a post-idealistic phase which resulted in a widespread and severe re-structuring, where 'survivors' have witnessed the decimation of their colleagues and have been left to pick up the pieces. 'Survivor syndrome' was identified in 1994 by a group of Personnel professionals who had carried out a national survey of the financial services industry: unsurprisingly, the employees who are left show decreased loyalty to the company and closer identification with colleagues and work groups. The antidote proposed by HR researchers and consultants is the drafting of a 'new, more appropriate psychological contract' between the company and its employees. Employment is replaced by 'employability' entailing 'personal career ownership' and 'a changing definition of loyalty' (Doherty and Horsted 1995).

In addition to the re-definition of traditional values, the climate of environmental and personal insecurity in which UK 'people managers' are asked to operate is hardly conducive to co-operation. As the management guru C. K. Prahalad acknowledges: 'Many HR professionals have found it difficult dealing with the implications of restructuring. After all, it's difficult telling your people they are the most important resource when all they see is that they are the most expendable resource' (Prahalad 1995: 34). Once again, 'people managers' are confronted with a dualism that leaves them victims of their own role. The solution, according to Prahalad, is in the enabling role of HR people who should become agents of change by helping the organisation to forget its past, and managers to rediscover dormant skills and learn new ones.

However, if HR is the 'biggest under-leveraged skill in a large company' (Prahalad 1995: 36), how are 'people managers' in fact supposed to act as a leverage for the rest of the organisation? And there is more. Corporate ethics have been increasingly placed under public scrutiny by cases exemplifying its absence, and Personnel professionals often find themselves in the position of being asked to support ethics plans which they have had no hand in creating (Pickard 1995: 24). As *PM* commands on 4 May 1995: 'Prepare to make a judgement.' The expressive illustration of a lighthouse emerging from a stormy sea which accompanies the feature replicates the front cover of the same issue where the block red-lettered caption reads: KEEPING OFF THE ROCKS: DO YOU NEED A BUSINESS ETHICS POLICY? This sea metaphor is not unique in the survival discourse paraded in many of the features in PM. For example, as Sumantra Ghoshal, another management guru argues, HR managers are called to give 'navigational support' to line managers in the rough sea of restructuring (MacLachlan and Thatcher 1995).

At the same time, however, it is possible to identify a parallel discourse of 'acid testing' for HR managers which provides suggestions as to how one can tell that personnel professionals are making a contribution to their companies. The 'acid testing' proposed sketches out the (ideal) UK human resources manager as an individual with involvement at board level on strategic matters and salary in line with other directors, responsible for the introduction of perform-ance contracts which include HR objectives, and for a working per-formance management system. Recognition of the contribution made by the HR function at all levels of the organisation is taken for granted in this ideal projection.

This contrasts sharply with the self-projection discourse of 'positive human qualities' applied to Italian personnel managers, according to which the struggle for recognition rests on a complete re-thinking of the professional and human qualities expected of them. The list is daunting, and includes items such as 'attention to customer's perceptions', 'service', 'co-operation', 'transparency', 'competence' and 'coherence'. The new Personnel profession must rid itself of its most jealously guarded possession – that is (exclus-ive) access to information and knowledge – which should instead be granted to groups and individuals within the organisation. This poses a challenge to the hegemonic position of the old-type Per-sonnel function, which is now confronted with meeting employees face-to-face and working *with* them, rather than *against* them. The 'direction' ('la direzione') has finally been called out of its splendid isolation onto the daily scene of human dealings (Bordogna 1995).

The personal qualities of personnel professionals in Italy could not be tested more effectively than in the treatment of disabled employees, subsumed under the patronising legalese of 'protected categories'.[14] The pragmatic morale of this 'caring discourse' (let's change the disabled into a resource for the company, rather than simply putting up with them as a cost), effectively turns it into a piece of corporate ethics. Nevertheless, it is primarily the (ideal-istic?) picture of the 'caring' personnel manager that comes across; i.e. the manager who is willing to create new roles for the disabled, to mediate between them and the resistance or outright rejection of the organisation, and to act as the 'person-in-the middle' or, in the writer's own words, the man 'between the hammer and the anvil' ('fra l'incudine e il martello') (Pasini 1995).

As mentioned above, 'caring' is simply the flipside of 'control' in this Janus-like construction of personnel management. An article in the 1995 May–June issue of *DdP* ('How to manage dismissal suc-cessfully') depicts the personnel manager in the stressful role of the 'messenger of dismissal', and stresses that the calculated efficiency of the 'ritual of dismissal' must not leave anything to chance, or to emotion. The article prescribes the following procedure. Phase 1: the message is communicated in a 'serious and solemn' voice within the first five minutes of the meeting; Phase 2: the employee reacts by shutting himself or herself off (i.e. the message is not immediately processed); Phase 3: on registering the damning nature of the announcement, the person reacts in one of the ways featuring in the standard checklist mentioned above. At this point, variations in the procedures are anticipated. (For example, if the blow is visibly too hard for the employee to bear, the manager is advised to repeat the ritual from Phase 1 in the very near future (Manzoni 1995).) The dismissal routine, detailed in an emotion-free narrative for the manager, who is clearly expected to be 'on top of it', in fact belies the turmoil that engulfs both parties at a time when corporate interests must be safeguarded at the price of shattering somebody's life. Here the 'caring' attitude of the personnel manager is tested to breaking point. Cynically, managers could turn this experience to their own advantage, should the time ever come when they find themselves on the other side of the desk. However, there is a substantial difference, as the magazine implies in a number of articles, between the non-managerial staff and the *quadri* and *dirigenti* (roughly translatable as middle managers and executives). While both are prime victims of acquisitions, mergers, restructuring and so on, only the latter are caught in the safety net of 'outplacement'. For the others, the 'human resources revolution' (read: savage staff cuts) perpetrated to safeguard organisational functionality means 'separation' (read: dismissal) between the organisation and the individuals dismissed.

Outplacement,[15] or dismissal with a softer landing, is, in the words of an Italian human resources executive, 'an excellent way of managing a softer exit of good personnel from the company' ('Il ricorso all'outplacement è un ottimo modo per gestire in maniera morbida l'uscita del personale comunque valido dall'azienda') (Lusvarghi 1995). Somewhat ironically, trust between the outplacement consultant and the 'exiting' manager is quoted as the essential ingredient for a successful outcome of the operation. Outplacement is as much about providing an alternative to redundancy as it is about relational policies. Internally, the anxiety of personnel directors is reduced, as is the resentfulness of the managers on their way out, and the knock-on effect on staff morale. Externally, the company's image as a 'caring' organisation is boosted.

'Control' and 'care' are still set against each other even in this most delicate phase of the managers' working life, a small-scale version of the dualism that they will have experienced in their mediating role between attention to the individual and attention to corporate aims and objectives.

6. CONCLUSION

This chapter has proposed a socio-semiotic perspective on generic text types, extended to accommodate a cognitive dimension which is seen as accounting for the (conscious or unconscious) process of choice-making at the level of discourse. This process underlines the verbal construction of the personae of the human resources/personnel professionals to which both reader and writer contribute by drawing from their experiential baggage, thus making the act of interpretation not only historically and socially situated, but also 'possible' in the first place.

The analysis of three 1995 issues of *People Management* (*PM*) and *Direzione del Personale* (*DdP*), the magazines of the British and Italian official associations of personnel professionals, has concentrated on the Rhetorical Framing and Thematic Profiling of the two publications as tokens of human resource management. In particular, two thematic clusters have been isolated for detailed investigation on how the personnel profession is constructed linguistically in the two cultural contexts. It appears that the accepted differences between the two countries are synthetically captured in the titles of the magazines themselves, where the more sympathetic (British) 'People Management' confronts the traditional (Italian) 'Personnel Direction'.

In the mid-nineties, Italian personnel professionals were still in the throes of defining a role that reconciled the humane, emotional and psychological aspects of dealing with people – i.e. the 'caring' half of the profile – with the traditional 'control' exercised by the old-style 'directional' approach that had ensured personal privileges in the past but which was recognised as being dysfunctional, if not obnoxious, in modern organisations. Their British counterparts were far more concerned with the issues generated by the ongoing economic crisis. For them, it was often a question of coping with redundancies and 'survivors', in a post-restructuring phase that also tested their skills and questioned their roles, although in an obviously different way from their Italian colleagues. Self-representation and self-projections are overlapping discourses in the narratives of the two magazines, where they perform the balancing act of constructing the Personnel profession as trapped in the 'control–care' dilemma described not only in *PM* and *DdP*, but also in some of the more perceptive management literature.

NOTES

1. The two magazines in question, *People Management* and *Direzione del Personale*, are published by the Institute of Personnel Management (IPM) and by the Associazione Italiana per la Direzione del Personale (AIDP), respectively, and are the official magazines of the personnel profession in the two countries.

2. 'In most general terms, contextualization . . . comprises all activities by participants which make relevant, maintain, revise, cancel . . . any aspect of context which, in turn, is responsible for the interpretation of an utterance in its particular locus of occurrence' (Auer 1992: 4).

3. It is envisaged that these parameters will be employed at all three levels of rhetorical analysis, i.e. textual, thematic and lexical. This chapter illustrates a first application of some of them to the interpretation of specialist magazines.

    This matrix is meant to be 'expandable' in that further research into genre that follows less traditional approaches is likely to contribute other parameters. The textual realisations are also a tentative list.

4. In this chapter, the terms 'writer' and 'reader' will be used throughout in preference to other pairs (e.g. coder–decoder, producer–consumer, etc.) in the awareness that their definitions must account for the mutual non-exclusive understanding of their functions.

5. In her article, Elaine Chin discusses Martin Nystrand's model in some detail. In particular, its underlying construct, the 'principle of reciprocity', is relevant to the stance in favour of a more socio-cognitive orientation in genre analysis advocated in this chapter. According to this principle, '[m]eaning is accomplished when readers enter into the space that writers have created through texts, when readers close the 'circuit' open to all possible meanings by constructing one interpretation during a single act of reading' (Chin 1994: 454).

6. In this chapter it will not be possible to include a discussion of the lexical choices although the concordanced texts of the six selected magazines have revealed some interesting patterns. In a recent study of lexical nets in spoken business discourse (Collins and Scott 1997), the authors employ a computer-aided analysis that is potentially compatible with the understanding of keywords and semantic clusters held by the author of this chapter (see also Barbara and Scott, this volume).

7. PM is a fortnightly publication whereas DdP is bi-monthly. For the analysis, a selection was made of the first issues of PM for each alternate month in the first half of 1995, January, March and May, and the first three issues of DdP (Jan–February, March–April, May–June) in the same year.

8. It is interesting to comment on the title of the publication itself. *Direzione del Personale* has traditionalist overtones, reminiscent of early management doctrines. 'To direct personnel' is a far cry from the 'human resources management' of today: 'direction' is juxtaposed with 'management' and 'personnel' with 'human resources'. Whether the word choice reflects a real improvement is arguable. What is certain, is that discourse labels have changed to reflect a change in perceptions, if not in actual practice.

9. The range of features which appear in the magazines is influenced not only by the materials sent in by the contributors but also by the policy of the editorial office. In this comparative analysis, the interest lies in highlighting the themes common to both magazines, which are also likely to reflect common concerns of the profession in the two countries as reflected in the national press (see section 5.2.2 for an illustration of intertextuality).

10. The linguistic shift in some quarters, from 'personnel' to 'human resources' arguably follows on from this 'discovery' and, at least in Italy, it is datable to the eighties. Against this background, the choice of title of the Italian magazine, *Direzione del Personale*, faithful to the older 'control' model, is highly significant and possibly indicative of an attempt to maintain the *status quo* despite the linguistic shift just mentioned.

11. The IDP official magazine was called *Personnel Management* before changing its title to *People Management* in January 1995.

12. Interestingly, the Italian magazine, unlike the British one, also carries cartoons, some of them quite sarcastic, alongside the 'serious' treatment of topical issues in HRM.

13. Significantly, then, 'Trust and Understanding', the caption on the front colour cover of the January–February issue, is represented by a man and a child wearing dinner suits and holding hands. The man looks down at the child as he walks. A picture of fatherly reassurance which leaves no room for speculation on gender issues!

14. According to the Italian law, individuals from these categories, most of whom bear a physical or mental disability, must represent 15 per cent of the 'able' workforce of any company. Resistance to employment of the disabled incurs heavy penalties. Top management is notoriously reluctant to become involved in legal disputes, and delegates any dealings on these issues to Personnel.

15. Outplacement is the alternative to crude dismissal offered to senior managers and executives who are placed 'in the care' of an agency

external to the company which acts as a job-seeking intermediary on their behalf.

REFERENCES

Armstrong, Geoff (1995) A magazine to champion the contribution of people. *People Management* (12 January): 24.

Auer, Peter (1992) Introduction: John Gumperz's approach to contextualization. In Peter Auer and Aldo di Luzio (eds), *The Contextualization of Language*. Amsterdam and Philadelphia: Benjamins, pp. 1–38.

Bargiela-Chiappini, Francesca and Harris, Sandra (1997) *Managing Language: The Discourse of Corporate Meetings*. Amsterdam and Philadelphia: John Benjamins.

Bazerman, Charles (1994) *Constructing Experience*. Carbondale and Edwardsville: Southern Illinois University Press.

Bordogna, Roberto (1995) Fiducia e comprensione, risorse strategiche per lo sviluppo dell'impresa. *Direzione del Personale* (Jan.–Feb.): 20–5.

Briggs, Charles L. and Richard Bauman (1992) Genre, intertextuality and social power. *Journal of Linguistic Anthropology* 2 (2): 131–72.

Chin, Elaine (1994) Redefining 'context' in research on writing. *Written Communication* 11 (4): 445–82.

Collins, Heloisa and Scott, Mike (1997) Lexical landscaping in business meetings. In Francesca Bargiela-Chiappini and Sandra Harris (eds), *The Languages of Business: An International Perspective*. Edinburgh: Edinburgh University Press, pp. 183–208.

Cook, Guy (1990) Transcribing infinity: problems in context presentation. *Journal of Pragmatics* 14: 1–24.

Dee Proctor, Jo (1995) Getting teams off the ground. *Personnel Management* (4 May): 28–35.

Devitt, Amy J. (1993) Generalizing about genre: new conceptions of an old concept. *College Composition and Communication* 44 (4): 573–86.

Doherty, Noeleen and Horsted, Jim (1995) Helping survivors to stay on board. *People Management* (12 January): 26–8.

Douglas, Mary (1994) The genuine article. In S. Riggins and S. Harold (eds), *The Socialness of Things: Essays in the Socio-Semiotics of Objects*. Berlin: Mouton de Gruyter, pp. 9–22.

Gunnarsson, Britt-Louise (1995) Studies of language for specific purposes: a biased view of a rich reality. *International Journal of Applied Linguistics* 5 (1): 111–34.

Halliday, Michael A. K. and Ruqaiya, Hasan (1985) *Language, Context and Text: A Social Semiotic Perspective*. Geelong, Vic.: Deakin University Press (reprinted 1989, Oxford: Oxford University Press).

Kress, Gunther and Threadgold, Tracy (1988) Towards a social theory of genre. *Southern Review* 21 (3): 215–43.

Legge, Karen (1995) *Human Resource Management: Rhetorics and Realities.* London: Macmillan Press.

Lolli, Massimo (1994) Come cambia la funzione del personale. *Direzione del Personale* (Sept.–Dec.): 15–18.

Lusvarghi, Gabriella (1995) Cambiare lavoro. Da problema a opportunità con l'outplacement. *Direzione del Personale* 23–5 (May–June).

MacLachlan, Rob (1995) Our aim: to be a guide through bewildering times. *People Management* (12 January): 25.

MacLachlan, Rob and Thatcher, Michael (1995) HR's role 'to navigate through restructuring'. *People Management* (12 January): 18.

Malinowski, Bronislaw (1923) The problem of meaning in primitive languages. In C. K. Ogden and I. A. Richards (eds), *The Meaning of Meaning: A Study of the Influence of Language upon Thought and the Science of Symbolism.* London: Routledge and Kegan Paul, pp. 296–336.

Manzoni, Roberto (1995) Come gestire con successo la risoluzione del rapporto di lavoro. *Direzione del Personale* (May–June): 20–2.

Nystrand, Martin (1989) A social-interactive model of writing. *Written Communication* 6: 66–85.

Pasini, Emilio (1995) Inserimento al lavoro di handicappati. L'esperienza di una società. *Direzione del Personale* (March–April): 17–21.

Piccardo, Claudia, Varchetta, Giuseppe and Zanarini, Gianni (1992) Car makers and marathon runners: in pursuit of culture through the language of leadership. In P. Gagliardi (ed.), *Symbols and Artifacts: Views of the Corporate Landscape.* New York: Aldine de Gruyter, pp. 255–70.

Pickard, Jane (1995) Prepare to make a moral judgement. *People Management* (May): 22–5.

Prahalad, C. K. (1995) How HR can help to win the future. *People Management* 34–7 (12 January).

Rafoth, Bennett A. and Rubin, Donald L. (1988) *The Social Construction of Written Communication.* Norwood, NJ: Ablex Publishing.

Rossi, Riccardo (1995) Corso accelerato per il responsabile delle risorse umane. *Direzione del Personale* (Jan.–Feb.): 31–3.

Silverstein, Mike (1992) The indeterminacy of contextualization: when is enough enough? In Peter Auer and Aldo di Luzio (eds), *The Contextualization of Language.* Amsterdam and Philadelphia: Benjamins, pp. 55–76.

Swales, John and Priscilla, Rogers (1995) Discourse and the projection of corporate culture: the Mission Statement. *Discourse & Society* 6 (2): 223–42.

Villa, Danilo (1995) Si scrive 'esternalizzazione', si pronuncia 'spin off'. *Direzione del Personale* (March–April): 13–15.

Watson, Tony J. (1986) *Management, Organisation and Employment Strategy.* London: Routledge.

Witte, Stephen (1992) Context, text, intertext: toward a constructionist semiotic of writing. *Written Communication* 9 (2): 237–308.

SEVEN

Words of women: a study of executives' rhetorical strategies

Carol David

1. INTRODUCTION

Only recently has the public language of women become the subject of research. Scholars generally agree that because women have traditionally held subordinate positions in society, they have developed communication strategies consonant with their exclusion from public life, and these rhetorical strategies have been seen as inferior to the logocentric rhetorical tradition and as lacking the power needed for leadership. This chapter will examine the rhetorical strategies of two CEOs to determine if women with power in the business community use different strategies from their male counterparts.

Before comparing women's and men's business speeches, the chapter selectively reviews linguistic and rhetorical research on gender and language and identifies attributes of male and female rhetorical strategies. The discussion of data focuses on the speeches of Charlotte Beers, former CEO, now Chairman [*sic*] Emeritus, of the multinational advertising firm Ogilvy & Mather, and of Marcia Hanson, CEO of AmerUs Bank, a Midwestern retail banking and consumer lending organisation. The principal texts examined are two ceremonial speeches delivered by these CEOs, but some evidence is also drawn from their language in company videos. A series of memos Hanson writes to her employees in preparation for an upcoming retreat provides background information on her management style. The analysis of the language of these texts will highlight how the CEOs develop personality and project power in their professional rhetoric. For this study, ten high-level female executives were contacted. All responded to a request for copies of their speeches, but several answered that they did not write out their speeches and two refused to take part. Because Charlotte Beers and Marcia Hanson sent the largest portfolios of speeches and supplementary documents, their texts were selected for analysis. Their willingness to share personal information may indicate a bias towards collaborative relationships, tendencies which show in the language they use.

2. WOMEN'S AND MEN'S RHETORICAL STRATEGIES

Andrea A. Lunsford writes that the realm of rhetoric has been almost exclusively male. It 'has never recognized the forms, strategies, and goals used by many women as "rhetorical"' (Lunsford 1995: 6). She describes traditional rhetoric as 'competitive, agonistic, and linear', as opposed to one that might include 'often dangerous moves', such as personal references and 'valuing – indeed insisting upon – collaboration' (1995: 6).

Karlyn Kohrs Campbell offers an additional description of what could be a feminine rhetoric. She explains that rhetorical strategies known as consciousness-raising grew out of small group sessions developed in the feminist movement of the sixties. Although consciousness-raising was associated with small groups, it might also be used to describe a style of public speech where women use personal experience as evidence and structure 'arguments inductively to develop conclusions out of a series of instances'. Women could speak 'as peers sharing experience, not as authorities brandishing academic credentials' (Campbell 1994: xix). Campbell adds that not all women have chosen this strategy; it is only that many seem to use elements of it.

3. WOMEN'S AND MEN'S STYLE

Pedagogical advice on rhetorical style has traditionally been framed in male terms. Since the time when practical rhetoric was taught in colleges in the United States, textbooks have prescribed the 'plain style' with its emphasis on vigorous and forceful prose. Other advice given to student writers is to use active verbs and avoid weak modifiers and qualifiers. Joanne Wagner, who analyses the teaching of rhetoric at four of the elite Seven Sisters colleges (Smith, Vassar, Wellesley, Mount Holyoke) in the late nineteenth century, explains that Herbert Spencer in his 1852 volume *The Philosophy of Style* emphasised economy as the primary goal, basing his judgement on the objectives of science (Wagner 1995: 187). Wagner laments the plain style's emphasis on features more associated with male rhetoric, which fail to define or even allow for women's personalities to develop.[1]

The English language contains many male biases in grammar and diction, some particularly salient in business discourse. In addition to the pronoun dilemma, which requires the awkward 'he or she' reference, other male hegemonies include generic groups – freshman, airman (without a feminine equivalent); titles – chairman, councilmen; greetings – Dear Sir, Gentlemen (without a feminine equivalent). When business metaphors do occur, they are typically male, related to competition and action, sports and war. Company stories, for example, are often told in heroic terms, creating myths of epic proportions (Mitroff and Kilmann 1975: 18). One forum that allows for a greater display of figurative language is the ceremonial speech. Research has shown, for example, how Michael Walsh, former CEO of the conglomerate Tenneco, embeds an extended epic metaphor into a speech describing the financial turnaround that he brought about in his company (David and Graham 1997; see further discussion below). Syndicated columnist Ellen Goodman believes that the sports jargon in public language is unnatural to women and its proliferation in business and political language excludes women's experience (Goodman 1996: 9A). Certainly the dominance of male terms in public language reflects the preponderance of male figures and positions in public life.

While male speakers, accounting for most heads of state, political figures, CEOs, ministers and news commentators, have had ample opportunities to disseminate male rhetorical styles, women have had little chance to introduce an alternative rhetoric to public speech. Wagner explains that in early rhetorical studies presented to women, male strategies were unquestioned, and women were taught to model them rather than adopt strategies of their own (Wagner 1995: 191). Little change has taken place since that time, and women in executive positions still have primarily male models of public speech as objects of study. Linguist Cheris Kramarae states the problem succinctly: 'Women and men are not equally able to say what they want, when and where and how they want' (Kramarae 1981: 19).

4. MALE AND FEMALE PUBLIC SPEAKERS

For the most part, women public speakers have been confined to topics on 'women's issues': suffrage, women's rights, children, social problems. Several examples of female public figures demonstrate the problems that women have met in their efforts to exhibit power in public language. Eleanor Roosevelt, for instance, was a pioneer in political life.[2] Her speeches used aphorism and biblical allusions. She undermined her own authority to gain male power-figures' acceptance, and to fulfil audience expectations she avoided controversy and did not counterattack or name her opponents (Petersen 1994: 385–7).

In contrast to Roosevelt, Geraldine Ferraro, who in 1984 was the first woman to run for the office of vice president, used a rhetoric patterned on the confrontational and tough male style. Because incumbent Ronald Reagan was seen as a strong male figure who held the line against the Soviets, Ferraro could play a 'feisty, argumentative' part as antagonist in opposition to the 'soft' lines Mondale and the Democrats had defined in the election (Blankenship 1994: 192). In her speeches she did not avoid a confrontational tone (Blankenship 1994: 204); however, she and Mondale soundly lost the election, and although many women admired her courage, she was labelled as strident and aggressive by much of the public. Other women attempting to use power more directly have faced frustration and failure – the failure, for example, of Hillary Clinton's health-care initiative.

Thus, women in public life have been placed in a tight bind. If they choose male rhetorical strategies, they are criticised for being strident. Yet there is no clearly developed women's style that represents their individual personalities and the power of persuasion. A woman in an executive position must develop a language of power, but to answer expectations of feminine behaviour, she must demonstrate a relational and collaborative persona. She must, in short, develop a feminine rhetoric of power in a culture where feminine power has been an oxymoron.

Men have an easier task. Not only is a male style inherent in the language, but men have a long rhetorical tradition to draw from, even a firmly established business rhetoric. In a ceremonial speech written for his inner circle of managers, newly appointed CEO Mike Walsh exhibits the force of epic symbolism that defines him as a new leader with power and agency. In presenting his new managerial style, which includes a horizontal organisational system and team concepts, he evokes a setting of sports and war. Walsh creates an action-packed, suspense-filled narrative, symbolism that contradicts the actual day-to-day negotiations taking place in an office and boardroom, but the speech, made about males to an inner circle of males, is dramatic and motivating (David and Graham 1997). Another CEO, Lee Iacocca, who was well known during his tenure with Chrysler and once a potential presidential candidate, often addressed issues in national politics. For instance, he digressed into the evils of Japanese trade tariffs and problems with unions. He supported traditional American values of individualism (Seeger 1994). Although he used some sports metaphors, his style was rougher than Walsh's. His was a shirt-sleeves language, sometimes with mild profanity; he often spoke to the male world of auto-manufacturing in a gruff male language. These male voices spoke with the authority granted to them by their positions and, although they project individual personalities through their language, they are bolstered by a tradition of male dominance.

In the research on rhetorical strategies, linguists have contributed studies on the conversational strategies of women and men, which might also appear in public language. Although linguists have linked specific conversational strategies to women, Mary Crawford cautions that these strategies have not always been compared in situations where the speakers' intentions were the same (Crawford 1995: 17). In fact, men and women in the same situations and power positions may use similar strategies. Linguists generally agree that power is the key issue which defines the strategies speakers choose. As Mary Ritchie Key states in her book *Male/Female Language*, 'Male and female behavior can only be undersood within the matrix of the power structure of the total society' (1996: xiv). Because males have assumed positions of power, females have tended to develop more affiliative relationships and conversational styles that have been labelled as indirect, co-operative and emotional. These strategies are different from the communication styles of males which, as linear and analytic (Lunsford 1995: 6), are associated with leadership.

Because this study examines texts of two women holding CEO positions, and therefore positions of power, we can make some comparisons between the traditional male rhetorical strategies that researchers have identified as logical, competitive and authoritative and women's strategies: their use of emotional expressivity and narrative (Campbell 1994: xix; Kramarae 1981: 15–18); indirection; a polite, collaborative tone (Lakoff 1990: 204–5; Lunsford 1995: 6). It will be of interest to discover if these female executives apply rhetorical and linguistic strategies that project women's individuality and power.

5.   THE DATA

Epideictic speeches, because they are given at ceremonial occasions, allow for the study of texts which may contain figurative language and individual styles. Although they often reinforce traditional values (Perelman and Olbrechts-Tyteca 1971: 51), business speakers do use them to introduce change in organisations and promote their own ideology, as shown above in the rhetoric of Walsh and Iacocca. Both of the speeches analysed below fall under the broad genre of epideictic speeches, but Beers' speech is addressed to an internal audience of managers and Hanson's is an external invited speech presented to a business faculty. The following section analyses the texts, concentrating on rhetorical strategies, including the content and arrangement of the argument (which might suggest women's interests and inductive arrangements), and choice of evidence (which might be narrative or personal experience). It also addresses 'women's style,' including metaphorical language, which might evoke images more specific to their experience than sports and war; and tone, which could be non-combative and co-operative. Additionally, the speakers' personae and deliveries as shown in company videos are briefly described. The method employed is modelled on the rhetorical scholarship which examines particular texts within their rhetorical situations.

5.1.   Charlotte Beers' executive rhetoric

In 1992, coming from a position as head of a single-office firm in Chicago, Charlotte Beers joined Ogilvy & Mather, a firm with 270 offices world-wide. Ogilvy & Mather had been acquired in a hostile takeover by a British group in 1989 and was experiencing financial difficulty and loss of clients. Four years after Beers joined Ogilvy &

Mather the company showed a dramatic turnaround. Beers' efforts brought in American Express and Jaguar accounts (Sellers 1996: 48). The principal analysis examines a speech given to Beers' top managers six months after she joined the company. The speech, entitled 'Ogilvy & Mather 1993 Worldwide Strategy', was delivered extemporaneously and then written for distribution to management. Written speeches are often prepared by speech writers, but as Tarver explains in his analysis of Iacocca, there is no doubt that the speech represents the ideas and personal approach of the author (Tarver 1994: 215). (References, unless designated otherwise, are to this text, which is reproduced in part in Appendix A.)[3]

The strategy speech divides into an introduction; the description of the three strategies she proposes: targeting clients, establishing a new concept of working with brands, and cutting costs; and a brief closing. Her purpose is to introduce her initiative for handling clients' accounts, one she labels 'brand stewardship'. While the term 'brand management' is common in advertising, her special twist on the concept carries with it a new, personal, and emotional relationship with clients' brands; in the term 'stewardship' she evokes a nurturing, almost religious tone. Rather than detailing procedures in this speech, Beers uses language to build a culture the initiative needs to gain approval. As a ceremonial speech as well as a summary of strategy, the text contains certain features Karlyn Kohrs Campbell and Kathleen Hall Jamieson identify in presidential inaugurals: the speaker attempts to bridge from past to present by showing that traditional values will obtain, honouring past heroes and referring to general rather than specific goals (Campbell and Jamieson 1986).

In the introduction Beers appeals to the past by recalling the founder of the company, David Ogilvy. Ogilvy's image serves her purpose to urge unity in the large multinational company; he is the guiding presence whose voice is heard 'in all the halls of O&M'. She begins the speech as follows:

> 'We know the words, we just can't hear the music' (J. Plumeri). Our founder gave us words to live by. Today we have to set to music or rehear some of the words around which David Ogilvy built this remarkable agency.
>
> David's phrase *One Agency Indivisible* is music I'd like to hear in all the halls of O&M. *One Agency Indivisible*. This is a commanding idea as big as our company. From this idea of unity have come remarkable benefits to Ogilvy & Mather.

She revisits his influence three times in the speech. He is 'our inspiration', 'the David Ogilvy legend', 'the spirit of David's fierce honesty'. This reference also assures the audience that the new CEO is an admirer and a loyal follower of the founder and thus they need not worry about major changes of direction in the firm. She charts an optimistic path for her upcoming success: 'I think we have hit bottom and are poised for recovery'. She does announce directly that there will be changes: 'that change is expected, needed and possible'.

After this introduction she addresses in the next two strategies the primary message of the speech, outlining features for establishing relationships with clients and an attitude about working with them. Using metaphors which evoke personal rather than professional relationships, she defines the new culture. The language she chooses establishes an extended metaphor of romantic love and religious nurturing between upper management and employees and between the company and clients and the consumers and brands. The emotional terms she uses to do this occur throughout the speech. Top management has a 'passionate belief in our people . . . our brand O&M', which she terms our 'beloved' company. The audience can expect from her and top management 'an enthusiasm – a love of – caring about – advertising'. The staff are 'in love with our work'. They have 'started dialogue, courtships' with companies. They will 're-woo' them. The agency will establish the brand as an intimate part of the consumers' lives. Beers emphasises the creative abilities of her staff by the use of anaphora, or repetition – 'We give, we are in, we know, we seek, we are prepared':

> Though the client has mastered much to bring us a product – always juggling the relationship between costs and value to the user – the product does not become a BRAND until it has found a place in the minds and hearts of consumers.
>   That's how we give the product value by knowing where it will fit into the user's life. This is the beginning of the creative process for we are in a long and loving dialogue with these users. We know how to ask the questions that generate insights and emotions beyond the facts. We seek out their unmet needs, their wishes. We are prepared to understand subtleties like self esteem and a thirst for romance and dreams.

If the sales staff demonstrates their 'zest' and 'admiration of our work', the clients will become our 'missionaries'. Our account people should be 'stewards of the brand'.

Unlike male metaphors, as typified in the speech by Michael Walsh referred to in section 4, she does not glorify the actors; her speech evokes a mood of love and nurturing; it does not describe action. Her tone is serious and deliberate, and her persona, as shown in her training film, suggests a teacher – in her black suit and white collar, the same image she presents in a cover picture in *Fortune* magazine (1996). She maintains a certain distance from the subject, as if she is explaining rather than persuading, which keeps the emotional element controlled.

5.1.1. Gendered rhetoric

The speech contains some features of male rhetoric. Beers uses a traditional logical, deductive arrangement, outlining the items in the order they are announced and ending with the financial report, which lowers the impact of the emotional elements of the speech. However, Beers also uses many features identified as female strategies. She explains rather than argues, even though at the time the speech was given it was important that her new ideas for the company be accepted. Because the initiative proposes an emotional promotion of clients' brands, the description includes many emotional terms. In part, the language is the backbone of the new strategies and therefore it is not imported to provide an emotional speech. However, she does propose the initiative by describing the emotion involved in the work and worker relationships – for instance, speaking of a passion for the company and employees. She uses extended metaphors of love and stewardship (a term associated with males but in this context of love and communion it becomes a nurturing female quality). The terms could be viewed as cloyingly sweet; *Fortune* reports that she met with some resistance from her staff, even Ogilvy himself, in supporting emotion as the underlying relationship with brands (Sellers 1996: 48), but the determined tone and focused delivery keep the emotions from becoming intense.

Beers' proposal for personal relationships among employees supports current findings that women value personal and collaborative relationships (Lunsford 1995: 6). Her attitudes about collaboration are revealed directly in a speech she presented to the Chicago women's group two years after the strategy speech. 'So as a recipe for success, are you looking for a few good leaders, a decent number of managers and a cluster of followers? I don't think so. That's the antithesis of "empowerment", a word I'm weary of . . . but collaborative still has a lot of potency to me' (Beers 1995: 2). In this speech to women, many of whom she has known and worked with in the past, she describes her experience selling her campaign. Providing narrative examples, she discloses doubts, misdirections and failures along with the final epiphany. In another speech upon receiving the Matrix Award (given to women for excellence in communications), she shows that bravery does not belong exclusively to men: 'As the world these days teaches you that your skills are nurturing, to be nourishing, to be collaborative, let me remind you that it is also your natural heritage to lead, to be bold and brave' (Beers 1996: 7). As these speeches demonstrate, her public speaking language is personal and emotional.

5.2.   Marcia Hanson's executive rhetoric

Marcia Hanson, president and CEO of AmerUs Bank, moved from a position of president of Firstar Bank to her present position in 1995. She holds an undergraduate degree in English and a PhD in developmental psychology. Before entering the banking field she held teaching and administrative jobs in academe. The speech is an invited address given at a large Midwestern university for the final ceremony of the College of Business's annual Business Week. The audience is a primarily male business faculty and the state Board of Regents. The speech is entitled 'Business ethics speech'. (All references, unless otherwise designated, are to this speech, which is reproduced in part in Appendix B.) Other references are to a series of memos Hanson has written and a video produced for employees.

The text falls under a subcategory of epideictic speeches which Seeger lists as Iacocca's 'speeches to external constituencies' and subdivides by topic (1994). As a talk on business ethics, Hanson's text resembles speeches identified in Seeger's book as topics on general business problems. Iacocca addresses economic issues such as fair trade, the budget deficit, and foreign competition with the Japanese, espousing his philosophy and values. Hanson's speech has a similar purpose of defining her philosophy, specifically on the ethics of management styles. She describes good and bad management systems and styles and relates them to general principles of developmental psychology.

In the speech, Hanson compares new horizontal management systems, which usually organise employees into teams and involve them in decision-making, with old, hierarchically structured systems. Salient in the speech is an emphasis on employees as agents of their own destinies. She states directly that allowing employees to develop themselves and their skills gives them 'employability rather than employment'. Management provides 'no promises'. Although the horizontal structures, with their team concepts, have been equated with values of co-operation, Hanson stresses individuality: 'The realization that each of us, in the end, is a free agent represents a degree of freedom and responsibility we have never had before.'

She begins the speech with an introduction recalling a personal experience, her graduation from college. She references the image of business that many college students held in the 1960s, an image that she and the audience know still exists today. By dismissing this image and presenting herself as an insider in both business and academe, she is able to criticise business practices without offending the audience:

> When I graduated from college in 1967 with my liberal arts degree and my sixties idealism, I truly believed that the term 'business ethics' was an oxymoron. Little did I imagine that eleven years later I would be entering the exciting world of business where I had previously assumed all manner of evil resided.
>
> I'm not really sure where we got our skepticism of business. I am sure, however, that we all looked with great disdain on those poor souls who chose to major in business administration. Those of us who didn't get shipped to Vietnam flocked into teaching or the peace corps or graduate school where, in many instances, our idealism and naiveté had a rude encounter with reality. We found that ethical behavior had, in fact, no relationship with a liberal arts education. And as we struggled with the rest of the nation to find purpose and meaning in our country's involvement in Southeast Asia or the riots and burning of our inner cities, we began to understand that ethics is not a matter of right and wrong or black and white, but rather it is a tapestry with many shades of gray.

She also introduces a theme of national politics that will continue throughout the speech, connecting her business examples to public events and giving stature to her remarks. Later, she returns to personal references, explaining that she has been a manager for the past twenty-eight years and her examples will come from 'situations I have personally experienced'. She announces that her topic will be business ethics, 'the smaller issues of day-to-day work interactions', which she later refers to as 'the level of personal interaction' which requires difficult ethical choices. The speech develops inductively with the argument structured in two main parts. The first and longest section includes the comparison of management systems. The second section addresses the development of ethical integrity, both in early childhood and later in the business world.

Her evidence supporting 'new management systems' is developed through examples illustrating unethical management practices which have taken place in old systems. The 'first scenario' describes a hierarchically structured company where the manager does not share information and consequently employees are suspicious and accusatory. The second example presents a hypothetical case of downsizing and considers unacceptable reactions. Her third scenario recognises the struggle of Shannon Faulkner, the first female cadet at the military academy, the Citadel. Hanson uses this experience to illustrate the loss of individuality in a hierarchical organisation such as the military. In a single paragraph she addresses the positive values of the new, horizontal management systems and follows with five questions centring on the ethics of the old system. She does not question the implications of the new system, which we assume she implements in her company, although some critics have pointed out that extended responsibilities for employees can lead to inequities, among them long working hours (Steingard and Fitzgibbons 1993). These new systems have been developed by males, based roughly on W. Edwards Deming's Total Quality Management (TQM), which he designed for a male Japanese business culture. Whether they are more favourable to women than the old systems might depend upon how they are implemented.

The metaphors of the speech evoke images of personal and family relationships and of developmental psychology. She dismisses the paternalism associated with the old management system, calling it a 'paternalistic caretaker', 'a kind of parent', where workers were members of an 'extended family of sorts'. Managers were like 'good parents, looking out for their employees' interests by making critical decisions for them'. New styles of management are framed in language that evokes independence and growth: employees will receive information to be 'more involved in making key decisions'. She frames her management philosophy in psychological terms:

> We are probably all fed up with the current political rhetoric about family values – particularly when it is used to condemn or exclude certain members of society. But it's hard to argue that a firm

grounding in principled thinking does not begin at home, in the way individuals who love and care for us from birth treat us, themselves and each other. Very often, the source of dysfunctional behavior in the work setting emanates from an adaptive behavior learned early in life. She acknowledges that negative experiences can still be salvaged through intervention. The workplace supplies intervention, 'fostering this development' by facing ethical dimensions directly. Workshops are an important means of growth where she may engage in 'processing experience with my people to help them – and me – understand it more fully'. Describing ethical development in the language of psychology is not surprising, considering her background. Her commitment to personal interactions is carried out both in language and business operations. For example, in a series of memos she exhibits careful and deliberate planning for an upcoming retreat directed at company strategy. Hanson imports a facilitator for the meetings, explains the personalities involved to him, provides all attendees with a carefully constructed agenda for the workshop and describes social activities to take place afterwards. Her procedures forecast a personal and dialogic session.

5.2.1. Gendered rhetoric

Hanson's support of TQM management systems and her preference for independence suggest traditional male values. Also, the overall tone of the speech is unemotional and scholarly, suitable for the audience of primarily male faculty and administrators. However, her rhetorical style includes new metaphors more associated with 'women's rhetoric'. In a way, in fact, she reverses the values of TQM supported by Michael Walsh in his speech, which presented teamwork in competitive war and sports metaphors. Hanson presents independence in a nurturing language of growth and development. Rather than glorifying war in military metaphors, she is highly critical of military hierarchy. In her example of Shannon Faulkner, she includes a criticism of 'military leaders [who] have mastered the techniques of breaking down individual identity, instilling discipline, and building a sense of unity out of diverse personalities through the use of physical and mental conditioning and, in some cases, adversarial haranguing'. She warns that 'when these techniques are employed with a sense of mean-spiritedness and dominance, which they often are, the resulting environment can become hostile and threatening for employees'.

The inductive arrangement of her argument and the further in-directness of five questions that point to unethical assumptions in hierarchical systems create a change from the linear, deductive male style. Furthermore, providing support by example and including her own experience are rhetorical features identified as female. In the metaphors of family and childhood development she applies her own educational expertise, and in recommending consciousness-raising workshops she employs a collaborative concept which Camp-bell explains was explored in women's groups in the sixties. While she presents a strong argument, her tone is not dictatorial. Rather, it is softened by a number of tentative phrases, examples of the polite-ness strategies identified by linguists Brown and Levinson (1987), which Graham and David have shown occur in egalitarian organ-isational cultures (Graham and David 1996: 14). Hanson uses 'I believe', 'I hope', 'I have not read anything about . . .', 'I will leave it to each of us as individuals to think more about how we feel about each of these contracts.' Her delivery of a speech to employees in a 1997 video portrays confidence and control, but like Beers, her per-sona suggests a teacher who presents the data for analysis.

6. DISCUSSION

Both women are devoted to business ideology; they expect their employees to understand the bottom line. Nothing in the content of their work suggests that they would support the ideology of Nancy C. M. Hartsock, a political scientist who enunciates a new order for business, basing it on female experience and biological destiny (Hartsock 1985). Both promote traditional business values of hard work and company loyalty. They are in control of the situation and topic, and are determined and focused in their presentation. In addi-tion, both women take risks in their speeches, a quality associated with males. For instance, Beers introduces an initiative which is overwhelmingly emotional and asks her management, most of whom are male, to endorse it. Hanson, in speaking to an external audience whose values she does not know, supports a TQM system without examining opposing views; she also sharply criticises the military. All of these rhetorical strategies suggest little difference from the traditional strategies created and used by males. However, more women's than men's strategies are present in their rhetorical style.

Each demonstrates a distinct personality in her texts. Beers brings to her speeches a background in advertising. When she announces in her video that the key to brand stewardship is emotion 'because there is no place else to go' (Case Study in Brand Stewardship at American Express 1996), she speaks from her past experience. Her persona displays a pedagogical tone – she teaches her plan. In her strategy speech announcing her upcoming plans, Beers is cautious, adhering closely to the characteristics identified as typical of inaugural addresses. Two years later, the 'Leadership' speech is less restrained. In this address to women, some of whom she has worked with in the past, she is more personal and more bold, disclosing through narrative her own disappointments and victories.

Hanson too projects metaphors unique to her expertise and values rooted in developmental psychology. Furthermore, as Lee Iacocca often did, she takes a stand on a national issue, in this case the problems arising from the first woman's enrolment in a male military academy. She offers a strong, almost one-sided view of her position on management, but she softens it with a tone that suggests inquiry rather than conclusions. Even though Hanson argues for horizontal over hierarchical management systems, she seems to ask her audience to consider the implications of the two. Her strategy is to ask and not to dictate.

With predominantly female strategies, is it possible to display power? In the first place, these executives hold power in their positions, the power that organisational theorist William Halal calls 'the power of influence' (Halal 1984). The context these executives operate within is different from that of the women protestors of the suffrage and the feminist movements, who faced audiences that may have been hostile to the speakers' very presence. These women leave little doubt about their professionalism or legitimacy to speak. While the style of the speeches would not be characterised as 'forceful' or 'strong', as stylistic advice has often prescribed, it is convincing. Their voices are persuasive but not authoritarian. Their power is not in force but in honesty and commitment. These executives persuade but do not coerce.

7.   CONCLUSION

These speeches allow for the comparisons between genders that Crawford calls for (in section 4 above), basing them on speakers in similar positions of power. Furthermore, the texts allow compar-isons because they conform to genres identified in epideictic cor-porate speeches. For instance, Beers' strategy speech, delivered soon after she assumed the job of CEO, falls within a sub-genre called the presidential inaugural, which Campbell and Jamieson have ana-lysed and which David and Graham have applied to speeches of CEOs, terming it 'the executive inaugural' (1997). Beers, like Michael Walsh, is new to her position, and speaks to an internal audience of managers, assuring them that company values have not changed but motivating them to adopt the new order and its goals. But where Walsh calls forth images of action, Beers creates metaphors of love and connection. Hanson's invited speech outlining her philo-sophy and values conforms to a sub-genre composed of speeches delivered to special constituencies, defined in Seeger's studies of the rhetoric of Lee Iacocca (1994). Both Iacocca and Hanson refer to their personal experience and make use of narrative examples to support their opinions and beliefs, but where Iacocca uses short, pithy examples in almost explosive bursts, Hanson elaborates and analyses to show causes and effects. The two strategies result in a difference in tone – one, forceful and authoritative; the other, in-structive and inquiring. Classifying the types of corporate speeches is important in any analysis because, as Seeger points out, speeches such as these must conform to the expectations of the genre and the audience. Seeger believes that 'Iacocca's success as a communicator may be attributed in part to his ability to speak to the constraints of the genre while at the same time making these generic addresses fresh' (Seeger 1994: 23).

The same might be said of the success of Beers and Hanson. Both follow the requirements of the genre yet develop original styles. Although both CEOs use a variety of strategies identified by rhet-orical and linguistic scholars as typical of both men and women, the number identified as women's strategies appears to be greater and the personalities that emerge are decidedly feminine. These women are able to generate new rhetorical strategies of a sort that Foss, Foss, and Trapp contend will 'revise and reformulate tradi-tional notions of rhetoric' away from what Sally Miller Gearhart has called the 'conquest model' of persuasion (Foss *et al.* 1991: 284).

In content and argument, one text, while using a linear, deductive arrangement, explains an emotional initiative. Another text argues for a management plan that includes independence for workers, but the argument contains an inductive, non-linear arrangement. Both women endorse collaborative procedures in company operations. In the use of evidence, both reference their personal experience; one text supports the argument entirely by elaborated narrative examples. The language choices display the most salient differences from males' style of competitive sports and war metaphors; these texts contain metaphors equated with women's interests and values: romantic love; nurturing and stewardship; connectedness; and psychological growth and development. The tone heard throughout the texts avoids dictatorial or authoritative language. Both women instruct. They are polite, sometimes deferential. One uses tentatives, showing open-mindedness, and the other discloses self-doubts. In addition, both women evidence their own personalities and values while at the same time projecting a power of commitment to their topics and connectedness to other people. Although these are women's strategies, it is not that males would never use them; it is rather that these women in power seem to use them comfortably and frequently.

APPENDIX A[4]

'We know the words, we just can't hear the music' (J. Plumeri). Our founder gave us words to live by. Today we have to set to music or rehear some of the words around which David Ogilvy built this remarkable agency.

David's phrase *One Agency Indivisible* is music I'd like to hear in all the halls of O&M. *One Agency Indivisible*. This is a commanding idea as big as our company. From this idea of unity have come remarkable benefits to Ogilvy & Mather. One agency meant that respect and nourishment for Direct as well as Advertising created the most successful partnership of this kind in the world today. In Asia and Latin America, one agency also means public relations or design.

One Agency means we get off planes wearing, carrying something Red. I used to feel this was a little much, but after you've been in a number of O&M offices with the signature red somewhere in evidence, it feels like home. Our clients tell me they feel the same way.

Indivisible means a shared set of beliefs about what matters. But we are, at times, a house divided. In the turbulent times in the agency's recent history, in the absence of a sense of unified purpose, there is a readiness to pursue selfish interest, to over-protection of turf, to political maneuvering. All these are symptoms not only of a lack of common purpose, but also of obsolete structures, occasionally, the wrong people in the wrong jobs, and failure to deal with the takeover.

Can we realistically ask you to put the company and our work over your own personal interests or that of your own unit or division? Yes, if you believe there's a benefit to you eventually and your leaders are doing it. As one of your leaders, I owe you a point of view on this . . . let me define what I think my job is. My absolute first priority is to magnify your ability to do a superior job for your clients, for your agency.

Every time I see a client, open a new business door, promote, hire, fire, I am trying to create an environment in which you and your work thrive. You can expect this of all of the top managers at O&M. And you can ask us to do our jobs with confidence, style, zest, urgency, integrity, with a passionate belief in our people, our brand O&M. Your job is to deliver on the promises we all make and in your own management role to offer the same to your team.

Because there's another saying around O&M I don't want to set to music . . . Gentlemen With Brains. It's not what you think. I'm not reacting to the Gentlemen part. After all, I've been a Chairman for a number of years. What I don't like about this phrase is the implication that we will reward courtesy before candor. Brains aren't enough – it's the price of entry. It's brains applied that make a difference in an active, imaginative, discerning way.

We are, at times, a company that takes too long to say what we think, or simply won't listen to what our own people think. A company that thinks talking about it is doing it. That our clients feel is somewhat uninvolved, distant. People believe that we have awesome skills, but they have to dig them out of us.

As we approach planning for '93, we also need to assess where we are in our life cycle. My assessment of where we are is fed by highly concentrated meetings with some 200 of our key clients, long hours with key managers, the clarity granted (at times) to an outsider like myself, plus a few new business pitches – plus memos from David Ogilvy.

My view of where we are is intended to represent Worldwide. I recognize that there are many exceptions. I think we have hit bottom and are poised for recovery. Poised but not assured. It's a fragile state and what you choose to do as you implement your strategy for 1993 makes a critical difference to our future. You will direct, through your behavior and actions, the newly defined Ogilvy. For it's at this time, at bottom, that change is expected, needed and possible. Your job is to manage that change. Our job is to give direction for change. But change in a company so well resourced, so fundamentally sound, so legendary in reputation requires care. And I tried to exercise care in laying out the '93 plan.

I start with this idea. Activate the Assets. Let's get up front and center those assets, often latent, of our beloved company. Let's leave behind any and everything we've outgrown, don't believe in, can't use, even people who can't embrace our plan.

For 1993 we have only three strategies. You can reorder them. You must put your own tactics against them. If necessary, you can add a fourth – but no more. People simply cannot absorb more. It's like putting too many claims in a 30 second spot. Keep it simple, which is another way of saying highly focused. Your people need to know after you define your own '93 strategy what to do and what's expected of them.

Is it obvious that one of our very great assets is our client list? Behind that client list lies another asset not so obvious. Because I've had the advantage of many one-on-one conversations with our key clients, I can tell you that we have a wealth of goodwill. Clients, people, ex-O&Mers, non-clients wish us well, want us to succeed, love the David Ogilvy legend, our brand. You can't buy goodwill, you can't even earn it, but it's ours to activate.

One of the key reasons I came to O&M was our client list. Probably true for you too. It is the envy of our competition. It is the great fear of our competitors that we'll figure this out. To date, they are not unduly alarmed, because they've grown faster, smarter, made more opportunities with our clients than we have.

Consider these facts: We have an astonishing number of clients who are in first place. This means they'll do the acquiring, the growing, the world brands. It's much harder to succeed with the companies who have only mid-level brands. These clients have the resources, talent and energy to succeed. And many have a profound belief in the power of advertising.

APPENDIX B[5]

When I graduated from college in 1967 with my liberal arts degree and my sixties idealism, I truly believed that the term 'business ethics' was an oxymoron. Little did I imagine that eleven years later I would be entering the exciting world of business where I had previously assumed all manner of evil resided.

I'm not really sure where we got our skepticism of business. I am sure, however, that we all looked with great disdain on those poor souls who chose to major in business administration. Those of us who didn't get shipped to Vietnam flocked into teaching or the peace corps or graduate school where, in many instances, our idealism and naiveté had a rude encounter with reality. We found that ethical behavior had, in fact, no relationship with a liberal arts education. And as we struggled with the rest of the nation to find purpose and meaning in our country's involvement in Southeast Asia or the riots and burning of our inner cities, we began to understand that ethics is not a matter of right and wrong or black and white, but rather it is a tapestry with many shades of gray.

Given this reality, I would like to exercise the license granted to me as speaker to focus my remarks somewhat more broadly on the topic of 'workplace ethics', as I believe that it is easy for us to focus on those ethical issues which are likely to make headlines, like whether or not it is ethical for corporate executives to receive double digit compensation increases when their companies are losing money and laying off thousands of workers. . . . In some respects these issues are easier to talk about than the ones we all encounter in our day-to-day work interactions. . . .

What I would like to do today is describe a number of work scenarios – situations I have personally experienced – that demonstrated that the ethics of the workplace is part of everyone's experience. . . .

Before I begin, I need to put my comments this afternoon in a context for you, because I believe my experience has a great deal of influence on how I perceive the ethical dimensions of the scenarios I am about to describe. I have been working for the past 28 years. Eleven of those years were spent in education; seventeen in business. I have held management positions during 16 of the past 28 years, so my perspective is heavily influenced by the expectations of a manager.

My first scenario is about a manager of a large division of a company, one that manufactures the highest profit margin product in the company. His management practices include withholding information from his subordinates and from his manager. . . .

Let me share another scenario with you. This one, in one form or another, is likely to touch each of us at least once during our work lives. For whatever reason, an enterprise is faced with the need to drastically cut expenses and reduce capacity in a significant way. . . .

Another scenario: I followed with interest, as I'm certain many of you did, Shannon Faulkner's struggle to be accepted to the Citadel in South Carolina and her subsequent resignation. . . .

As we were reminded by the Shannon Faulkner experience, the military has a long tradition of teaching recruits to subordinate themselves to the good of the whole. While you and I may take issue with this practice, military leaders have mastered the techniques of breaking down individual identity, instilling discipline, and building a sense of unity out of diverse personalities through the use of physical and mental conditioning and, in some cases, adversarial haranguing.

I have not read anything about the appropriate uses and limitations of these techniques, although at least one article must have been written. I have, however, witnessed and experienced firsthand the impact of using some of these techniques in the workplace, a somewhat inappropriate application, in my opinion. When some of these techniques are employed in the workplace, discipline and decorum may result, but individual self esteem and personal professional growth are often undermined. And when these techniques are employed with a sense of mean-spiritedness and dominance, which they often are, the resulting environment can become hostile and threatening for employees. And, yes, I believe there are ethical dimensions to such behavior.

My final workplace example focuses on a significant shift in assumptions which has occurred in the workplace over the past decade. . . . I am referring to the shift from employer as paternalistic caretaker who guarantees a job for life in exchange for lifetime loyalty and a commitment to show up every day to a new contract between employer and employee – one founded on mutual respect, honesty and no promises.

There are very different assumptions underlying each of these contracts, assumptions that I believe have ethical dimensions. Under the old contract, the employer was a kind of parent. Workers were members of an extended family of sorts. Jobs were somewhat narrowly defined; what was expected of employees rarely required spontaneity and flexibility. Employees had policies and procedures to depend on for structure and definition. Managers, like good parents, were charged with looking out for their employees' interests by making critical decisions for them, keeping them from being bothered by information they didn't absolutely need to know, and providing them with long-term job security.

Contrast that with the new relationship between employer and employee, one that focuses on a commitment to employability rather than employment. Employees are expected to take responsibility for continuously improving their own skill base. Opportunities for advancement are more often lateral than upward. In many situations, teams are replacing hierarchy, and employees are given information because they have become more involved in making key decisions.

For those of us who grew up with the expectation of the old contract, the reality of no promises is scary. At the same time, the realization that each of us, in the end, is a free agent represents a degree of freedom and responsibility we have never had before. . . .

I will leave it to each of us as individuals to think more about how we feel about each of these contracts, but suffice it to say, in much of the world of work, these changes are occurring, and so also must the underlying principles with which we approach each other as workers.

As I have painted these workplace scenarios, I'm sure some of you have squirmed in your seats and wanted to say 'Yeah, but . . .' There is, for example, the issue of intention. If it is my intention to protect my co-worker from facing unemployment, am I really doing something unethical when I propose across-the-board cuts rather than targeted reductions? Is the intention of providing an employee with the peace of mind inherent in job security less noble than making an employee responsible for keeping his or her own skill base current? If it simply never occurred to me as a manager that I should communicate with my staff about our strategic initiatives and how they impact our work, am I to be held accountable if their work undermines a key strategy? Should I, as a manager, be held accountable if my management style threatens a subordinate's self esteem – especially if I didn't mean anything I said as a personal attack?. . . .

I want to conclude my comments today with a few thoughts about what we can do to foster a more ethical workplace.

We are probably all fed up with the current political rhetoric about family values – particularly when it is used to condemn or exclude certain members of society. But it's hard to argue that a firm grounding in principled thinking does not begin at home, in the way individuals who love and care for us from birth treat us, themselves and each other. Very often, the source of dysfunctional behavior in the work setting emanates from an adaptive behavior learned early in life.

This does not let us off the hook, however, nor should it discourage us from trying to influence children, adolescents and adults to develop more ethically-informed perspectives. Developmental psychologists have asserted for decades that moral perspective can be enhanced through deliberate intervention. From this I draw encouragement that we can influence individuals in the classroom and in the workplace to grow beyond the limitations of early childhood experience and develop more ethically complex and responsible ways of interacting.

A key to fostering this development is to confront ethical dimensions in the workplace very directly and talk about them openly with employees. Sometimes people who are subjected to the impact of certain behavior or are in the middle of reacting to things around them cannot see the web within which they are intertwined. As a manager, I believe very strongly in processing experience with my people to help them – and me – understand it more fully. With my former employer, for example, I personally facilitated a series of workshops which examined the changes occurring in our organization as a result of the new contract between employer and employee that is emerging. . . .

NOTES

1. Miriam Brody condemns the male characteristics associated with style even more strongly in her book *Manly Writing* (1993). She points out that historically, in defining style, research has not only ignored women but also disparaged them. For instance, an elaborated writing style has been compared to female dress. In the classical period a decorative style was seen as effeminate, and Quintilian, in a doubly offensive comparison, associated adornments of language with the eunuch – effeminate, ornate and over-decorated, and corrupting – unlike the straightforward and natural style (Brody 1993: 20). Brody explains that later, during the Enlightenment, the richly ornamented clothing of women became a sign of disguise and deception. Thus, male features of style were valorised – natural, virile, straightforward – and they have continued to be the standards in textbook advice.

2. In addition to her role as first lady, she became the first female US delegate to the United Nations and she engaged in a lifetime of public works and appearances. She lived in a world that expected women, as Debra L. Petersen explains, to engage in 'fulfilling social and familial responsibilities and to further their husband's political career only in behind-the-scenes activities' (Petersen 1994: 383). Roosevelt's strategy was one of indirectness so that she might maintain the appearance of the wife and mother and still take part in public issues. She used ploys, such as knitting at conferences, publishing daily menus at the White House, and entertaining UN delegates at tea.

3. In this speech Beers defines the new mission and introduces the upcoming initiative she has designed. Also referenced is a video of a training session made for American Express and two additional speeches, one, entitled 'Leadership in Our Time', delivered in 1995 to the Chicago Network, a women's business group, and one, 'The Matrix Award', given to a professional group, Women in Communications, on receiving their Matrix Award. Although advertising is an industry dominated by males, Ogilvy & Mather does employ a number of women in senior partner positions (Sellers 1996: 56). The audiences for the internal speech and the training video included both genders but mainly males.

4. The following is taken from Charlotte Beers' 'Ogilvy & Mather 1993 Worldwide Strategy' speech given to upper management. Because of the confidential nature of the speech, only the introduction is included.

5. Business Ethics Speech – Marcia Hanson, 22 September 1995, Iowa State University, Ames, Iowa. The edited text covers the sections quoted in the analysis.

REFERENCES

AmerUs Bank (1996) Marcia Hanson Video. Des Moines, IA: AmerUs Bank.

Beers, Charlotte (1993) 'Ogilvy & Mather 1993 Worldwide Strategy'. Address delivered to Ogilvy & Mather management, New York.

Beers, Charlotte (1995) 'Leadership in our time'. Keynote address delivered to the Chicago Network, Chicago.

Beers, Charlotte (1996) 'The Matrix Award'. Address delivered at Award Ceremonies for Women in Communications, New York.

Blankenship, Jane (1994) Geraldine Ann Ferraro. In Karlyn Kohrs Campbell (ed.), *Women Public Speakers in the United States, 1925–1993*. Westport, CT: Greenwood Press, pp. 190–206.

Brody, Miriam (1993) *Manly Writing: Gender, Rhetoric, and the Rise of Composition*. Carbondale, IL: Southern Illinois University Press.

Brown, Penelope and Levinson, Stephen (1987) *Politeness: Some Universals in Language Use*. Cambridge: Cambridge University Press.

Campbell, Karlyn Kohrs (1994) Introduction. In Karlyn Kohrs Campbell (ed.), *Women Public Speakers in the United States, 1925–1993*. Westport, CT: Greenwood Press, pp. xi–xxiii.

Campbell, Karlyn Kohrs and Jamieson, Kathleen Hall (1986) Inaugurating the presidency. In Herbert W. Simons and Aram A. Aghazarian (eds), *Form, Genre, and the Study of Political Discourse*. Columbia: University of South Carolina Press, pp. 203–23.

Case Study in Brand Stewardship at American Express (1996) Video. New York: Ogilvy & Mather.

Crawford, Mary (1995) *Talking Difference: On Gender and Language*. London: Sage Publications.

David, Carol and Graham, Margaret Baker (1997) Conflicting values: team management portrayed in epic metaphors. *Journal of Business and Technical Communication* 11 (1) 24–48.

Foss, Sonja K., Foss, Karen A. and Trapp, Robert (1991) *Contemporary Perspectives on Rhetoric*, 2nd edn, Prospect Heights, IL: Waveland Press, Inc.

Goodman, Ellen (1996) Kemp jargon: trapped in training camp. *The Des Moines Register*, 9A (17 August).

Graham, Margaret Baker and David, Carol (1996) Power and politeness: administrative writing in an 'organized anarchy'. *Journal of Business and Technical Communication* 10 (1): 5–27.

Halal, William E. (1984) The legitimacy cycle: long-term dynamics in the use of Power. In Andrew Kakabadse and Christopher Parker (eds) *Power, Politics and Organisation: A Behavioral Science View*. New York: Wiley, pp. 47–64.

Hanson, Marcia (1995) Business Ethics Speech. Speech delivered at Business Week, Iowa State University, Ames, IA. Des Moines, IA: AmerUs Bank.

Hartsock, Nancy C. M. (1985) *Money, Sex and Power: Toward a Feminist Historical Materialism*. Boston: Northeastern University Press.

Key, Mary Ritchie (1996) *Male/Female Language with a Comprehensive Bibliography*, 2nd edn. Lanham, MD: The Scarecrow Press, Inc.

Kramarae, Cheris (1981) *Women and Men Speaking*. Rowley, MA: Newbury House Publishers, Inc.

Lakoff, Robin Tolmach (1990) *Talking Power: The Politics of Language*. New York: Basic Books.

Lunsford, Andrea. A. (1995) On reclaiming rhetorica. In Andrea A. Lunsford (ed.), *Reclaiming Rhetorica: Women in the Rhetorical Tradition*. Pittsburgh: University of Pittsburgh Press, pp. 3–8.

Mitroff, Ian I. and Kilmann, Ralph H. (1975) Stories managers tell: a new tool for organizational problem solving. *Management Review* 64 (7): 18–28.

Perelman, Chaim and Olbrechts-Tyteca, Lucie (1971) *The New Rhetoric: A Treatise on Argumentation*. Trans. John Wilkinson and Purcell Weaver, South Bend, IN: University of Notre Dame Press.

Petersen, Debra L. (1994) Anna Eleanor Rooosevelt. In Karlyn Kohrs Campbell (eds.), *Women Public Speakers in the United States, 1925–1993*. Westport, CT: Greenwood Press, pp. 379–94.

Seeger, Matthew W. (1994) Lee Iacocca as business statesman. In Matthew W. Seeger (ed.), *'I Gotta Tell You': Speeches of Lee Iacocca*. Detroit: Wayne State University Press, pp. 15–25.

Sellers, Patricia (1996), Women, sex & power. *Fortune* (5 August), pp. 42–56.

Steingard, David S. and Fitzgibbons, Dale E. (1993) A postmodern deconstruction of Total Quality Management (TQM). *Journal of Organizational Change Management* 6 (5): 27–42.

Tarver, Jerry (1994) Information, motivation, and audience adaptation in addressing general business problems. In Matthew Seeger (ed.), *'I Gotta Tell You': Speeches of Lee Iacocca*. Detroit: Wayne State University Press, pp. 209–46.

Wagner, Joanne (1995) Intelligent members or restless disturbers. In Andrea A. Lunsford (ed.), *Reclaiming Rhetorica: Women in the Rhetorical Tradition*. Pittsburgh: University of Pittsburgh Press, pp. 185–202.

PART III:

BUSINESS GENRES AND THEIR LANGUAGE

EIGHT

'Can we count on your bookings of potatoes to Madeira?' Corporate context and discourse practices in direct sales letters

Miriam van Nus

1. INTRODUCTION

Organisations are increasingly using direct mail letters to offer products and services or to establish and maintain relations with their clients. Research into such letters has provided valuable insights into the textual ways in which organisations aim to achieve such goals (Mann and Thompson 1992). Although a number of studies have taken characteristics of the immediate context of text production and interpretation into account and have indicated how, for instance, the sender–receiver relationship may have had an effect on the structure of the letters, a systematic investigation of the influence of the organisational environment on sales offers as products of corporate discourse practices is long overdue.

The relationship between the corporate context and the writing process has been explored in several studies concerning other forms of business writing. Swales and Rogers (1995) demonstrate how organisational culture shapes (and is shaped by) its mission statement (Odell 1985). Driskill (1989) discusses the influence that factors internal and external to the organisation may have on the effectiveness of business texts and shows how language standards applied by regulatory bodies in industry and the risk of lawsuits affect advertising copy. Studies such as these present case studies involving individual organisations; other studies focus on describing classes of business texts. Yates and Orlikowski (1992) give a diachronic account of the memo genre and describe how the genre has been influenced by technological developments. Bhatia (1993), in a description of sales and application letters, which he views as instances of the 'promotional genre', indicates how a concern with the business

181

environment can be incorporated into a genre-analytical approach to business texts. From a similar perspective, Louhiala-Salminen (1997) discusses features of business faxes and shows how the sender–receiver relationship affects their textualisations (see also Akar and Louhiala-Salminen, this volume).

The purpose of this chapter is to illustrate how the corporate context shapes one particular type of business text, direct sales letters. In order to do so, discourse practices with respect to the production and distribution of these letters are discussed in some detail.

2. THE CORPORATE CONTEXT

2.1. Background

Approaches to the concept of 'context' vary in a number of ways. They differ, for instance, with respect to (1) the static or dynamic nature of the concept, according to which context is either a stable influence on text production and interpretation, or a dynamic construct that changes in the process of text production and interpretation; or (2) its cognitive, linguistic or social basis, whereby context is viewed as knowledge, text or situation (Schiffrin 1994; Van Dijk 1997). Irrespective of the suggested nature or basis of the concept, these approaches have all put forward ways to describe 'context', and to identify contextual components.

A distinction is often made between the 'linguistic' context of utterances (the co-text or local context) and their 'situational' context. The description of the situational context may be restricted to the immediate textual environment in which utterances are produced and interpreted, but it may also include background knowledge that is brought to bear on the immediate situation. A number of studies recognise at least these two situational levels of context in addition to the linguistic context of utterances: a 'context of situation' and a 'context of culture' (Halliday and Hasan 1985), 'encounters' and 'forms of life' (Frentz and Farrell 1976, discussed in Miller 1984), 'the specific context' and 'culture' (Givon 1984) and a 'here and now' situation and 'general knowledge of social situations' (Schiffrin 1994).

On account of the recurrence of immediate situations and of texts as communicative products of these situations, an 'intertextual contextual component' may also be distinguished in addition to the 'linguistic context' and the 'situational context' – see Halliday and

Hasan (1985) and applications in Gunnarsson (1990) and Fairclough (1992). This component reflects the way in which members of a community draw on textual conventions when producing and interpreting texts (Selzer 1993). These conventions, the result of past experiences with texts which were the product of comparable situational contexts, constrain text producers and provide expectations for receivers.

Similarities between texts that result from comparable immediate situations, which may be referred to as 'generic intertextuality' (Devitt 1991), have resulted in classifications of types of texts using criteria such as lexico-grammatical surface features, structure and purpose (Ventola 1989; Swales 1990; Paltridge 1995). Of these three criteria, Swales (1990) argues that 'purpose' (cf. 'exigence' in Miller's (1984) terminology, or 'function' in Leckie-Tarry (1995)) provides a sound basis for the definition of genre and an explanation for any similarities regarding the other two criteria mentioned above. Genres then become 'ways of using language to achieve different culturally established tasks, and texts of different genres are texts which are achieving different purposes in the culture' (Eggins and Martin 1997: 236). The definition indicates that the understanding of the purpose of a genre should not be restricted to the speaker's intentions. As Miller (1984) points out, it is possible that a speaker's intentions do not meet the conventional expectations of other participants regarding the nature of the situation. Instead, '[t]he exigence provides the rhetor with a socially recognizable way to make his or her intentions known. It provides an occasion, and thus a form, for making public our private versions of things' (1984: 158). To sum up, the purpose of a genre is a social purpose, a way through which a society's activities are performed, and through which communicators can achieve their own individual purposes.

2.2.   The corporate situation: an operationalisation of 'situation'

To date, few studies have extended the notion of situational or intertextual context to the business world. Bhatia (1993) describes the ongoing situation of a text and its wider context and makes these specific to the business world. He refers to the 'institutional context' of business texts whose components include elements of the immediate context, such as sender, receiver, sender–receiver

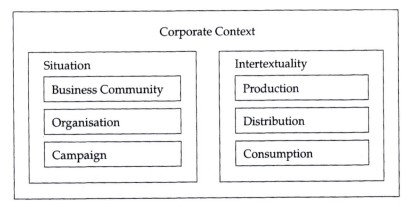

Figure 8.1:   A model of corporate context

relationship, and features of the community in which the texts are used, such as its 'social structure, interactions, history, beliefs, goals' (1993: 23). Driskill (1989) adds another contextual layer, and presents a model of the corporate context in which she distinguishes between 'external and internal sources of meaning'. External sources of meaning are part of the external environment of an organisation. They include 'society, government, competitors, resources, [and] markets'. Driskill's internal environment includes aspects of an organisation such as its 'size, structure, technology, culture, individuals, roles, and forms of argument or reasoning' (1989: 130). The present study adopts the two contextual layers identified by Driskill (1989) and adds a third layer, the 'marketing communication campaign', which is the immediate situation of direct sales offers. The terms used for the three layers of the new model proposed here are 'business community', i.e. external environment, 'organisation' (i.e. internal environment) and 'campaign' (see Figure 8.1).

2.3.   Corporate genres: an operationalisation of 'intertextuality'

The idea that cultures can be characterised in terms of their genre repertoires – i.e. the recurrent activities performed through language – has only recently been extended to specific (professional) discourse communities. Swales (1990: 24–7) identifies a repertoire of genres as one of the defining characteristics of a discourse community. The corporate world 'possesses' genres to accomplish commercial aims. One, or several, genres may be employed in marketing communication campaigns. Discourse practices with respect to particular marketing genres can be described in terms of their conventional production, distribution and consumption processes (Fairclough 1992). Production and consumption practices constitute the ways in which genre texts conventionally achieve their social purposes (see section 4). The distribution practices of genre texts are operationalised in this study as practices with respect to format (type of document) and medium selection (see section 3).

The model of corporate context resulting from the combination of the two structural components of 'situation' and 'intertextuality' discussed so far is illustrated in Figure 8.1.

With reference to direct mail, the dimension of 'marketing communication campaign' may involve the use of direct sales letters. The texts are shaped by aspects of the campaign (e.g. type of offer, target group), the organisation (e.g. organisational culture) and the wider business community (e.g. advertising regulations), including the marketing communication practices established within the organisation and across organisations.

3. DISTRIBUTION

3.1. Background

Several media and formats may be selected to distribute genre texts (Bhatia 1993). Sales offers can be made through personal selling, advertising, and direct media such as direct mail (i.e. personalised advertising distributed by mail) (Floor and Van Raaij 1994). In the present study, information regarding the selection of direct mail and direct mail formats was collected by means of a questionnaire. The influence of a number of different variables at the levels of 'business community', 'organisation' and 'campaign' on these selection processes was identified. Figure 8.2 presents the corporate context hierarchy in which 'sector' comprises the situational level of the business community. 'Organisational features', 'marketing plans' and 'marketing communication plans' together form the level of the

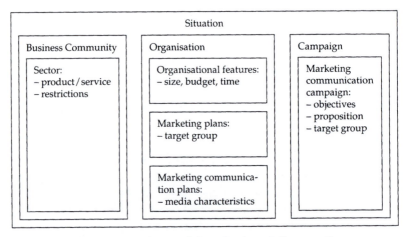

Figure 8.2:   Corporate context and the selection of direct mail

organisation and 'marketing communication campaign' constitutes the level of the campaign – see Floor and Van Raaij (1994) for their marketing communication hierarchy which formed the basis for the questionnaire.

3.2.   Direct mail selection

A survey was held among 600 Dutch organisations, providing business-to-business services in the following sectors: (1) transport; (2) finance and economics; (3) insurance; (4) production and techno-logy; (5) automation; and (6) company management, with a 35.7 per cent response rate. The survey indicated that sectors differed with respect to media selection in general and direct mail selection in particular. The nature of the services provided had an influence on the selection of direct mail, which might have been due to the level of adaptability of the services provided to the wishes of clients (standard versus tailor-made), the level of specialisation and the frequency of purchase. To give an example, standard services were offered to prospective clients through direct mail more often than tailor-made services. Furthermore, there were restrictions on mar-keting communication in certain sectors which affected the selec-tion of direct mail. As indicated by respondents working in certain financial institutions, some sectors simply did not allow any form of advertising.

It also turned out that smaller organisations tended not to select direct mail to communicate with their clients. According to some respondents, the organisation had to be especially geared to direct mail campaigns, which meant that dedicated staff were required to plan and execute campaigns. They explained that especially the follow-up to campaigns required readjustments.

The nature of the services provided brought with it a particular target group. If this group consisted of a limited number of (potential) clients, companies chose not to use direct mail but personal forms of communication. Smaller networks of clients can easily be contacted personally. Respondents also reported that direct mail has certain advantages and disadvantages that were set for or against its use. Some respondents regarded it as an efficient medium since a single campaign enabled companies to provide information quickly to a large number of business contacts. Some considered direct mail a good way to establish the first contact quickly. It was also considered a good method to maintain relations with clients, when the clientele was too big to do this on an individual basis. The main disadvantage of direct mail put forward by several corporate users was the ineffectiveness of the medium, due to its being insufficiently targeted. Direct mail was also said to be unpopular with clients and environmentally unfriendly, and mention was also made of the costs and time involved in planning and executing campaigns.

At the level of the marketing communication campaign, a small target group was likely to be one of the reasons why the medium was not used by a number of companies. Furthermore, direct mail seemed to be predominantly associated with generating new business (one possible campaign objective). It was often used in communication campaigns which aimed at eliciting requests for further information which could eventually lead to new business, a tactic known in marketing as 'an open proposition'.

With respect to format, the respondents indicated that their organisations primarily sent out letters, brochures/leaflets and what is referred to in marketing as 'response vehicles', such as reply cards. Pilon (1990) suggests that direct mail shots can consist of a number of different formats, such as letters, cards, leaflets, brochures, catalogues, books, booklets, magazines, newsletters and reports. However, as the findings of the survey indicate, only a few of these formats were actually listed as frequently used by respondents.

4.   THE PRODUCTION OF DIRECT SALES LETTERS

4.1.   Analytical categories

Production practices were operationalised in section 2.3 as ways in which genre texts conventionally achieve their purposes. The communicative purpose of a genre was, therefore, taken as the starting point of the analysis of direct sales letters as instances of genre texts. This purpose is achieved through the presence and patterning of textual units (Bhatia 1993). Two types of textual units can be identified: structural units, which give the text the format of a letter, and functional units, which have a particular function in the discourse and contribute towards achieving the communicative purpose of the genre texts. Nickerson (1994) proposes a categorisation of communicative acts according to their contribution to the letter. Her categories comprise acts whose main function is 'transactional' (i.e. aimed at the exchange of information), acts which are 'interactional' (i.e. maintain relations between sender and receiver) and acts which give the text the structure of a letter. The latter are labelled as 'structural units' in this study; both her transactional and interactional acts are categorised here as 'functional units' (see sections 4.2 and 4.3).

Louhiala-Salminen (1997) chooses to capture all acts in the single category of 'rhetorical moves'. Bhatia (1993), whose analysis includes only a small number of units which would be classified here as 'structural', takes a similar approach. A distinction between structural and functional units in the analysis of direct sales letters is useful, however, since it enables a discussion of textual units both in terms of the structure of the letter (e.g. the 'lead' of the letter) and their discourse function (e.g. offer of service).

4.2.   Structural units

The structural units included in the analysis that follows are presented in many correspondence coursebooks as standard elements of the format of a business letter. The structural unit called 'lead' has been added to Table 8.1. Lamers (1991: 170) discusses the importance of this first unit of the body of the letter and advises writers of direct mail letters to start their letters with a so-called 'reader's benefit' before offering any products or services (e.g. 'waarom

Table 8.1:   Standard structural units of business letters

Letterhead	carries company information such as name, address
Inside address	gives name and address of receiver
Reference	encodes the letter for filing purposes
Date	includes date and town from where the letter was sent
Salutation	signals the beginning of the letter
Subject line	prepares for the body of the letter
Preclose	prepares for the close
Close	closes the letter
Signature	includes information about sender such as name, position
Postscript	gives additional information after the close of the letter

begrijpt u ook niets van computers?'/'why don't you understand anything about computers either?').

Most of these elements are stable functional units: e.g. a letter-head always identifies the sender's company. Some other units can fulfil a variety of functions. A subject line may refer to the offer made in the letter (e.g. 'Administrative systems for horticultural centres'), but it may also present the company (e.g. '[Name] – For All Your Automation Problems').[1]

Table 8.2:   Functionally stable structural units

Letterhead	identifies the sender
Inside address	identifies the receiver
Reference	identifies the letter
Date	indicates date and place of sending
Salutation	greets the receiver
Close	greets the receiver
Signature	identifies the sender

Table 8.2 lists the structural units which are also stable functional units. These units are not always included in analyses of business letters. Connor *et al.* (1995) state that as they occur in most letters, they do not add anything to the understanding of a particular type of letter. In direct mail, however, the units listed in Table 8.2 do make an important contribution towards the success of the letter.

Letters which are personalised (i.e. which include the name of the receiver) and dated are more likely to be successful (Lamers 1991). This warrants a close examination of these units.

Subject lines, leads, precloses and postscripts have varying functional roles. Applying Bhatia's (1993) moves analysis of sales promotion letters to a small set of letters, Van Nus (1996) found that subject lines 'established credentials' in letters sent to prospective clients (e.g. '[NAME] WORKS WITH ENERGY ON THE NEWEST TECHNOLOGY'). The subject lines of letters sent to existing clients, however, either presented the offer or offered an incentive (e.g. 'To the Amsterdam Concert Hall for Christmas – for free!'). Furthermore, postscripts, in letters to both existing and prospective clients, contained information which could motivate the receiver to respond: thus, incentives were offered or pressure tactics used (e.g. 'Respond quickly, the number of places available is limited').

4.3. Functional units

Bhatia (1993) presents a textual analysis of the structure of sales promotion letters in terms of 'moves' and 'strategies'. Segments may, for instance, 'establish the credentials of the company' [move] by 'indicating an awareness of the needs of the receiver' and/or by 'referring to the expertise of the company' [strategies]. Bhatia describes moves as units which have particular communicative functions: 'each move serves a typical communicative intention which is always subservient to the overall communicative purpose of the genre', and strategies as realisations of 'a particular communicative intention at the level of a move' (1993: 30).

Like Bhatia, Swales identifies discourse functions at two levels, moves and steps, and adopts a moves analysis which unfolds as a linear structure, with no indication of functional relations. On the contrary, Mauranen (1993) proposes a hierarchical approach to text structure analysis. Drawing on principles of genre analysis and rhetorical structure theory, she argues that writers of research papers express a main point or claim which they use to try to convince the reader. The writer's rhetorical strategy is shown in the textual patterning around this claim. An analysis of these text patterns leads to the identification of rhetorical moves, which are functional units defined in terms of their contribution to supporting the writer's main claim.

The present study also adopts a hierarchical approach to text analysis, and considers texts as hierarchies of acts through which the text's communicative purposes are achieved (Paltridge 1995). Genre texts are analysed as sequences of 'communicative acts', which realise 'generic moves'. A move may consist of one or more acts. One of the moves represents the primary purpose of the text and forms the pivot of the hierarchical structure of the text. The way in which other moves support the pivotal move is determined, in this study, by an analysis of the rhetorical relations within and between moves using rhetorical structure theory (Mann et al. 1992).

The textual features on which Mauranen's (1993) framework relies in order to identify the nature and boundaries of functional units include reference, theme, modality, tense, typography and re-flexivity. Van Leeuwen (1993) identifies 'moves' and 'stages' using a similar list of features such as mood, person, tense and theme. In this study, reference, metadiscourse and mood have been selected as indicators of functional units and for their contribution to per-suasive discourse.[2]

5.   THE BACKGROUND AND THE DATA

Gulien & Co. Nederland BV is the Dutch subsidiary of an inter-national ship broker's firm.[3] It has offices in the main ports in the Netherlands and represents shipping companies providing line ser-vices from Dutch ports to several overseas ports and vice versa. Gulien & Co.'s most important service is that of a booking agency: businesses contact Gulien & Co. when they wish to transport cargo using any of the shipping companies that Gulien & Co. represent.

In order to draw attention to the services they provide, Gulien & Co. Nederland BV telephone and visit their (potential) clients. They provide information on line services by advertising in trade magazines and by sending out press releases and direct mail letters. They started sending direct mail letters, which they suggest is unu-sual for the industry, in 1992, at a time when they did not employ any sales representatives. Although they do so now, they still con-tinue to send out direct mail letters because this enables the com-pany to reach a large number of clients at once. The letters are sent to groups of clients to offer new services or renew interest in exist-ing services. The clients are invited to book cargo transportation, or to ask for quotations or for further information regarding shipping lines.

The subsidiary initiates approximately twenty direct mail campaigns per year, a number which it expects to increase in the near future. The letters are written by employees in the marketing and business development department. The recipients of the letters are selected on the basis of variables such as port, carrier and type of cargo. These prospective clients have in the past booked cargo transportation, asked for quotations or general information, or have been visited by representatives. Nine letters were selected for analysis from a set of nineteen sales letters which the company had provided: three of these offer existing services, three offer new services, and three offer new services to prospective clients only. The classification was made using information provided by the company and explicit references in the text. Gulien & Co.'s letters generally offer new and/or existing services to both existing and prospective clients, but in some notable instances, as in the letters selected for analysis which offer new services to prospective clients, specific groups of clients are targeted.

6. THE FINDINGS

The following sections present the findings with respect to the two types of units. Section 6.1, on structural units, discusses textual components such as salutation, postscript and lead. Section 6.2, on functional units, first discusses boundary indicators such as reference, metadiscourse and mood, before presenting the functional units that were actually found in the letters analysed (section 6.3).

6.1. Structural units

The letters identify the company in their letterheads, and specify the receivers in their inside addresses. When the inside addresses contain attention lines selecting one particular reader, the salutation repeats the name of this person ('Geachte Heer Visser'/'Dear Mr Visser'). Inside addresses with attention lines specifying a department rather than a single person, or ones without an attention line, have corresponding salutations reading 'Geachte Dames en Heren'

('Dear Ladies and Gentlemen'). None of the letters has a reference code. Six letters close with 'Met vriendelijke groet' ('With kind regards'). Five closes are preceded by a preclose, which expresses the company's readiness to receive bookings by thanking the client in advance for the bookings yet to be placed ('Bij voorbaat dank voor uw steun en vertrouwen!' / 'Thanks in advance for your support and trust!'). Signatures contain the name of the company and the name of the sender. Eight letters add the position of the sender. Direct mail writers are generally advised to add postscripts to repeat the essential message of the body of the letter (Lamers 1991). However, only one of the letters analysed contains a postscript, offering to send further information about one of the shipping destinations.

Eight letters present the letter's subject matter in a subject line following the salutation. This is an 'orientational' unit, indicating to the receiver what offer is going to be made in the letter: e.g. 'export/verschepingen naar Rusland' ('export/shipping to Russia'). The only letter which does not contain an orientational subject line presents information that seems at first to be in subject-line position (see Example 1). It is in bold print, capitalised, underlined and typographically separated from the remainder of the letter. However, it clearly serves a different function in comparison to the orientational subject lines of the remaining eight letters: it wishes the reader a 'Happy New Year', and does not indicate what the letter is going to be about. Two letters have orientational subject lines which are followed by similar interpersonal moves. (The English translations [E] follow the examples in Dutch.)

[1]   Geachte Heer Visser,

NAYA SAAL MUBARAK
Of te wel: <u>gelukkig nieuwjaar</u> in het Hindi, de meest gesproken taal in India.

1997 wordt vast een gelukkig en een gedenkwaardig jaar in de indiase maritime historie, want: Indian Sea Services (ISS), India's trotse nationale lijn, begint [. . .]

[E1]   Dear Mr Visser,

NAYA SAAL MUBARAK
Or, in other words: 'Happy New Year' in Hindi, India's main language.

> 1997 will be a happy and memorable year in Indian
> maritime history, for: Indian Sea Services (ISS), India's
> proud national line, will launch [...]

Three letters open by directly addressing the reader and commenting on the message. One of these letters presents a kind of summary of the letter before it starts the body of the letter proper (see Example 2).

[2]   Geachte Heer Dijkstra,

Export/verschepingen naar Rusland via Sint Petersburg

Laten we eerlijk zijn: 'Rusland' is voor ons nieuw. Daarom zenden we deze brief aan alle exporteurs die wij kennen van onze andere vaargebieden. Als u (nu al, of straks) naar de Russische Federatie exporteert en de inhoud van deze brief voor u van belang is, dan hopen wij, dat u met ons kontakt wilt opnemen!

Na een diepgaande voorbereidende studie begon Euro Sea Services recent met [...]

[E2]   Dear Mr Dijkstra,

Export/shipping to Russia via St Petersburg

Let's be honest: 'Russia' is new to us. That is why we are sending this letter to all exporters whom we know from our other shipping areas. If you are currently exporting to the Russian Federation or intend to do so in the near future and the contents of this letter is of interest to you, we hope you will contact us!

After a thorough preparatory study, Euro Sea Services recently launched [...]

The interpersonal moves that open the letters are analysed as instances of 'the lead'. The only letters which do not contain these moves in their leads are those offering existing services. It seems that when a certain rhetorical effort is required – that is when letters introduce new services – the writers of the letters prefer to establish a relationship with their audience before actually offering the service. Table 8.3 summarises the findings related to structural units in the selected documents.

Table 8.3: Occurrence and realisation of structural units

Structural units	Number of letters	Realisations
Subject line	8	present subject matter
Lead	7	establish relations
	2	offer service
Preclose	5	thank
Postscript	1	offer additional information

6.2. Functional units

6.2.1. Reference

The most frequent reference chains, occurring in all the letters analysed, are those formed by references to the sender (Gulien & Co.), the receiver, the carrier represented by Gulien & Co. and cargo destinations (see Table 8.4). References to the sender and the reader are predominantly pronominal references. The sender is generally referred to using exclusive 'we' (e.g. '[. . .] hopen wij u wat milder te stemmen met zonnige en exotische Zuidzee bestemmingen' / '[. . .] we hope to put you in a better mood with sunny and exotic South Sea destinations'). The only exception occurs in one letter in which the sender is twice identified as 'Gulien & Co.'. In this letter, the sender produces a new shipping line for the reader and takes great pains to present this line as reliable ('Als we er geen vertrouwen in hadden, waren we er niet aan begonnen' / 'If we had not felt sure, we would not have started it'). By using the full company name, the sender may attempt to offset the unfamiliarity of the newly introduced shipping line with Gulien's familiarity and reliability.

References to the sender and the receiver do not occur as frequently as references to destinations and carriers. One letter which offers an existing service contains only a single reference to the receiver. Receiver references are always pronominal. References to destinations and carriers are more diverse. These reference chains show lexical recurrence, nominal groups with the same referent ('ESS' – 'de Europese rederij' / 'ESS' – 'the European carrier'; 'Sint Petersburg' – 'dé haven van de Russische Federatie' / 'St Petersburg' – 'the Russian Federation's main port'), and whole/part relations ('het Midden Oosten' – 'de Rode Zee' / 'the Middle East' – 'the Red

Table 8.4: Occurrence and realisation of references

References	Average number per letter	Realisation
Sender	3.6	pronouns and name company
Receiver	4.6	pronouns
Carrier	6.0	name company, NP same referent
Destination (port)	12.7	place names, NP same referent

(NP = Noun Phrase)

Sea'). Especially the letters offering existing services are, judging by the proportion of references, destination-orientated. Letters offering new services to prospective and existing clients have proportionately more references to sender, receiver and carrier. However, there do not appear to be any differences in reference patterns. There may be a difference of emphasis in the letters (i.e. some letters appear to be more destination-orientated), but the patterns are very similar, moving from receiver references at the start of the letter, to destinations and shipping lines when these are presented and evaluated, to references to Gulien & Co. and the receiver when response is solicited at the end of the letter. Table 8.4 lists the frequency and realisation of references to the sender, receiver, carrier and destination.

6.2.2. Metadiscourse

The textual elements classified here as metadiscourse are elements whose primary function is to make a contribution not to the propositional content of the text, but to the processing of the text. They guide the reader by providing textual markers such as illocution markers ('In conclusion, . . .') and internal connectors ('However') (Crismore *et al.* 1993; Mauranen 1993).

None of the letters sent by Gulien & Co. contains illocution markers. Internal connectors appear to be used by the sender to draw attention to the offer or to information which the sender hopes will motivate the reader to consider the offer. 'Want' (for) introduces the service twice, and once introduces a selling point (see Example 1). 'Dus' (so) occurs twice and introduces selling points (Example 3); 'en' (and) occurs in sentence-initial position three times (out of a total of seven occurrences), urging the reader to continue reading about the qualities of the carrier or the service. 'Maar' (but) also

Table 8.5: Occurrence of connectors in sentence-initial position

Connectors	Number	Initial
dus (so)	2	–
daarom (therefore)	1	1
maar (but)	5	3
en (and)	7	3
want (for)	3	–

occurs in initial position, where it introduces the offer as a solution to a problem once, and twice seems to refute the assumption readers might make on the basis of the preceding text that the offer is not relevant to them, as in Example 4.

[3]   Op de lijn varen thans de moderne ijsklasse-schepen (dus tweeënvijftig/52 weken per jaar inzetbaar!) Petrova Renkov en Urida Nova van elk rond de 7.000 Ton deadweight.

[E3] On this line the modern ice class ships (so running fifty-two/52 weeks a year!) Petrova Renkov and Urida Nova now sail, each about 7,000 tons deadweight.

[4]   Hoewel de schepen een capaciteit van zo'n 375 teus hebben, mikt Euro Sea Services in eerste instantie vooral op het vervoer van konventionele-lading [. . .] Maar natuurlijk vervoert Euro Sea Services graag uw 'shipper's own' containers.

[E4] Although the ships have a capacity of about 375 TEUs, Euro Sea Services primarily focuses on shipping conventional cargo [. . .] But Euro Sea Services is happy, of course, to carry your 'shipper's own' containers.

There do not appear to be any differences between the three sets of letters with respect to the use of internal connectors to draw the reader's attention to particular textual elements. As shown in Table 8.5, connectors often occur in sentence-initial position. This is the case in all three sets of letters analysed.

6.2.3. Mood

All the letters end with soliciting and/or enabling reader response, which in several letters coincided with changes in mood. In five

Table 8.6:   Occurrence of interrogatives and imperatives

Mood	Response	Attention
Interrogatives	5	3
Imperatives	2	–

letters this involves the use of interrogatives (see Example 5); two
letters present an imperative (see Example 6).

[5]   Héél hoog in het vaandel van ESS staat: **SERVICE**. Mogen
       wij u die verlenen?
[E5]   ESS feel very, very strongly about: **SERVICE**. May we offer
       it to you?

[6]   BEL! alstublieft voor verdere informatie en boekingen met
       Joost Vliegenthert: **123456789**.
[E6]   CALL! please for further information and bookings Joost
       Vliegenthert at **123456789**.

[7]   Maar wat betekent dit voor u?
[E7]   But what does this mean for you?

Other changes in mood occur when the reader's attention is drawn
to textual elements, such as the evaluation of the service offered, as
in Example 7. Table 8.6 shows the frequency with which interrogatives and imperatives were used to solicit response and to draw
attention.

6.3.   Acts and moves

The analysis of boundary indicators has resulted in the identification of acts that occur in the letters. The acts are categorised as
being either transactional, interactional or metadiscursive. Transactional acts are representatives; that is, they tell people how things
are. Interactional acts can be expressives (of feelings and attitudes),
directives (trying to get people to do things), and commissives (com-
mitting ourselves to doing things) (Schiffrin 1994; Coulthard 1985).
A third category, of metadiscursive acts, was added to the selected
speech act categories (Gunnarsson 1990).

Table 8.7:   Categorisation of acts based on boundary indicators

Metadiscourse	Transaction	Interaction
Orientation	Essential details service	Offer service
Attention	Essential details response	Evaluation
Occasion		Solicit response
Further information		

Metadiscursive acts communicate something to the reader about the letter. They provide information about the subject matter of the text ('orientation'), draw attention to the text ('attention'), indicate which occasion gave rise to the text ('occasion'), and indicate how the reader may obtain further information about the matter presented in the text ('further information') (Pander Maat 1994). Most letters contain orientational subject lines (see section 6.1). In addition, some letters use orientational subheadings. Most letters also contain attention-getting devices. These generally appear at the start of the letter, as in Example 8 (see also Example 7).

[8]   **Is dit zomer . . . ?**
[E8]   **Is this summer . . . ?**

[9]   Meer details vindt u op de achterzijde van deze brief.
[E9]   For more details, see the back of this letter.

Two letters explain at the start why the letter was being sent to the reader, e.g. Example 2. Finally, three letters indicate to the reader that further information about the offer will be provided (as in Example 9).

Transactional acts provide the factual information which the reader needs in order to consider the offer – e.g. dates and prices (essential details service), and to respond – e.g. phone number (essential details response) (see Examples 10 and 11). All the letters analysed contain examples of these acts.

[10]   Euro's volgende afvaart is de 'EuroStar' oov 14 november a.s. van Rotterdam (laatste laadhaven) naar Dakar, Abidjan, Tema, Lomé en/of Cotonou (b.v.a.).
[E10]   Euro's next sailing is the 'EuroStar' (barring unforeseen circumstances) 14 November next from Rotterdam (last loading port) to Dakar, Abidjan, Tema, Lomé and/or Cotonou (in case of sufficient demand).

[11]   123456789: – Chris Schouten   (toestel 123)
[E11]   123456789: – Chris Schouten   (extension 123)

The main purpose of these acts is understood to be to provide information. The interactional acts in Examples 12–14, on the other hand, commit the sender to providing a particular service (Example 12, offer service), or express the sender's attitude (Example 13, evaluation), or aim to elicit a response from the reader (Example 14, solicit response).

[12]   [. . .] hopen wij u wat milder te stemmen met zonnige en
         exotische Zuidzee bestemmingen, zoals:
         Hawaii   Honolulu
[E12]   [. . .] we hope to put you in a better mood with sunny
         and exotic South Sea destinations, such as:
         Hawaii   Honolulu

[13]   Wij hebben veel vertrouwen in de voorzichtige, gedegen
         aanpak van Euro Sea Services (europese- en russische
         belangen, waaronder rederijen en banken).
[E13]   We have a lot of confidence in the careful, thorough
         approach of Euro Sea Services (European and Russian
         interests, including shipowners and banks).

[14]   Mogen wij (weer) op uw boekingen van aardappelen en
         uien naar Madeira rekenen?
[E14]   Can we count (again) on your bookings of potatoes and
         onions to Madeira?

To conclude, the fictitious letter that follows (Example 15) exemplifies the moves realised by the acts that have just been discussed. As it is a fictitious letter, only an English version is provided.

[15]   Dear Mr Cooper,
         Export/shipping to the Arab Gulf   orientation

         Tomorrow you will read this in *Transport*:   occasion

         EURO SEA SERVICES launches a weekly   offer service
         full-container service direct from
         Rotterdam to the Arab Gulf.

         What does this mean for you?   attention

         A considerable improvement of shipping   evaluation
         possibilities to **the Arabian Gulf**.

- the shortest sailing time on the market:
  only 6 days!
- direct bills of lading to **11 ports** and
  many inland destinations

The first official departure: MS 'Maria Yulova' on 5 December from Rotterdam, and subsequently every week on Wednesday	essential details service
For more details, see the back of this letter.	further information
Will you help us make a success of this full-container service of ESS?	solicit response
123456789: Dirk Janssen for all information, rates and bookings with Euro Sea Services to the Arabian Gulf.	essential details response

With kind regards,

Gulien & Co. Nederland BV
Jeanne Hoogma (Sales & Marketing)

7. CONCLUSION AND SUGGESTIONS FOR FUTURE RESEARCH

The findings from the analysis of Dutch direct sales letters presented in this chapter compare very closely with Bhatia's (1993)
discussion of sales promotion letters sent by Singaporean companies
and Western multinationals. This suggests that there are similarities
in the ways in which sales offers achieve their communicative purposes across countries. In other words, discourse practices in the
production of sales offers appear to be shared cross-culturally. The
approach adopted in this study differs from Bhatia's in its attempt
to base the analysis of the structure of genre texts on specific linguistic features. Following Mauranen (1993) and Van Leeuwen
(1993), reference, metadiscourse and mood were selected as indicators of text structure which provide information about a number
of lexico-grammatical features of the sales offers analysed. Future
research should concentrate on the internal structure of moves and
on the structure of the letter, both in terms of obligatory and optional
moves and in terms of the relations between moves. Furthermore,

a comparison of letters sent to existing and prospective clients should be carried out to show how the relation between sender and receiver affects textual organisation.[4]

The model of corporate context presented in this chapter extends the notion of 'context' to the business world, thus providing a model suitable for the analysis of business documents. It specifies 'context' at three different situational levels ('business community', 'organisation' and 'campaign'), at which particular variables can be distinguished (see Figures 8.1 and 8.2). In addition, the model includes the notion of 'generic intertextuality' and can be used to show how situational variables influence practices with respect to the distribution, production and consumption of genre texts. The study of the distribution of direct mail letters has revealed how the selection of direct mail is the result of many different factors, ranging from the size of the organisation to sector restrictions. Variables other than those directly associated with direct mail campaigns (such as the target group or the type of offer made) can be selected to test whether these have an influence on textual conventions. The production of the letters may be sensitive to factors at the levels of 'organisation' and 'business community' as well (Abelen et al. 1993).

The process of consumption (the third component of intertextuality) remains to be investigated (see also Introduction). Much business writing research to date has tended to focus on the production of texts and the relationship between the production process and the corporate context (Mirel 1993). Whether texts meet the expectations of their readers and which components of textual variation influence the effectiveness of texts for different target groups represent important questions for business writing research in general and business writers in particular (see Davies et al. this volume). These are among the most pressing concerns emerging from the direct mail survey reported in this chapter, in which many respondents point out that they need to rely on intuition rather than empirical data regarding the effectiveness of their texts.

ACKNOWLEDGEMENT

I would like to thank Dirk Visser for providing me with data and a wealth of additional information about Gulien & Co. I would also like to thank Catherine Nickerson and Francesca Bargiela-Chiappini for their very helpful comments on an earlier draft of this chapter.

NOTES

1. See Pander Maat (1994) for a discussion of 'orientation' and 'attention' with respect to subject lines.
2. See Cook (1992) on pronouns in advertising, Crismore *et al.* (1993) on metadiscourse in persuasive writing, and Frank (1989) on the use of questions in direct sales letters.
3. To safeguard anonymity, pseudonyms are used throughout this chapter.
4. See Frank (1989) for a comparison of questions in unsolicited and solicited American direct mail letters.

REFERENCES

Abelen, Eric, Redeker, Gisela and Thompson, Sandra A. (1993) The rhetorical structure of US-American and Dutch fund-raising letters. *Text* 13 (3): 323–50.

Bhatia, Vijay K. (1993) *Analysing Genre: Language Use in Professional Settings.* London: Longman.

Connor, Ulla, Davis, Kenneth W. and De Rycker, Teun (1995) Correctness and clarity in applying for overseas jobs: a cross-cultural analysis of US and Flemish applications. *Text* 5 (4): 457–75.

Cook, Guy (1992) *The Discourse of Advertising.* London and New York: Routledge.

Coulthard, Malcolm (1985) *An Introduction to Discourse Analysis,* 2nd edn. London: Longman.

Crismore, Avon, Markkanen, Raija and Steffensen, Margaret S. (1993) Metadiscourse in persuasive writing: a study of texts written by American and Finnish university students. *Written Communication* 10 (1): 39–71.

Devitt, Amy J. (1991) Intertextuality in tax accounting: generic, referential and functional. In Charles Bazerman and James Paradis (eds), *Textual Dynamics of the Professions: Historical and Contemporary Studies of Writing in Professional Communities.* Madison, WI: University of Wisconsin Press, pp. 336–57.

Driskill, Linda P. (1989) 'Understanding the writing context in organisations. In Myra Kogen (ed.), *Writing in the Business Professions.* Urbana, IL: National Council of Teachers of English/The Association for Business Communication, pp. 125–45.

Eggins, Suzanne and Martin, James R. (1997) Genres and registers of discourse. In Teun A. Van Dijk (ed.), *Discourse Studies: A Multidisciplinary Introduction.* London: Sage, pp. 230–256.

Fairclough, Norman (1992) *Discourse and Social Change.* Cambridge: Polity Press.

Floor, Ko and Van Raaij, Fred (1994) *Marketing-communicatiestrategie*. Houten: Stenfert Kroese/Educatieve Partners Nederland.

Frank, Jane (1989) On conversational involvement by mail: the use of questions in direct sales letters. *Text* 9: 231–59.

Frentz, Thomas S. and Farrell, Thomas B. (1976) Language action: a paradigm for communication. *Quarterly Journal of Speech* 62: 334.

Givon, Talmy (1984) *Syntax: A Functional Typological Introduction*. Amsterdam/Philadelphia: John Benjamins.

Gunnarsson, Britt-Louise (1990) The LSP text and its social context: a model for text analysis. In Michael A. K. Halliday, John Gibbons and Howard Nicholas (eds), *Learning, Keeping and Using Language: Selected Papers From the 8th World Congress of Applied Linguistics*. Sydney, 16–21 August 1987, vol. II. Amsterdam/Philadelphia: John Benjamins, pp. 395–414.

Halliday, Michael A. K. and Hasan, Ruqaiya (1985) *Language, Context and Text*: Aspects of Language in a Social-semiotic Perspective. Oxford: Oxford University Press.

Lamers, Hendrik A. J. M. (1991) *Handleiding voor Pr- en Reclameteksten*, 2nd edn. Muiderberg: Coutinho.

Leckie-Tarry, Helen (1995) *Language and Context: A Functional Linguistic Theory of Register*, edited by David Birch. London and New York: Pinter.

Louhiala-Salminen, Leena (1997) Investigating the genre of a business fax: a Finnish case study. *The Journal of Business Communication* 34 (3): 316–33.

Mann, William C., Matthiessen, Christian M. I. M. and Thompson, Sandra A. (1992) Rhetorical structure theory and text analysis. In William C. Mann and Sandra A. Thompson (eds), *Discourse Description: Diverse Linguistic Analyses of a Fund-Raising Text*. Amsterdam/Philadelphia: John Benjamins, pp. 39–78.

Mann, William C. and Thompson, Sandra A. (eds) (1992) *Discourse Description: Diverse Linguistic Analyses of a Fund-Raising Text*. Amsterdam/ Philadelphia: John Benjamins.

Mauranen, Anna (1993) *Cultural Differences in Academic Rhetoric: A Textlinguistic Study*. Frankfurt am Main: Peter Lang.

Miller, Carolyn R. (1984) Genre as social action. *Quarterly Journal of Speech* 70: 151–67.

Mirel, Barbara (1993) Beyond the monkey house: audience analyses in computerized workplaces. In Rachel Spilka (ed.), *Writing in the Workplace: New Research Perspectives*. Carbondale and Edwardsville: Southern Illinois University Press, pp. 21–40.

Nickerson, Catherine (1994) Business letter writing in English by non-native (Dutch) speakers. In David Marsh and Liisa Salo Lee (eds), *Europe on the Move: Fusion or Fission?* Proceedings of the 1994 SIETAR Conference at the University of Jyväskylä, Finland, pp. 221–6.

Odell, Lee (1985) Beyond the text: relations between writing and social context. In Lee Odell and Dixie Goswami (eds), *Writing in Nonacademic Settings*. New York: Guilford, pp. 231–248.

Paltridge, Brian (1995) Analyzing genre: a relational perspective. *System* 23 (4): 503–11.

Pander Maat, Henk (1994) *Tekstanalyse: een Pragmatische Benadering.* Groningen: Martinus Nijhoff.

Pilon, Henk A. (1990) *Direct Marketing & Direct Mail: van Strategie tot Praktijk.* Leiden/Antwerp: Stenfert Kroese.

Schiffrin, Deborah (1994) *Approaches to Discourse.* Oxford, UK/Cambridge, USA: Blackwell.

Selzer, Jack (1993) Intertextuality and the writing process: an overview. In Rachel Spilka (ed.), *Writing in the Workplace: New Research Perspectives.* Carbondale and Edwardsville: Southern Illinois University Press, pp. 171–80.

Swales, John M. (1990) *Genre Analysis: English in Academic and Research Settings.* Cambridge: Cambridge University Press.

Swales, John M. and Rogers, Priscilla S. (1995) Discourse and the projection of corporate culture: the mission statement. *Discourse and Society* 6 (2): 223–42.

Van Dijk, Teun A. (ed.) (1997) *Discourse Studies: A Multidisciplinary Introduction.* London: Sage.

Van Leeuwen, Theo (1993) Genre and field in critical discourse analysis: a synopsis. *Discourse and Society* 4 (2): 193–223.

Van Nus, Miriam (1996) Persuasive strategies in Dutch direct mail. Paper presented at the 11th World Congress of Applied Linguistics, 4–9 August 1996, University of Jyväskylä, Finland.

Ventola, Eija (1989) Problems of modelling and applied issues within the framework of genre. *Word* 40 (1/2): 129–61.

Yates, Joanne and Orlikowski, Wanda J. (1992) Genres of organizational communication: a structurational approach to studying communication and media. *Academy of Management Review* 17 (2): 299–326.

NINE

Towards a new genre: a comparative study of business faxes

Didar Akar and Leena Louhiala-Salminen

1. INTRODUCTION

In 1987 Jenkins and Hinds published an article in which they compared the rhetorical structures of business letters written in English, French and Japanese. At that time, business letters were still 'the method' for written business communication, and textbooks abounded with sample letters and sample phrases, to be used in 'standard' situations. Ten years have passed since Jenkins and Hinds, and the business scene has changed: technological advances have introduced new media for information exchange and globalisation appears to be a reality for most industry sectors and businesses. But there is one aspect of Jenkins and Hinds' article that is still typical of applied linguists' papers and articles on business communication: a defensive stance, a kind of 'this may seem uninteresting but it isn't'. This apologetic position is, however, totally unnecessary, as research into business communication in general, and especially English business communication from the Second Language (L2) user's point of view, remains a sparsely populated area, in sharp contrast to the widespread and highly significant role played by English as the language of international business.

2. PREVIOUS RESEARCH

Jenkins and Hinds (1987: 328) write, 'such ritualized and formulaic writing may give the impression that these forms are uninteresting to study rhetorically', and they go on to claim that the content of a business letter is often a close paraphrase of a sample letter published in a textbook or other source. They do, however, manage to justify their research by saying that the formulaic phrases of business letters are based on 'the underlying assumptions about meaning and the communicative nature of the event', which makes the ready-made expressions of business letters, and cross-cultural comparison, worthy of study after all (Jenkins and Hinds 1987: 328). In fact, we might claim that 'underlying assumptions about meaning' are always present in all communication, and the success of that communication is based on shared knowledge. Ten years ago, the members of the business discourse community knew that the use of formulaic phrases like those identified by Jenkins and Hinds conveyed politeness and deference; i.e. the underlying assumption of their meaning was shared. Today's messages certainly carry shared meanings too; only the forms and wordings seem to have changed.

In the past ten years, the technology used in communication has advanced rapidly. The following quotation from Michael Kinsley in the December 1996 issue of *Forbes* magazine illustrates the speed of changing technology:

> Nineteen eighty-nine was the year you stopped asking people, 'Do you have a fax machine?' and started asking: 'What is your fax number?'. Nineteen ninety was the year you started being annoyed (and, by around Christmastime) incredulous that anyone in the business or professional world would not have a fax number. Similarly 1996 is the year you stopped asking people, 'Do you have e-mail?' and started asking, 'What is your e-mail address?'.

It is evident that little research has been conducted as yet on business communication after the appearance and proliferation of the fax machine, not to mention electronic mail. Among the few studies that exist, Connor and Helle (1996), Hedderich (1997), Louhiala-Salminen (1995) and Warwick (1992), confirm that in international business the fax is the most frequently used medium for the transmission of business messages. There are other studies on written business communication which include fax messages, but which do not distinguish them from the other texts in the data, such as letters or e-mail messages. For example, in her contrastive study of American and Japanese persuasive business communication, Connor (1988) analyses data consisting of letters, faxes and e-mail exchange between an American and Japanese manager. Similarly Firth (1995) includes phone conversations, telex and fax messages in his study of international business negotiations, and Yli-Jokipii (1994) analyses the requests in business discourse found in a corpus of letters regardless of the medium of transmission. Yli-Jokipii describes the fax messages in her data as having a high sensitivity to situation and to the power status of interactants. However, she also notes that the physical qualities of fax messages are 'unconstrained', lacking any distinctive form, as 'diverse genres, such as pictures, elaborate graphs and drawings, and also hand-written notes' can be transmitted by a fax (Yli-Jokipii 1994: 40). She further contends that the sensitivity to rhetorical requirements in fax messages is low, as exemplified by the fact that they do not contain introductory paragraphs preceding the request to the same extent as postal letters. On these grounds, she claims, faxed messages do not constitute a separate genre. This may indeed have been true for the corporate world in the mideighties, the period during which most of Yli-Jokipii's data were written, prompting her to comment, 'the fax machine is a new device in its current corporate use, and the terminology surrounding it has not been fully established' (Yli-Jokipii 1994: 40). However, her observations no longer seem to apply to the business world in the nineties.

Louhiala-Salminen's (1995) study confirms that the business practitioners who send and receive faxes feel that, along with the form, the style and the whole 'event' of writing has changed. They emphasise that writing a fax is enjoyably easy, it does not have to be 'perfect', and by no means does it have to be grammatically correct, as long as the message gets across. In other words, efficiency is the key element.

The comparative study on business faxes presented in this chapter builds on earlier reports on the changing nature of written business communication – e.g. Connor and Helle (1996); Louhiala-Salminen (1995, 1996); Warwick and Bertini (1995) – and on further research conducted separately by the authors.[1] It seems clear that the traditional concept of the 'business letter' is already outdated, and thus the question 'is the business letter a genre?' has, in fact, become irrelevant – for more on the genre status of business letters, see, e.g., Jenkins and Hinds (1987: 342); Swales (1990: 61); Louhiala-Salminen (1995: 39). In the authors' data, the formulaic phrases that Jenkins and Hinds studied ten years ago appear only occasionally, and always together and in combination with chunks of informal 'chatting'. The aim of this chapter is therefore twofold: (1) to characterise fax messages sent and received in international business; (2) to look for evidence of a new genre. In order to address these concerns, a well-established approach to genre analysis will be adopted – Swales (1990) and Bhatia (1993) – and the form and content of a set of Finnish and Turkish fax messages will be investigated. The discussion of formal features will focus on the fax cover sheet, while the analysis of the content will include the identification of the communicative purposes, the rhetorical moves deployed to achieve these purposes, and any patterns of intertextuality.

2. THE CONTEXT[2]

The Finnish data for this study were collected from FINEX, a small Finnish export company established in 1990. FINEX operates as an 'export department' for small and medium-sized Finnish companies manufacturing specialised products, but lacking export know-how or resources. These manufacturing companies, which have all operated for a long time on the Finnish market, are now looking for new markets outside Finland, and they therefore buy export services from FINEX. The two project managers, who are also the owners of the company, act as export managers for them. They have extensive experience of all aspects of international business, and they are constantly in close contact with the companies that they work for, a fact which is a distinctive feature of FINEX's day-to-day communication. FINEX at the time of writing employs two export professionals on a full-time basis, and uses part-time and secretarial and translations services. FINEX works for eight manufacturers whose products they sell abroad.

TUREX, the Turkish company in this study, is also a small size import–export company specialising in leather goods. Their business activities include importing raw materials from various East or Southeast Asian countries, manufacturing clothing items in Turkey, and selling these finished products to Western European countries and to the former Soviet Union republics. Germany and Russia are their principal markets. In their transactions, they either have direct contact with the companies they work with, or they work through intermediary firms. The owners of the company are the ones who carry out most of the correspondence. They also employ secretarial and technical staff. Like FINEX, TUREX's typical business activities include constant contact with the international business world through fairs and exhibitions, visits to and from other countries with which they have business, and continuous phone and fax correspondence.

3. THE DATA

The Finnish data consist of sixty-nine fax messages sent to or from FINEX. This is the total fax exchange by the company during the week of 24 March to 29 March 1996, which was described by our informants as an ordinary week with no special events, but pleasantly busy. In the Finnish data, most of the message exchange took place between FINEX and the Finnish principals at one end, and between FINEX and the international customers at the other. Of the sixty-nine messages, twenty-seven were sent to FINEX, and forty-two were sent from FINEX during the week. The faxes were written in five languages, but the majority were in Finnish and in English. Finnish was used between FINEX and the Finnish principal companies, and English was used between FINEX and the international customers, who represented sixteen countries in Europe, Asia and America. Almost all of the English messages were written by non-native speakers of English.

The Turkish data consist of ninety-two messages written in the period 1991–1996.[3] These messages consist of sixteen incoming and seventy-six outgoing messages and are all written in English. The countries with which TUREX corresponded in this set of data were Korea, Taiwan, New Zealand, Germany and Italy. All the texts were written by non-native speakers.

4. FORMAL FEATURES OF FAX MESSAGES

Fifty-eight of the Finnish fax messages are short, one-page documents and only two or three paragraphs long. Nine are two pages long, one is three pages and one is fifteen pages in length. Similarly, ninety-one of the Turkish data consist of one-page documents, and there are only three faxes which are two pages long, and two faxes which are three pages long.

In both sets of data, faxes are generally written on the company's fax cover sheet, or the company letterhead with the company name, the logo and the contact data are printed on the top or at the bottom. The fax cover sheet is the most distinctive feature associated with fax messages. These sheets contain a header with information about the receiver, the sender and the document that is being sent. Even when the messages appear typed or handwritten on a blank sheet, the lines in a standard header are usually copied.

At first glance, a fax header is similar to a memo header, because it imports all of the items found in a memo header, i.e. 'to', 'from', 'subject' and 'date' lines. Some firms opt to add reference lines for filing purposes, specifying the reference numbers under which the previous communications have been filed by both the receiving and sending parties. In addition to the 'to' line which identifies the receiving company, the fax-specific 'attention' line identifies the primary reader of the fax. Since it is usually the case that in a company one fax machine is shared by several employees or departments, it is therefore necessary first to identify the company (the right fax machine, in other words) and then to provide the information to route the message to the primary reader. These two levels are not necessary in inter-office memoranda which do not have an 'attention' line, because they are addressed and delivered directly to the appropriate reader. In order to accommodate the technological characteristics of the fax machine, a 'number of pages' line is added to the standard header. Since the transmission of the data by telephone is liable to be affected by technical problems, as a measure of caution the number of the pages sent in that particular transmission is given in the 'number of pages'.

Orlikowski and Yates (1994) argue that the form of the text together with the communicative purpose are the identifying features of a genre, and they maintain that some genres have such a distinctive form that form alone is enough to identify that genre. They give the special heading used in memos as an example. 'Form', in their account, refers to readily observable features of communication, including structural features, medium and language system. From Orlikowski and Yates's perspective, it may be concluded that the established formal conventions in fax messages identified so far, point to a new, distinctive genre.

4.   CONTENT FEATURES OF FAX MESSAGES

In search of the generic nature of the fax, the content of the English language data was examined in more detail. Using the framework introduced by Swales (1990) and developed by Bhatia (1993), the 'main purpose' of each message was identified, and the 'rhetorical moves' used to achieve the purpose were analysed. Naturally, the general, all-encompassing purpose of business messages is to achieve

Table 9.1: Breakdown of purposes found in the English-language data

	Finnish	Turkish
Request	39	41
Inform	36	29
Confirm	–	11
Complain	–	12
First contact	13	1
For your information	6	1
Order	6	5

the goals of a buying–selling negotiation, but underneath this 'umbrella', seven sub-purposes could be identified (see Table 9.1): (1) making a specific request; (2) giving specific information (often in reply to an inquiry); (3) confirming; (4) complaining; (5) establishing first contact; (6) sending a document for the recipient's information; (7) placing an order.

Some of the messages included more than one purpose, but it was still fairly easy to detect the main purpose – i.e. the actual reason why the fax had been written – because in many cases (especially in the Finnish data which cover five consecutive days) it was possible to follow a chain of events, including replies to earlier faxes, and replies to replies. Additional information was also provided whenever necessary by the managers of both companies, after the data had been collected.

As Table 9.1 shows, in addition to those 'purposes' common to both the Finnish and Turkish data, there are some which were found only in one set of data. This difference is most probably due to the different time spans the data cover, rather than social or cultural differences. As already mentioned, the Finnish data cover only one week's correspondence, during which no conflicts or complaints occurred. The Turkish data, on the other hand, cover a five-year period, which is long enough for complaints and conflicts to occur. Apart from these easily accountable differences, both data sets include requests, for-your-information messages, orders, confirmation of orders, and first contact messages.

In these seven 'purpose' categories, a total of eighteen different rhetorical moves were identified, which were used to achieve the purpose of the message. Table 9.2 (in the Appendix) shows the 'moves'; 'x' indicates that the move was found in all the faxes in that category, whereas '(x)' means that the move was identified, but not found, in every single instance of that category.

In the following section several examples from both the Finnish and Turkish fax messages will be discussed in order to illustrate the rhetorical structure of texts with different communicative purposes.

4.1.   Example 1: a request

Example 1 (in the Appendix) represents purpose category no. 1 in Table 9.1: that of 'specific request'. It was written by one of the FINEX project managers, addressed to a Czech customer. Seven different 'moves' were identified, of which (1) the recipient's contact data, (2) salutation, (16) closing and (17) signature were found in all messages except the for-your-information (FYI) faxes. Move (3) refers to a previous contact or something that has happened before ('Meanwhile you have received . . .'). It is typical of request faxes for reference to earlier events to be made in a very direct way at the beginning of the fax text; for example : 'We have still the aluminium cases ready for shipment in our stock. Did you get the import approval?' or 'Your order is ready for despatch!', thus reminding the recipient where they now stand in the business transaction. In Example 1, move (10), 'specific request', consists of a set of questions that FINEX would like to receive replies to ('We would like to hear . . .', 'Would you also be interested . . .', 'Are you going to participate . . . ?').

4.2.   Example 2: a for-your-information (FYI) message

Faxes forwarded 'for your information' are frequent in the Finnish language corpus. In fourteen cases the message itself is a simple 'tiedoksesi', a Finnish word meaning 'for your information', written on the faxed document that the sender wanted the receiver to see. The document itself was often in another language, usually English. The FINEX project manager frequently translated or summarised a foreign language message by writing the Finnish translation by hand on the document and he would then send it as an FYI note.

This is a typical message strategy in the communication from FINEX to the principals, since the FINEX project manager knows several languages, while most employees of the manufacturing companies know only Finnish.

Of the FINEX English messages only two are FYI messages, but both of them contain interesting examples of features typical of fax communication. One of them was originally a fax message from a Swiss customer to an international transportation company, complaining about a broken thermostat in a certain delivery from Finland. At the end of the message the writer had typed 'cc.' and the name of the FINEX representative. The original fax was then photocopied, the FINEX project manager's name was circled by hand, and arrows were drawn pointing to the name. In this way, the 'for your information' move was realised without using any lexical items, as the circle around the name and the surrounding arrows served the same purpose. This is both a fast, efficient method of getting the message across, and a good example of an alternative typographic convention used in forwarding the message.

Example 2 (in the Appendix) is the second FYI fax. It illustrates two points. First, it indicates very clearly how intertextuality (see below) is utilised in fax communication, and it also shows how well aware a message writer is of the expectations of the receiver; i.e. that a fax message is expected to be different from a letter message. The original message does not belong to the present database as it was not faxed but mailed by FINEX to a Norwegian recipient, together with some information about a trade fair and a visitor's card. The same letter was also faxed to the same addressee with a simple, handwritten message scribbled in the upper right-hand corner of the sheet: 'fax for your information'. In the mailed message, the writer adopted a proper, formal letter-writing style ('We are pleased to inform you . . . Enclosed please find . . . We would very much appreciate meeting you . . .'). The fax message, on the other hand, is handwritten, with no capital letters, no salutation and no signature. It is evident that the letter writer is consciously aware of the expectations of the addressee; the layout and the tone of the message are all the same as a textbook example of 'the model business letter'. When faxing the same sheet, however, the same norms are not followed. The writer instead trusts the receiver to pick out the information from the faxed letter and does not even add a separate cover sheet, writing only 'fax for your information' by hand, on the formal letter.

4.3.   Example 3: a complaint

Example 3 (in the Appendix) is a complaint from TUREX, sent to a supplier who had delayed a delivery three times and had thus caused TUREX to lose business. As in all other complaint faxes in the database, this particular one starts with reiterating information known by both interactants. The first sentence aims to establish credentials by stating TUREX's annual production figure which validates their credibility, and presents them as a customer which the receiver should want to keep. After this move, as a hint of goodwill on the sender's side, TUREX refer to their previous business with the receiver which they give as the reason for their latest order. To counterbalance this goodwill move, however, they also mention the existence of competitors. After this groundwork, the specific complaint about the delayed delivery is finally made. Typically, all the complaints in the data are justified by declaring the negative consequences for the sender's business. In this case, TUREX had fallen behind in their production schedule and had already lost some business. However, the goal of such complaint messages is not simply to accuse the supplier, but rather to find a solution to the problem. In this fax the suggested solution ('immediate partial shipment') is couched in no uncertain terms as a threat ('we shall not work with you in future').

5.   INTERTEXTUALITY PATTERNS

The term 'intertextuality' was introduced by Kristeva (1986) in relation to Bakhtin's work. According to Bakhtin, all utterances (or texts) are linked to prior texts they respond to, as well as future texts that they anticipate. Thus, texts ('utterances', in Bakhtin's terminology) are, to some extent, constituted by elements from other texts. Moreover, this is not limited to other texts only; like genres and registers, discourse conventions can also be integrated into a text.

Drawing upon the concept of links to other texts and discourse conventions, Fairclough (1992) distinguishes between two types of intertextuality: 'manifest' versus 'constitutive' intertextuality. 'In manifest intertextuality, individual other texts are explicitly present in the text under analysis. [. . .] The constitutive intertextuality of a text, on the other hand, is the configuration of discourse conventions that go into its production' (1992: 271). The notions of 'manifest' and 'constitutive' intertextuality can be successfully applied in distinguishing a particular set of texts, as shown by Paltridge (1995). They also provide a useful tool for describing faxes, as these exhibit consistent patterns of bringing prior and anticipated texts into the present text. As the discussion below indicates, 'manifest' intertextuality is realised in references to previous communication, while 'constitutive' intertextuality involves the incorporation of oral language features in the written mode.

As parts of an ongoing communication process, many texts explicitly cite the prior text to which they are responding. The most common realisation of 'manifest intertextuality' in the faxes is the reference to previous communication, such as a previous fax or telephone conversation, or a face-to-face meeting, as in the following examples.

[1]   Thanks for your fax of today . . .

Following our phone conversation on Friday 19 May 1995 we confirm that we will give you tomorrow shipment address and bank name.

After our meeting in Paris fair on Sept 18 we are still waiting for your proforma invoice for delivery October 10.

A reference to previous events also occurs in Example 1 in the Appendix as move no. 3: 'Meanwhile you have received the ABC.' The majority of the faxes in the database, specifically 73 per cent, start with strategies such as thanking for the previous fax, or giving the reference number and the date of previous correspondence in order to establish the frame of reference. Thus, the present text is connected to other text(s) and co-exists with them.

Bringing previous texts into the present can also be used strategically for rhetorical purposes, as in the case of the complaint message analysed above (Example 3 in the Appendix). Here, the previous attempts which are obviously known to the reader are reiterated in order to ground the complaint and the requested resolution of the problem. The incorporation of the prior text, sometimes in its entirety, as discussed above in relation to the FYI messages in the Finnish data, is also found in Turkish messages. It is common practice to send back the same fax putting a comment on it, particularly when the purpose is the exchange of information. In the data, 18 per cent of the faxes include at least two, and in some cases even three texts. In one such example which includes three texts, the writer requests information on five subjects which he minimally specifies in phrases, not even in sentences, in the first text. In reply, the reader provides the required information in a handwritten form adjacent to each point, and he also asks for further information concerning one of the points, on the same text. In turn, the first writer sends the same text for the third time, noting on it the information that the other respondent asked for. According to an informant from TUREX, the same text is often exchanged several times with additions, especially when the participants have an established business relationship. When the relationship is new, on the other hand, the company sends a new text each time they correspond. Additionally, in certain situations such as the confirmation of reservations at hotels, the convention is to fax the confirmation on the same text as the original request, regardless of the relationship between the respondents.

Thus, the patterns of 'manifest' intertextuality, found in the data, are easily identifiable and, to a great extent, conventionalised. Among the emerging patterns of 'constitutive' intertextuality which are less obvious, one worth discussing is the transfer of oral language features into the written mode. The distinction between oral and written language has always been recognised, but the nature of that distinction has remained contentious. The traditional view about the spoken versus written language is a dichotomous one in which oral and written language stand in clear opposition. In the eighties, Tannen (1982) and Chafe (1982) presented another perspective in which oral and written texts form a continuum, with academic prose as an example of the written end and informal chat of the opposite end. Chafe (1982) argues that spoken and written language differ along two parameters: 'fragmentation' versus 'integration' on the one hand, and 'involvement' versus 'detachment' on the other. The former parameter, which involves the organisation of idea units, stems from the time constraints that the interactants meet when they produce a text. The latter parameter – that is, the degree of 'involvement' as opposed to 'detachment' – depends on the relationship between the speaker/writer and the audience. Chafe (1982: 45) argues that 'speakers interact with their audiences, writers do not', which entails, first, a considerable amount of shared knowledge regarding the environment of the conversation; second, 'immediate feedback' from the listener concerning his or her comprehension; and third, more concern on the part of the speaker for 'experiential involvement' than for consistency.

The fax messages described so far in this chapter fit Chafe's depiction of the relationship between the speaker and the listener, with the possible exception of experiential involvement. To begin with, the parties corresponding through fax messages have indeed a mutual understanding of the context, which results in a tendency to use deixis, and a highly contextual language. For example, it is not uncommon for a message to start with a demonstrative pronoun such as 'this', as in the extract below, without an immediate antecedent in the text. However, the message is still understood within the general context of the ongoing communication.

[2]⁴   Thanks for your fax on Mar 22,
       This mid brown color was planned for Mar 10, then delayed
       to Mar 19 then to 26. So, we cannot blame our customer
       because of canceling our order.

From the text, it is not clear which mid-brown color the writer is talking about; however, within the context of the particular business transaction, and probably also in the previous fax to which the writer refers, 'this' has an antecedent. Similarly, the following example also contains an unbound deictic element.

[3]   Thanks for your fax on Aug. 10 ref. 2432
      We do believe that for nubuck 'A' you can offer a CandF
      price of $2.00/SF by sea for such quantities we are planning

'Such' in the example above does not refer to anything in the text *per se*, but it has an antecedent outside the text, which is known to both interactants. It is not only the quantity that is known, but also the fact that the quantity is large enough to ask for a discount. In this respect, the deictic item is used as it would be in spoken language.

    The second characteristic of oral language, according to Chafe ('immediate feedback') is also to be found in fax communication in that the feedback from the respondent is received significantly faster than it would be with traditional media. Moreover, a delay in the response, or lack of one, may lead to various rhetorical manoeuvres to get the other party to respond, as in Example 4:

[4]   Today this is the 5th fax message to ask you payment of
      same shipment. We still have no information!

The writer who has not received a response even uses an exclamation mark to signal his frustration, and this is hard for the reader to ignore. In this example, the third component of Chafe's characterisation of spoken language ('experiential involvement'), also finds expression in fax communication.

6. CONCLUSION

The majority of the fax messages in both the Finnish and the Turkish data illustrate a marked evolution from the patterns and styles of traditional business and administrative correspondence still taught in schools. The style is predominantly informal in both sets of data, with a large number of sentence fragments and technical abbreviations. This 'faxy' character is further reinforced by the common use of distinctive fax cover sheets. Business faxes have well-defined intended audiences, and as such, they form a part of transactional, indeed at times palimpsestic, sequences of communications which are driven by both interactants towards the negotiated settlement of business affairs. This also means that faxes tend to be prepared by and addressed to decision-makers rather than to make their way to and from a 'typing pool'.

The current social, economic, and technological changes in Turkey and Finland as well as elsewhere, in addition to the effects of post-modernism and globalisation, would suggest that new media and traditional correspondence can neither be easily combined nor differentiated. Fairclough argues that the changes taking place in contemporary societies are reflected in quintessentially hybrid texts which 'mix together discourses and genres in creative and often complex ways cutting across conventional boundaries within and between orders of discourse' (Fairclough 1996: 13). He mentions the example of computer-mediated communications leading to the emergence of new genres which combine features of speech and writing, conversational discourse and public discourse. The discussion of intertextuality in fax messages given here clearly demonstrates that Fairclough's observations also apply to faxes. The old genres of business communication, requests, applications, complaints, offers and so on, remain true to their communicative and rhetorical purposes. None the less, they are affected by new technology and new business practices, and also, perhaps, by new types of business personae. As a result, a new set of conventions for conducting business is emerging that is mediated by the particular features of the message system. This development is clearly demonstrated in the case of communication by fax.

APPENDIX

Example 1: fax from FINEX to a Czech customer

---

(1)	CZECH Systems	1996-03-27
	Mr Josef Koubek	
	Plan 123	
	1234 Plzen	
	Telefax 123-45-12345	
(2)	Dear Mr Koubek,	
(3)	Meanwhile you have received the ABC 123 stretchers.	
(10)	We would like to hear your comments to our products and your plan for the next future. Would you also be interested in our stretcher tables in order to load the stretcher in ambulance? Are you going to participate in the Fair in Praque in April?	
(15)	Look forward to hearing from you.	
(16)	Best regards SUVIO & CO.	
(17)	signature Sini Suvio Export: P.O. Box 12 FIN 12345 Vuorio, Finland Tel. 358-12-121212 Fax: 358-12-131313	

---

(1) contact data, (2) salutation, (3) reference to previous contact, (10) specific request, (15) preclosing, (16) closing, (17) signature. (Numbers refer to rhetorical moves listed in Table 9.2.)

Table 9.2:   Rhetorical moves identified for each purpose

	Specific request	Inform	Confirm	Complain	First contact	FYI	Order
1 Receiver contact data	x	x	x	x	x		x
2 Salutation	(x)	(x)	(x)	(x)	(x)		(x)
3 Reference to prev. com.	(x)	x	x	x			x
4 Establishing credentials				(x)	(x)		
5 Goodwill	(x)	(x)		(x)			
6 Give info	(x)	x	x	x	x		(x)
7 Order							x
8 Confirm		(x)	x				
9 Specify products and terms		(x)		x			x
10 Specific request	x			(x)			
11 FYI						x	x
12 Complain				x			
13 Threat to change terms				x			
14 Resolution of conflict				x			
15 Preclosing	(x)	(x)	(x)	(x)	(x)		(x)
16 Closing	x	x	x	x	x		x
17 Signature	x	x	x	x	x		x

(An x indicates a move identified in all the faxes in that category; an (x) refers to a move identified in *some* of the faxes in the category.)

Example 2: a message from FINEX to a Norwegian
customer; originally mailed, this version faxed

BURKS AS
Box 12
Nyby
N-12345 Vikberg
NORWAY   1996-03-25
Fax: 994–47–12345

                        (11)   fax for your information
                                     (*handwritten*)
Attn. Terje Vik
Re: ABC
        Dear Mr Vik,
        We are pleased to inform you that we will now at last
        start distribution of the ABC in Finland.
        We are sorry for the delay in starting the marketing but
        now we have received the permission for sale.
        We will translate the text of dressings and then start the
        advertisements.
        As we informed you, the bigger presentation will be in
        May at the S & S Fair in Turku. Enclosed please find
        more information regarding the Fair and the visitor's card
        for you.
        We would very much appreciate meeting you at the Fair.
        Looking forward to hearing from you.
        Best regards
        FINEX
        (signature)
        Sami Suvio

---

(11) for your information. (Number refers to rhetorical moves
listed in Table 9.2.)

Example 3: a message from Turex to a Korean supplier

---

(1) TO: YJO Enterprise
ATTN: Mr YJO
(3) REF: your Fax 090/89 on Sept 30, 1994
(4) As you may know we are producing 100.000 leather jackets per year.
(6) (approximately 4.000.000 sf leather) We are currently using cow nubuck or lamb touch nappa instead of sheep which we have used in the past. As we
(5) have already worked with you in the past we preferred to start the business (6) with you, but we also placed trial orders with XYZ, ABC, and DEF which
(12) have satisfied us. You have already delayed your delivery by three times. Now we are in deep trouble with our customer because of our delivery time and we may loose our customer. Also we cannot understand that all of the colors in nubuck and lamb touch are continuously defective. We must tell you that we
(13) are very disappointed with you and we shall not work with you in future if
(14) the situation is not improved by immediate partial shipments. There is no need to tell that the quality must be as usual.
(16) Best regards.
(17) signature

---

(1) receiver's contact data, (3) reference to previous communication, (4) establishing credentials, (5) goodwill, (6) give information, (12) complain, (13) threat to change terms, (14) resolution, (16) closing, (17) signature. (Numbers refer to rhetorical moves listed in Table 9.2.)

NOTES

1. The writers have analysed current business communication in two widely different countries and cultures, Finland and Turkey (Louhiala-Salminen 1997; Akar 1998).
2. FINEX and TUREX are pseudonyms, not the real names of the companies. Also other names, all addresses and other identifying information

of all companies, people, events and products used in the text and examples have been changed. The rest of the text of the examples are as in the original.

3. The difference in the amount of data and the method of collection results from the fact that we started to collect data individually for two different projects. Prior to the data collection, several visits were paid to the companies, where access was obtained to their correspondence files, and interviews with the managers were carried out to complement the data.

4. The two examples are from the Turkish data. Text 1 in the Appendix provides an example from Finnish, the first word of which is 'Meanwhile'.

REFERENCES

Akar, Didar (1998) Patterns and variations in contemporary written business communication in Turkey: a genre study of four companies. Unpublished doctoral thesis, University of Michigan.

Bhatia, Vijay K. (1993) *Analysing Genre: Language Use in Professional Settings.* London: Longman.

Chafe, Wallace L. (1982) Integration and involvement in speaking, writing, and oral literature. In D. Tannen (ed.), *Spoken and Written Language: Exploring Orality and Literacy.* Norwood, NJ: Ablex Publishing Corporation.

Connor, Ulla (1988) A contrastive study of persuasive business correspondence: American and Japanese. In S. J. Bruno (ed), *Global Implicatons of Business Communications: Theory, Technology, and Practice.* Houston, TX: School of Business and Public Administration, pp. 57–72.

Connor, Ulla and Helle, Tuija (1996) 'How you like my fish?' Analysing writing in an international brokerage company, a case study. Paper presented at the AAAL Conference, Chicago, IL.

Fairclough, Norman (1992) Intertextuality in critical discourse analysis. *Linguistics and Education* 4: 269–93.

Fairclough, Norman (1996) Border crossings: discourse and social change in contemporary societies. In H. Coleman and L. Cameron (eds), *Change and Language.* Clevedon: British Association for Applied Linguistics, pp. 3–17.

Firth, Alan (1995) 'Accounts' in negotiation discourse: a single case analysis. *Journal of Pragmatics* 23: 199–226.

Hedderich, Norbert (1997) The demand for business German: a survey of German–American companies. *The Journal of Language for International Business* 8 (1): 41–52.

Jenkins, Susan and Hinds, John (1987) Business letter writing: English, French and Japanese. *TESOL Quarterly* 121 (2): 327–54.

Kristeva, Julia (1986) Word, dialogue, and novel. In T. Moi (ed.). *The Kristeva Reader*. Oxford: Basil Blackwell.

Louhiala-Salminen, Leena (1995) 'Drop me a fax, will you?' A study of written business communication. Reports from the Department of English No. 10, Jyväskylä, Finland: University of Jyväskylä.

Louhiala-Salminen, Leena (1996) The business communication classroom vs. reality: what should we teach today? *English for Specific Purposes* 15 (1): 37–51.

Louhiala-Salminen, Leena (1997) Investigating the genre of a business fax: a Finnish case study. *The Journal of Business Communication* 34 (3): 316–33.

Orlikowski, Wanda and Yates, Joanne (1994) Genre repertoire: the structuring of communicative practices in organisations. *Administrative Science Quarterly* 39: 541–74.

Paltridge, Brian (1995) Working with genre: a pragmatic perspective. *Journal of Pragmatics* 24: 393–406.

Swales, John (1990) *Genre Analysis*. Cambridge: Cambridge University Press.

Tannen, Deborah (1982) *Spoken and Written Language: Exploring Orality and Literacy*. Norwood, NJ: Ablex Publishing Corporation.

Warwick, Brian (1992) Business correspondence by fax: an investigation into frequency of use, discourse structure and linguistic features. Unpublished Master's thesis. University of Aston, UK.

Warwick, Brian and Bertini, Sara (1995) Business correspondence by fax: some ideas on why and how to teach it. *English Teaching Forum*: 30–3.

Yli-Jokipii, Hilkka (1994) *Requests in Professional Discourse: A Cross-cultural Study of British, American and Finnish Business Writing*. Annales Academiae Scientiarum Fennicae Dissertationes Humanarum Litterarum 71. Helsinki: Suomalainen tiedeakatemia.

TEN

Homing in on a genre: invitations for bids[1]

Leila Barbara and Mike Scott

1. INTRODUCTION

In the context of business transactions there is a commercially important if hitherto little-studied genre, that of invitations for bids (IFBs), which we have found to enjoy some interesting characteristics. As bedtime reading, they are in themselves about as fascinating as the average insurance contract, but they are none the less of linguistic as well as commercial interest, both pragmatically as examples of unequal discourse and formally in terms of cross-linguistic features. To illustrate: one would imagine that an IFB would begin with, or at the very least contain, a description of what goods or services are to be bid for, yet this is far from being the case.

The aim of this chapter is thus to propose a description of the genre 'invitation for bids', concentrating on specific linguistic features, starting by showing that it belongs to the class of 'colony texts' proposed in Hoey (1986) and moving into a description of its components and lexical features. The IFBs studied are from four countries (Bangladesh, India, Jamaica and Brazil) and include texts in English and Portuguese.

2. GENRE

For Swales (1990: 45–58), criteria for a genre include:

1. being a class of communicative events;
2. sharing communicative purposes and an intended audience;
3. sharing restrictions on form and content recognised by the insiders in the relevant discourse community;
4. having a specific nomenclature recognised as in criterion (3).

IFBs meet these criteria:

1. As well as being communicative events, IFBs have the function of triggering, of being the starting point of a communicative activity – a buying–selling activity. They are not encounters in Hasan's (Halliday and Hasan 1989) terms, of course, not least because very little face-to-face communication takes place during the process of bidding.

2. IFBs have a clear communicative purpose: offering to buy goods and/or services. In this respect, the use of the word 'bid' reflects the main meaning found in dictionaries: 'activity performed in auctions to purchase goods, as bidders are invited and as one bidder will win by offering either the lowest price or best technical qualification (or a combination)' (*Longman Dictionary of Business English*).

3. As will be shown, IFBs are clearly highly restricted in form and content.

4. IFBs share a name and other lexical restrictions adhered to by the relevant discourse community in the commercial world.

Looking at the lexicon of IFBs from different countries, this chapter will concentrate on showing their shared restrictions on form and content – that is, on Swales's criterion (3).

3.   BACKGROUND NOTES

Specialised discourse has long (in so far as one can use this adverb in discourse analysis studies) been an object of concern and much work has been carried out in analysing both academic discourse and the discourse of other professional communities (Swales 1990). Thus there have been over twenty years of studies of doctor–patient interaction, for example. ESP practitioners have paid close attention to comparisons of features of specific text types.

Yet it was only in the 1980s that the discourse of business came to be studied more intensively. Prior to that there are studies, such as Mitchell's (1957) 'The language of buying and selling in Cyrenaica: a situational statement', which are essentially anthropological linguistics and do not concern standard international trade practices. As international communication has intensified, research has begun to concentrate on intercultural communication in work settings.

Thus a good number of analyses of intercultural, cross-cultural and corporate discourse can now be found – recent publications including Clyne (1994), Eilich and Wagner (1995), Piquè *et al.* (1996), Yamada (1997), Bargiela-Chiappini and Harris (1997). Nevertheless, a search through CD-ROM databases (using MLA, ERIC, ABI and sociological and economics abstracts) failed to turn up a single reference to IFBs. This is a hitherto unanalysed genre.

4. THE DATA

From the point of view of the participants in an interaction, texts produced in business situations can be classed as public or private. Public texts include leaflets of various kinds, house organs, several types of reports and so on. These are non-confidential documents and their readership is not narrowly specified. Private documents, on the other hand, are those such as minutes of meetings and reports on staff selection interviews, that may circulate within the organisation or between organisations, but are usually accessible only to a limited number of people.

Invitations for bids are not as private as minutes or details on staff, but they share some of the characteristics of the private category. For example, they are not normally circulated to those who are not potentially interested in the business. It is well known to discourse and conversation analysts, and to researchers in business language, that it is quite difficult to gain access to private types of documents. The IFBs analysed in this chapter were obtained through personal contacts and, though this sample size is very small, these documents are likely to be representative to some degree, given the geographical variation in their origin.

The documents studied are six IFBs issued by public companies interested in acquiring goods and/or services; three are in English, (from Bangladesh, India and Jamaica), and two are in Portuguese, from Brazil[2]. The reason for including texts in English is obvious, as it is the language used internationally for business; in international transactions it is not particularly important whether texts are produced by native speakers or non-natives. What is linguistically important is the degree of appropriateness to the situation and the degree to which the (often international) participants understand each other, both in interactional and content terms.

The choice of Brazilian Portuguese has to do with the contextual interests of the larger project of which this research is part. From a theoretical point of view the use of two languages provides some evidence to support the possibility that the language is not a variable that influences the main features of the genre. The data analysed, despite the sample size, in fact provide evidence that the genre is, in nature, language- and culture-independent. In other words, the features of the genre are shared by the relevant business sub-community world-wide.

Tables 10.1 and 10.2 contain a statistical profile of the data analysed. From Table 10.1 it can be seen that the longest of the three texts in English was the one from Jamaica at 8684 words. The sentences in the sample are of medium length at around 20 words, but with a great deal of variation (a standard deviation which exceeds the mean).

Table 10.1: Basic statistics of IFBs in English

	Bangladesh	India	Jamaica	Total
Running words	2513	6673	8684	17870
Different words	620	925	1376	1878
Sentences	107	278	380	765

Table 10.2: Basic statistics on IFBs in Portuguese

	Brazil 1	Brazil 2	Brazil 3	Total
Running words	5437	11975	14250	31662
Different words	1284	1973	2304	3818
Sentences	336	452	366	1154

The Brazilian texts are rather longer on average, which helps to explain the greater number of different word types (3818 compared with 1877 in the sample in English). This is also due to the fact that Portuguese is a more highly inflected language than English so more different word-forms are detected. As Tables 10.1 and 10.2 show, there is considerable variation in length, ranging from the shortest IFB from Bangladesh to one over five times as long from Brazil.

5. THE METHODOLOGY

The procedures for analysis relied on WordSmith Tools (Scott 1996), a suite of software tools for lexical analysis. A first step was to identify 'key words' (KWs) in the IFBs. The KeyWords tool in this suite identifies key words by comparing relative frequencies of each word in the text being examined, with the corresponding word in a reference corpus. Where the frequency is found to be outstanding, the word in question is considered 'key'.[3] Using this tool, it was possible to identify certain words as characteristic of IFBs. The reference corpus used for the texts in Portuguese was 4.9 million words of the *Folha de São Paulo* newspaper from 1994. The reference corpus used for the texts in English was 9.3 million words of *The Guardian* newspaper from the same year.[4]

The next step was to investigate these 'key words' by perusing the contexts in which they were found. The tool used for this was Concord, a concordancer which shows key-word-in-context (KWIC) concordances, and allows the user to investigate collocates, common word clusters or phrases and so on.

6. THE ANALYSIS

6.1. Rhetorical function

The aim of the bidding process is to acquire goods and/or services. The original expectation of this study was that the text would include a detailed specification of all the features of the goods or services being purchased, but this was not found in any of the documents. The beginning of an IFB has a performative function; it performs the act of opening the bidding process. From then on, IFBs are concerned with the detailed specification of the rights and duties of the parties involved in the bidding process. They are regulative documents therefore, their rhetorical function being to specify rights and duties. As such, very few assertions or descriptions can be found; the text is constitutive and instructional, so that informative moves are modalised, as they involve obligation or necessity. A few examples from the Indian IFB are quite representative:

[1] 1.1. . . . no other party . . . shall derive any rights from . . .
     3.1. . . . all goods . . . shall have their origin . . .
     4.1. . . . the bidder shall bear all costs . . .

These phrases clearly indicate either constitutive moves (what is meant by X in terms of the bidding process) or obligations, generally on the part of the bidder. At the same time they supply information to the prospective bidder. Not only is the format declarative, but it is also characterised by several modals. Unlike some other types of instructional texts, such as recipes, exercises in textbooks or school tests, which are modulated but not modalised, the sample suggests that the modulation in bids does not consist of imperative sentences. It is more like the format of rules of games or committee regulations, usually modalised with 'shall'.

The IFBs examined contain two clear types of modality. The types which focus on the purchaser are of the set 'give', 'allow', 'may', 'will'; those which focus on the bidder are of the type of 'permission' or 'obligation', with frequent use of 'shall'. Modals will be examined in more detail in section 8.1, but these preliminary findings clearly suggest unequal discourse. The language of IFBs reflects the power and the rights of the purchaser, who is explicitly allowed control over the process. The bidder has to meet many more obligations, characteristically signalled by 'shall' or an equivalent.

6.2.   IFBs as 'colony texts'

The initial part of the document – the introduction, the opening proper and some other sections – can, in most IFBs, be easily and usefully described using a traditional approach such as Swales's 'move analysis'. But these categories constitute a very small percentage of the whole of an IFB text (less than 5 per cent in most cases). A more fruitful description of IFBs can be achieved by employing Hoey's (1986) concept of 'colony text'. He characterises a major sub-set of texts as belonging to the category colony text. The name comes from biology: bees are a species which act in some regards as a colony and in others as individuals. Colony texts, unlike mainstream texts, are composed of a number of sections which can operate more or less independently, even if they tend to be found within a common 'hive'. Interestingly, of Hoey's nine characteristics of 'colony texts',[5] only one (no. 5 – one component may be used without referring to the others) seems doubtful in the case of IFBs.

IFBs can be shown to have the following distinctive features of a 'colony text':

1. meaning not derived from sequence;
2. framing context;
3. sequencing system;
4. adding, removing or altering;
5. anonymity;
6. independent use;
7. intertextuality.

(1) Meaning not derived from sequence

In IFBs the meaning of the text does not depend on 'its parts being connected in one and only one way' and adjacent units do not form continuous prose, at least no more than non-adjacent units. Hoey (1986: 3) points out: 'Sections are frequently connected by heavy lexical repetition, but it is interesting to note that no other cohesive devices are ever used, unless one counts cross referencing'. Lexical or, indeed, phrasal repetition is quite obvious from concordance output such as Example [2] from the Brazilian texts:[6]

[2]
```
s o prazo de 5 (cinco) dias teis.  Será estabelecida a seguinte ordem, par
s o prazo de 5 (cinco) dias teis.  Será estabelecida a seguinte ordem, par
odução, sob qualquer forma. 10.4.5 Será lavrada Ata, constando todas as oc
odução, sob qualquer forma. 10.3.5 Será lavrada Ata, constando todas as o
         qualquer forma. 10.5.5. Será lavrada Ata, constando todas as oc
         das Propostas. 10.2.2.4 Será lavrada Ata, na qual devem constar
```

The model correctly predicts that 'several of the putative colonies listed contain groupings the integrity of which needs to be maintained although their components are not strictly sequenced'. Actually this feature 'brings colonies in line with "mainstream" discourses. Just as sub-discourses are embedded within larger discourses, so embedding occurs in colonies as well' (Hoey 1986: 5). An example is the table of contents that occurs in most lengthy 'mainstream' texts and in 'colonies'. Extract [3], from the Indian IFB, illustrates this need to preserve the integrity of a sequence:

[3] 13.1 Pursuant to Clause 9 the Bidder shall furnish as
        part of its bid, document establishing to the Bidder
        eligibility to bid and its qualification to perform the
        contract if its bid is accepted.

13.2 The documentary evidence of Bidder's eligibility to bid shall establish to the Purchaser's satisfaction that the Bidder, at the time of submission of its bid, is from an eligible source country as defined under clause 2.

13.3 The documentary evidence of the Bidder's qualifications to perform the contract if its bid is accepted, shall establish to the Purchaser's satisfaction:

(a) That, . . .
(b) That, ...
(c) That . . .

The three requirements (a), (b) and (c) might be in any order but must not be detached from 13.3. Clauses 13.3 and 13.2 could probably be in any order but must follow 13.1.

(2) Framing context

All the IFBs analysed display a title, which is part of the framing context of colony texts. Whether these titles 'provide a crucial context for interpretation of the sections that follow' (Hoey 1986: 10) in the IFBs remains to be shown. They are similar to the example which Hoey quotes, involving the title of an Act concerning badgers where, without the title and the prefatory material that follows it, 'one would be forced to interpret the sessions as recommendations or predictions rather than a statement of the law' (Hoey 1986: 10). Thus the IFB title, in combination with the introduction and the opening, perform the act of opening/starting the bidding process. The rest of the IFB is the instructional part.

IFBs contain other elements that help frame them. For example, like the prefaces of dictionaries, mentioned by Hoey, some have sections aiming at the definition of terms; these parts might seem to be there simply to help readers understand, but clearly they also have a legal function of protecting the purchaser against possible dispute.

(3) Sequencing system

Numerical sequencing is another feature of IFBs which is probably the most noticeable of the features of 'colony texts'. Nearly all paragraphs have a number – they may also have sub-section numbering using combinations of letters and numbers, as seen in the examples above. The numbering is essential, not only to preserve the sequencing but to show the (relative) autonomy of the items. For example, in the Indian IFB, section 18 is clearly independent of section 19 (which deals with the deadline for submission of a bid), but it seems that 18 to 18.4 form a whole 'bee', as in Example [4]:

[4]   18.   SEALING AND MARKING OF BIDS

18.1 The bidder shall submit the two parts of the bid as detailed in clause 9.1 (amended) separately. The bidder shall seal the original and copy of each part of the bid in an outer & inner envelope separately duly marking the envelopes as 'Original' and 'Copy' (Technical bid or price bid) as applicable.

18.2 The inner & outer envelopes of both the parts of the bid shall

(i)   be addressed to Purchaser at the following address: xxxxxx, Electricity (Projects), xx Floor, xx Block, xxx, xxx–xxx.

(ii)   bear (The Project name) IFB No. (Invitation for Bids) and the words 'Do not open before . . . . '

18.3 The inner envelope shall indicate the name and address of the bidder to enable the bid to be returned unopened in case it is declared 'late'.

18.4 If the outer envelope is not sealed and marked as required by clause 18.2, xxx will assume no responsibility for the bid's misplacement or premature opening.

It makes sense for the sections in Example [4] to follow one another, in the given sequence, and this is also marked linguistically by anaphoric linkage. However, items 18.3 and 18.4 show that the autonomy referred to above is relative, for they could as easily have been inversely ordered.

Numerical sequencing in section 21 of the same IFB appears to behave differently, as Example [5] illustrates:

[5]   21.   MODIFICATION AND WITHDRAWAL OF BIDS

21.1 The bidder may modify or withdraw its bid after the bid's submission provided that written notice of the modifications or withdrawal is received by xxx prior to the deadline prescribed for submission of bids.

21.2 The bidder's modification or withdrawal notice shall be prepared, sealed, marked and despatched in accordance with the provisions of clause 18. A withdrawal notice may also be sent by telex or cable but followed by a signed confirmation copy, postmarked not later than the deadline for submission of bids.

21.3 No bid may be modified subsequent to the deadline for submission bids.

21.4 No bids may be withdrawn in the interval between the deadline for submission of bids and the expiration of the period of bid validity specified by the bidder on the bid form. Withdrawal of a bid during this interval may result in the Bidder's forfeiture of its bid security, pursuant to clause 15.7.

Clauses 21.1, 21.2, 21.3 and 21.4 must come together as a group but could be put almost anywhere in the IFB and could come in any order. Therefore each of these items could be considered as an independent 'bee'. Clause 21.2 offers an interesting problem which provides another argument in favour of the claim that the IFB is a 'colony text'. Although the nominalised definite subject ('The bidder's modification or withdrawal notice') ties this clause to 21.1, it does so in a way which is not typical of mainstream discourse, where some elliptical wording would be expected, e.g. 'this notice', 'such a notice', or 'the modification or withdrawal notice', without the full lexical specification as found in the IFB.

(4)   Adding, removing or altering

The characteristic that components may be added, removed or altered after publication or in subsequent publications is expressly envisaged in two of the IFBs in English and one of the Brazilian IFBs:

[6] 19.2 XXX may, at its discretion, extend this deadline for the submission of bids by amending the bidding documents in accordance with clause 7, in which case all rights and obligations of XXX and bidders previously subject to the deadline will thereafter be subject to the deadline as extended. (India)

This potential for alteration is rather different from the case of updating or excising encyclopaedia entries in new editions, because it is motivated by quite different intentions on the part of the authors. However, there is a further type of re-editing in IFBs: the whole genre appears to be characterised by the 'borrowing' of clauses and sections from one IFB to another. This probably also occurs to some degree in other 'colony texts', such as dictionaries. Thus, except for the number in the title, the goods/services being bid for, and the date, most parts of IFBs can be reprinted in (or as) other documents, in accordance with the sixth property of 'colony texts' – components can be reprinted or re-used in subsequent work. Thus, a number of identical sentences were found in the Jamaican and in the Indian IFBs. But it must be clear that other documents represent other performative acts; reprinting as the same object is not possible. The items of an IFB are different from an article in a newspaper that can be reprinted in a book and still preserve its original identity.

(5) Anonymity

The property of 'colony texts' that they have no single author and/or are anonymous is difficult to determine in IFBs. IFBs from Brazil, for instance, could have had parts written by engineers or architects, parts by administrators, parts by economists and so forth. This IFB is unsigned, unlike some of the others. When they are signed, it is by the CEO of the company, a sign that it was probably written by a team of experts, which again reinforces the thesis that IFBs are colony texts.

(6) Independent use

But the fifth property, that one component may be used without referring to the others, does not seem to hold for IFBs. Anyone who is interested in bidding needs the whole document as it provides 'the rules of the game', although whether they are going to read it all in detail is another matter. In this respect IFBs are unlike dictionaries and phone directories. The fact that the bidder cannot plead ignorance of part of the bid makes IFBs much more similar to insurance policies, the Highway Code or statutes. As in the case of insurance contracts, bidders are probably less interested in the given than in the new (what is being bid, dates, where to get the relevant documents and to whom to address the bid). This helps to explain why some wordings appear to be used by companies as a template.

(7)   Intertexuality

Finally, there is the aspect of intertextuality which is also character-istic of IFBs, since they make a number of references to other docu-ments, which the bidder must purchase in order, first, to be able to prepare a bid and, second, to make the bid effective. Intertextuality is not mentioned by Hoey as a general characteristic of colony texts; nevertheless, such related documents would be 'sub-colonies' of the IFB, in terms of Hoey's description.

7.   COMPONENTS OF THE IFBS

As IFBs are long 'colony texts', a detailed analysis of IFBs could end up as a very long list of parts, with details of each. For example, the IFB from India has six sections subdivided into thirty-five items – with less than a page for each – and, of course, most of these are further divided into sub-items. As all the documents deal with the same topic – duties and rights – elements of meaning tend to recur in different parts. So, for analytical purposes, the elements are grouped in such a way as to provide some insight into the main content features of the genre.

Table 10.11 lists features of the IFBs examined and shows how consistent they are, as most elements occur in all IFBs. Sometimes they occur separately in different parts, at other times they are joined in the same part, and sometimes they are in the same sentence. One may have an element just briefly mentioned in the main IFB and the prospective bidder is referred to another document. The Bang-ladesh IFB is an extreme example of this synthesis: it is the shortest IFB, but it contains the same information as the others without details. A sample of it forms the Appendix. One sentence contains information about what is to be bid for and where the funding comes from. A quite different pattern, where extensive details are supplied within the IFB, is exemplified by the Jamaican IFB.

8.   KEY WORDS OF THE IFBS

In order to compare the two sets of IFBs, a complete list of 'key words' (KWs) was prepared for the three IFBs written in English.[7]

Table 10.3 shows the results. The second column, headed freq. 1, shows the frequency of each word in the collection of three English IFBs. The next column shows what this frequency represents as a percentage of the running words in these IFBs. The fourth column shows the frequency of the same word in our reference corpus (9.8 million words of *The Guardian* newspaper), and where appropriate the fifth column gives this as a percentage. The statistical test for 'keyness' was the Log Likelihood statistic (Dunning 1993), and all contrasts here were highly significant (p < .00000001). The presence of alternate forms such as 'bid', 'bids', 'bidder' and 'bidders' shows that the list is not lemmatised; arguably our set of ten can be reduced to seven different lemmas. 'Key word' lists in Portuguese tend to have even more duplication than this, since Portuguese has more inflected forms than in English.

Already in this small set of eleven word-forms belonging to seven lemmas, it is easy to spot that KWs are of different kinds. The forms 'shall' and 'or' would be most unlikely to be identified as 'key words' by human readers, nevertheless they are at the head of a list of over 300 KWs identified by a mechanical procedure and found to occur significantly (for each, p < .000001) more often than predicted on the basis of a reference corpus. Table 10.3 shows that 'or', which is a fairly common word, and which one would expect to be spread fairly consistently through most text-types in English, occurs about ten times more often than expected on the basis of the reference corpus. The Portuguese equivalent ('ou') shows a similar

Table 10.3: The top eleven key words in the English IFBs

Word	freq.1	as %	freq.2	as %
SHALL	295	1.65	377	
BID	264	1.48	863	
PURCHASER	158	0.88	21	
BIDDER	151	0.85	84	
BIDS	119	0.67	119	
OR	391	2.19	21309	0.23
SUPPLIER	105	0.59	120	
CONTRACT	126	0.71	844	
GOODS	83	0.46	482	
BIDDERS	51	0.29	51	
ANY	168	0.94	8486	0.09

outstandingness and appears in seventh place in the equivalent KW list for the Brazilian IFBs. As Portuguese verbs are inflected, the equivalent of 'shall' is not found in the top ten KWs, but the two forms 'deverão' (plural) and 'deverá' (singular) come in thirteenth and fifteenth place respectively. The analysis of the 100 top KWs from both sets of IFBs, broken down by category, reveals, as expected, that they are lexical words commonly associated with the business register.

8.1. Non-lexical key words: passives, 'shall', 'may' and 'will'

Some non-lexical items deserve further investigation in view of the role they play in the structure of the bids. For example, the verb 'to be' ('ser' in Portuguese) is largely used in passive constructions (407 out of 547 occurrences), very often modalised with 'shall' or 'will'. A directly parallel syntactic pattern obtains in Portuguese. Typical examples are:

[7]
```
and dated. d. The bid shall be signed in ink by the bidder or
.... proposal entries shall be permitted unless made before
cost of ocean freight shall be specified. In the event of
The successful bidder shall be required to furnish a
...... All proposals shall be quoted on the material/

(Bangladesh) This certificate required to be submitted ...
    (Jamaica) ... figured dimensions are to be followed ...
```

The frequent modalisation pattern suggests that in the passive constructions, the agents, whether implicit or explicit, are much more likely to be bidders than purchasers. This is usually the case with 'shall' ('dever' in Portuguese); the scope of the few occurrences with 'may' ('poder') may vary, being either the bidder/bid or the purchaser, as in:

[8]
```
(Brazil 1) ... os dois poderão ser apresentados em qualquer sistema ...
(both may be presented in any system)
(Brazil 1) ... apenas  poderão ser admitidos para desempate ... (may only
be accepted in order to break a tie)
```

'Shall' occurs in the following contexts:
  (1) in specification of features of the bids:

[9]   the bid shall contain . . .
      all copies of the bid shall be typed . . .

(2) in definitions of terms:

[10]   The term 'ASTM' shall mean . . .

(3) in specifications of obligations, positive or negative, of bidders:

[11]

```
        The Bidder  shall be prepared to furnish . . .
 The funds of IBRD  shall not be used to finance . . .
             Tests  shall be made . . .
            prices  shall be quoted
           bidders  shall be free to use ocean transportation through vessels
registered in any eligible source country (a good example of a restriction
is implied in the permission here)
```

(4) in a very few cases, where their rights are being specified, the purchaser becomes the subject of sentences with 'shall':

[12]   The purchaser shall have the right to request . . .

(5) to specify more general 'rules':

[13]   Materials manufactured in Jamaica shall be granted a
       margin of preference.

'Shall' is the most frequent modal used and is a key word; 'will' follows. When the agent is the purchaser, 'will' is the favoured modal. There are very few sentences with 'shall' and the purchaser as subject/topic. Where they do occur, these are very different from sentences that have the bidder as subject; they express rights and not duties and are related to rights to be exercised in the future, not to imperatives, as in:

[14]   The Purchaser shall have the right to . . .
       The Purchaser shall not be responsible for any costs . . .
       The Purchaser shall be entitled to . . .

The 100 top 'key words' in English and Portuguese suggest that, in this, the IFBs genre, there is a close match between modal use in the two languages. Thus, 'deverá' and 'deverão' follow the same pattern as 'shall': most of the 'dever' are in the future, just under half are in the passive and there is no occurrence of 'dever' with the purchaser as agent. An interesting frequent occurrence of 'dever' is found when it is fronted, as in:

[15]

```
Deverão ser incluidos todos os elementos . . .  ([literally] Shall be
included all  the elements)
Para implantaçáo do equipamento em . . . ., deverá ser previsto apenas
. . . (For the installation of the equipment in X, [there] shall be used
only . . . )
```

In both cases, special prominence is given to 'dever' that makes it clear that rules are being laid down as opposed to hypothetical eventualities envisaged.

Sentences with 'will' are often in the passive, like those with 'shall'; there are a few cases of explicit agent but in most cases the agent is omitted. Therefore 'shall' and 'will' behave in some sort of complementary distribution – one with the bidder and the other for the purchaser; one heavily carrying duties, the other evidencing futurity and expressing rights. These examples of passive 'will', where the purchaser is the implied agent, are from the Bangladesh IFB:

[16]
```
Only a complete response will be acceptable.
          . . . will be returned to the Bidder unopened.
          . . . will be sent to all prospective Bidders.
```

Active sentences can display the same functions:

[17]   (India) KBE will classify the bid . . .

Most uses of 'may' are of the allow type (modulation/deontic) when the bidder is involved and are of the possibility type, i.e. modalisation/epistemic when the purchaser is involved, although there are a few cases of modalisation with the bidder.

[18]
```
     A bidder may refuse the request without forfeiting its bid security
               (possibility-supplier)
     The bidder may offer similar materials and equipment (permission)
  The Purchaser may require the Supplier to furnish evidence . . .
               (possibility-purchaser)
     The Bidder may respond to only one . . . (permission/modulation)
```

There is also the subjunctive 'may', referring to an eventuality, as in 'as the Purchaser . . . may consider appropriate'.

8.2.   Non-lexical key words: 'of the'

The Brazilian IFBs have three prepositional clusters – 'deste', 'desta' and 'das' ('of this', and 'of the') – as key words. These introduce post modifiers or noun complements in complex noun phrases, frequently the bidder, the purchaser, elements being bid for or parts of the bid or the IFBs being referred to. This pattern led us to examine the occurrence of 'of the' in the invitations in English. Like 'shall', such items are hardly likely to spring to mind as key words. Through concordance analysis it became clear that they overwhelmingly came together, in complex noun phrases. First, these are legal documents which have to be explicit; second, as 'colonies', very little room is left for anaphora. Thus the occurrence of the preposition and the article in the English KW list does not mean two items but conjoined items, just as in Portuguese.

8.3.   Participants

Very high in the key word list for each language came the chief participants, the bidder and purchaser, often labelled in this way, functionally, but alternatively labelled using the company name (see Table 10.4).

Table 10.4:   Participant key words

English	Portuguese
Co. name; PURCHASER, PURCHASER'S	Co. name, LICITADORA (bidding)
BIDDER, BIDDERS, BIDDER'S, SUPPLIER, SUPPLIER'S	LICITANTE (bidder), LICITANTES (bidders), PROPONENTE (supplier), PROPONENTES (suppliers)

8.4.   Text structure and production

Table 10.5 contains the key words that have to do with the structure of the text. These words can be categorised in three sub-groups:

1. a sub-group of heading indicators that is not unique to but is necessary for colony texts (II, B, C, III, F, 10th, 20th);

Table 10.5:   Text structure and text production key words

English	Portuguese
Text structure key words	
II, III, B, C, F, S (= sections)	B, C, D, E, S (= sections), ASSINATURA (signature), ANEXO (appendix), ANEXOS (appendices), CLÁUSULA (clause), DÉCIMA (tenth), SUBCLÁUSULA (subclause), VIGÉSIMA (twentieth) CLAUSE, SECTION, THEREOF
Text production key words	
BID, BIDS, PROPOSAL TENDER TENDERS	PROPOSTA (proposal), PROPOSTAS (proposals)
CONDITIONS	CONDIÇÕES (conditions)
CONTRACT	CONTRATO (contract), (contractual), CONTRATUAL, CONTRATUAIS (contractual)
	CÓPIA (copy)
DOCUMENT, DOCUMENTS	DOCUMENTAÇÃO (documentation), DOCUMENTOS (documents)
DRAWINGS	
	ENVELOPE (envelope)
INSTRUCTIONS	INSTRUÇÕES (instructions)
INVITATION	EDITAL (invitation)
FORM	
	INVÓLUCROS (packages)
PRESCRIBED	
	PROPOSTO (proposed)
REQUIRED, REQUIREMENTS	
SCHEDULE	CRONOGRAMA (schedule)
SPECIFICATION, SPECIFIED, SPECIFICATIONS	ESPECIFICAÇÕES (specifications)
TELEX	

2. items which refer to elements of the text not by label but by names conventional in the discourse community (clause, section, appendix, signature);
3. the item 'thereof' which (despite the comment just made about anaphora) does operate anaphorically, linking clauses or sections.

A closely related set of key words relates to texts and the production of texts. This is not surprising, as the IFB process requires a detailed set of documents to be drawn up.

8.5. Bidding process

The next group of key words has to do with the process of bidding. These items occurred in the form of verbs, nouns, adjectives and adverbs.

8.6. Objects

This set of key words refers to the equipment that is to be supplied and installed: the object of the bid. The word 'item' in Table 10.7, which occurs in both languages, refers not to items in the text (where it would belong in Table 10.6) but to items to be supplied. It is

Table 10.6: Bidding process key words

English	Portuguese
APPLICABLE	
AWARD	
BIDDING	LICITAÇÃO (bidding), CONCORRÊNCIA (competition)
COMPARISON	ADJUDICAÇÃO (adjudication, comparison)
DEFAULT	
ELIGIBLE	HABILITAÇÃO (eligibility) ETAPA (stage), ETAPAS (stages) NOTIFICAÇAO (notification)
OPENING	
	RESCISÃO (rescision)
RESPONSIVE	
	RUBRICADOS (initialled)
SUCCESSFUL	
VALID, VALIDITY	

Table 10.7: Object key words

English	Portuguese
Specific objects (e.g. electrification), MATERIAL, MATERIALS, WORKS, EQUIPMENT, GOODS, ITEMS,	Specific objects (trains, stations, communications system), BENS (goods), DIMENSIONAMENTO (size), EQUIPAMENTOS (equipment), INFRAESTRUTURA (infrastructure), ITEM (item), ITENS (items), MATERIAIS (materials), OBJETO (object)

another of the small set of anaphoric words which through its superordinate nature forces the reader to refer forwards or backwards to trace its reference.

8.7. Participants' actions

Another set of key words has to do with participants' actions (see Table 10.8). Here again the match between the key words in English and in Portuguese is impressive.

8.8. Finance

Naturally this is important, but apart from 'per cent' we see little overlap in terms of specific items here, as shown in Table 10.9.

8.9. Setting and time

Table 10.10 (p. 248) concerns fundamental notions of 'where' and

Table 10.8: Participants' actions key words

English	Portuguese
DELIVERY	CONTRATADA (contracted) ENTREGA (delivery) ELABORAÇÃO (preparation), EXECUÇÃO (execution), ESCRITO (written), EMPREENDIMENTO (undertaking)
EVALUATED, EVALUATION FURNISH, FURNISHED	IMPLANTAÇÃO (setting up), GARANTIA (guarantee)
MANUFACTURE, MANUFACTURED PERFORMANCE	SERVIÇOS (services)
SUBMIT, SUBMITTED, SUBMISSION	APRESENTAÇÃO (submit), APRESENTADOS (submitted), APRESENTAR (submit)
SUPPLY	FORNECIDOS (supplied), FORNECIMENTO (supply), FORNECIMENTOS (supplies)
TRANSPORTATION	

Table 10.9: Finance key words

English	Portuguese
BOND, CIF (= cost, insurance, freight), CURRENCY, CURRENCIES, LOWEST, PRICE, PRICES, PAYMENT, QUOTED, RUPEES	COMISSÃO (commission), CENTO ([per] cent), COMERCIAIS PERCENT, (commercial), COMERCIAL (commercial), FINANCIAMENTO (finance), QUANTIDADES (amounts)

Table 10.10:   Setting and time key words

English	Portuguese
Countries and cities, ORIGIN	AREAS (areas)
DEADLINE, PERIOD, PRIOR	CONTADOS (counted), DATA (date), PRAZO (deadline), PRESENTE (present)

'when'. Tables 10.3 to 10.10 present graphically the following findings about IFBs as a genre. Firstly, most of the parts of the IFB as detailed in Table 10.11 are present as 'key words'. This is hardly surprising, since a key word procedure aims to identify 'aboutness' (Phillips 1989), a notion which relates to the reader's perception of text propositional meaning. Key words match well from one language to the other: both mini-corpora have similar lexical characteristics. In other words, the common function (to invite bids) and the common membership of an international discourse community override many language-systemic differences.

Table 10.11:   Bid elements

Elements Content of document	B'desh	India	Jamaica	Brazil 1	Brazil 2	Brazil 3
Title	x	x	x	x	x	x
Introduction		x		x	x	x
Bank named	x	x	x			x
Opening statement	brief	x		x	x	x
Table of contents		x	x	x	x	x
Details of contract	brief	brief	long	long	long	long
Force majeure			x			x
Definition of terms			x	x	x	x
International scope	x	x	x	x	?	x
Object						
Object of bid	brief	brief	brief	long	long	brief

Table 10.11:   Cont'd

Elements Content of document	B'desh	India	Jamaica	Brazil 1	Brazil 2	Brazil 3
Requirements						
Form of bid	x	x	x	x	x	x
Accompanying documents	x	x	x	long	long	long
Requirement to be sealed	x	x	x	x	x	x
How to submit the bid	x	x	x	long	long	x
Language of bid	x	x	x	x		x
Prices	x	x	x	x	x	x
Currency	x	x	x	x		x
Bid bond	x	x	x			x
Performance bond	x	x	x			x
Process						
Schedule	x	x	x	x	x	x
Further details available	x	x	x	x	x	x
Opening of the bid	x	x	x	x	x	x
2 stages	x	x	x	x	x	
Presence of bidders	x	x	x	x	x	x
Acceptance process	x	x	x	x	x	x
Result communicated	by post	by post	by post	published	published	published
Annulment of bidding			x	x		x
Defaults to 2nd bidder	x	x	x	x	x	x
Queries answered in writing	x	x	x	x	x	x
Changes in specifications	x	x	x	x		
Signature of contract	x	x	x	x	x	x

Secondly, several key words reflect the 'colony' status of IFBs; i.e. they give information about the structure of the genre. It remains to be seen if this feature is due to the colony type of the genre, or if it is present regardless of the type of text or genre. Thirdly, some key words give information about the interactional aspects of the genre and texts. A large proportion of IFB key words relate to the act of producing text, or to the sections of text. This is therefore a metalinguistic genre, which reflects the bureaucratic nature of its form and content.

9. CONCLUSION

The six invitations for bids representing the database have been analysed in three main ways. From a purely structural point of view, the IFBs are 'colony texts', although internally they sometimes preserve the structure of mainstream texts. This is supported by many factors, including the type of headings, which are characteristic of colonies, and the type of anaphora: predominantly 'non-mainstream'; i.e. 'colony anaphora', but within any given 'bee',[8] 'mainstream'. From the point of view of its parts and their content, it is clear that IFBs from different countries, regardless of language, share the same features, and again, regardless of language, the key words analysis showed that bids share most of the key vocabulary.

In this chapter, no systematic comparison was attempted between IFBs and other types of business or instructional texts which might have shown that the IFB is a sub-genre of either category of texts. Although the sample analysed does not comprise an extensive range of prototypical examples of IFBs, nevertheless there is substantial evidence to claim that the six documents all belong to the same genre, or sub-genre, in that they share the same topics, discourse community, purposes, structure and lexicon.

Both the language and the content of the IFBs reinforce the view that bidding is a highly ritualised process: the language and format reflect this in terms of formality. Proposals, which must be produced in writing only, are to be formally sealed, and to be opened in a public event (i.e. in the presence of bidders or their representatives). There are various possible reasons as to how the process may fail (a preponderance of negatives) and disqualify a bidder.

Bidding is a highly regulated ritual. The high degree of similarity between the IFBs in the two languages suggests that this may also be an international ritual.

APPENDIX: SAMPLE FROM BANGLADESH BID

SFD LOAN NO. XX/XXX
(NAME OF COMPANY)
PEOPLE'S REPUBLIC OF BANGLADESH

A   Notice and instruction to bidders:

1a Source of Financing: (Name of Company) has received a Loan from XXXXXX towards the cost of XX Program in Bangladesh, and it is intended that proceeds of this loan will be applied to payment under the contract(s) for which this invitation to bid is issued.

1b Sealed Tenders are invited by Director of Procurement (Name of Company), (Address), Dhaka, Bangladesh and the same will be received by him on or before 11.00 A.M. of 20–3–91. The tenders will be opened and read publicly at 11.30 A.M. on the same date. Any tender received subsequent to the time specified will not be considered and will be returned to the Bidder unopened. All bids/tenders shall remain valid for a period not less than one hundred twenty (120) days from the date opening. Tender documents may be obtained from the office of Director Procurement, (Name of Company), during the office hours on payment of Taka 2,500/ – (two thousand five hundred) only (non-refundable) in the form of demand draft/pay order in favour of '(Name of Company), Dhaka' for one set only.

2 Bids of Manufacturers or Suppliers:
    Manufacturers of the material(s) and/or equipment included in this invitation for Bids may bid directly in their own name, if qualified to submit proposal under the terms and conditions herein. Material and or equipment supplier's and

manufacturer's representatives or agents may also submit proposals if qualified under the terms and conditions herein. Such proposals however, must be accompanied by a certified letter(s) from manufacturer(s) and other evidence satisfactory to the Purchaser that the Bidder is authorized by the manufacturer to furnish and deliver the material and/or equipment for which a bid is submitted and that all material and/or equipment as supplied will be warranted by the manufacturer as required herein.

3 Description of Material:
The material and/or equipment to be procured is to be used in the construction, maintenance and operation of a system of Rural Electric 6.35/11 KV distribution lines serving rural areas in Bangladesh. The items specified in the material schedule(s) are to be delivered to the port of Chalna as designated in the Delivery Schedule.

NOTES

1. This research was developed within the DIRECT project, which studies the language of business communication, and which involves the University of Liverpool and the Catholic University of São Paulo (Pontifícia Universidade Católica de São Paulo), sponsored by The British Council, CAPES (Coordenação de Aperfeiçoamento de Pessoal de Nivel Superior of the Brazilian Ministry of Education) CNPq (Conselho Nacional de Desenvolvimento Cientifico e Tecnológico) and FAPESP (Fundação de Amparo à Pesquisa do Estado de São Paulo).
2. We wish to express our gratitude to those who entrusted the DIRECT project with some of their private correspondence, which made it possible to start a line of study which, it is hoped, will not only contribute to academic knowledge of business language or language in general but will be of use to those who are entering a job, or trying to learn or teach the job or the specific register.
3. That is, if a word is found to occur more often in a small text than its frequency in a reference corpus would suggest it should, it may be considered to be 'key'. See Scott (1996, 1997) for further discussion.
4. While these two newspapers are reasonably comparable with each other in terms of readership and coverage, it is evident that journalism has little in common with the type of texts being analysed here. The value of a reference corpus is that it provides a back-cloth against which

outstanding features of the text in question may be seen. Note that a reference corpus does not need to resemble the text one is analysing; indeed, one which resembles it greatly will prove problematic. A backcloth which is more useful (because more general) would be the British National Corpus, but as there is as yet no Brazilian National Corpus, it seemed more appropriate to use similar reference corpora for each language.

5. (1) the meaning of the whole colony text is not derived from sequence; (2) adjacent units do not form continuous prose; (3) there is a framing context; (4) there is no single author and/or the author is anonymous; (5) one component may be used without referring to the others; (6) components can be reprinted or re-used in subsequent works; (7) components can be added, removed or altered; (8) many of the components serve the same function; (9) there is alphabetic, numeric or temporal sequencing (Hoey 1986: 20).

6. To appreciate the fact of phrasal repetition, no translation is needed, but to make it easier for the reader to know what is being repeated, here are some translations. The key phrase 'prazo de 5 dias úteis' means 'period of 5 working days' and 'ser estabelecida a seguinte ordem' means 'the following order shall be established'. 'Sob qualquer forma' means 'in any way' and 'Será lavrada Ata, constando' means 'minutes will be taken, where . . . shall be specified'.

7. This was done by making a wordlist containing all words from the three texts, and comparing it, using the KeyWords tool in WordSmith Tools, with the reference corpus from the *Guardian* newspaper. The same procedure was used for the three IFBs from Brazil. Each list of KWs came up with over 300 items whose frequency in the IFBs was statistically ($p < .000001$) much higher than would be expected on the basis of the newspaper reference corpus.

8. Cf. section 6.2 for explanation of the 'beehive' analogy.

REFERENCES

Adam, J. M. (1989) *Longman Dictionary of Business English*. Harlow: Longman.

Bargiela-Chiappini, Francesca and Harris, Sandra (eds) (1997) *The Languages of Business: An International Perspective*. Edinburgh: Edinburgh University Press.

Clyne, Michael (1994) *Intercultural Communication at Work*. Cambridge: Cambridge University Press.

Dunning, Ted (1993) Accurate methods for the statistics of surprise and coincidence. *Computational Linguistics* 19 (1): 61–74.

Eilich, Karl and Wagner, Johannes (eds) (1995) *The Discourse of Business Negotiation*. Berlin and New York: Mouton de Gruyter.

Halliday, Michael A. K. and Hasan, Ruqaiya (1989) *Language, Context and Text: Aspects of Language in a Socio-semiotic Perspective.* Oxford: Oxford University Press.

Hoey, Michael (1986) The discourse colony: a preliminary study of a neglected discourse type. In Malcolm Coulthard (ed.), *Talking about Text,* Discourse Analysis Monographs, 13. Birmingham: English Language Research, pp. 1–26.

Mitchell, T. F. (1957) The language of buying and selling in Cyrenaica: a situational statement. *Hesperis,* Vol. 26, pp. 31–71, reprinted in T. F. Mitchell (1975) *Principles of Neo-Firthian Linguistics.* London: Longman 167–200.

Phillips, Martin (1989) *Lexical Structure of Text,* Discourse Analysis Monographs, 12. Birmingham: University of Birmingham.

Piquè, Jordi, Andreu-Besû, J.-Vicent and Vieira, David J. (eds) (1996) *English in Specific Settings.* Valencia: NAU Libres.

Scott, Mike (1996) *WordSmith Tools.* Oxford: Oxford University Press.

Scott, Mike (1997) PC Analysis of Key Words – and Key Key Words. *System* 25. 2. 232–245.

Swales, John (1990) *Genre Analysis.* Cambridge: Cambridge University Press.

Yamada, Haru (1997) *Different Games, Different Rules: Why Americans and Japanese Misunderstand Each Other.* New York and Oxford: Oxford University Press.

PART IV:

THE BUSINESS OF RELATING: EFFECTIVENESS, ADAPTATION AND EMOTION IN WRITING

ELEVEN

Spanish language billboard advertising in the US: are there effects on Anglos?[1]

Ellen E. Touchstone, Pamela M. Homer and Scott Koslow

1. INTRODUCTION

Billboard advertising, a form of outdoor advertising, is undergoing a renaissance in the US with outdoor advertising revenue growing 16.5 per cent since 1990 (Elliott 1996: D1). Furthermore, billboard advertising is increasingly being used to target the burgeoning 27 million (Zbar 1996) US Hispanics: 'out-of-home companies are stepping up efforts to reach Hispanics' (Davis 1994: S1). In fact, their estimated purchasing power of more than $228 billion (Strategy Research Corporation, in Zbar 1996: 27) is so attractive that Patrick Media Group, the largest outdoor media company in the US has even created a Hispanic sales and marketing group to work directly with advertisers wanting to target this group. The language used on these billboards – almost exclusively Spanish monolingual – is curious considering that census data indicate that much of the US Hispanic population is English-speaking or bilingual. Rodriguez (1997: M3) explains this finding, stating that 'in the marketing world, Hispanic is synonymous with Spanish'.

Although the use of Spanish monolingual versus Spanish/English bilingual copy in Hispanic-targeted advertising has been an area of active research (see Hernandez and Newman 1992; Koslow *et al.* 1994), much less is known of the reactions of non-Hispanics to the same advertisements. Due to the nature of Hispanic-targeted print or broadcast media, few non-Hispanics may see or hear Spanish-language advertisements. The more public nature of billboards, however, means that Anglos and other non-Hispanics may be unintentionally exposed to Spanish language billboard advertisements. The research reported here seeks to investigate Anglos' reactions to Spanish monolingual versus Spanish/English bilingual billboards. More specifically, the research questions examined are as follows:

1. Do Anglos react more negatively to monolingual Spanish billboards than to bilingual versions, and if so, how does this affect their attitudes towards the product?
2. Do monolingual Spanish billboards create and perpetuate a stereotype of US Hispanics as non-assimilatory? Conversely, do bilingual Spanish billboards create a more accurate image of the language situation of US Hispanics as dynamic and bilingual?

2. BACKGROUND

2.1. Ad-induced emotion and affect

Recently, considerable attention has been devoted to understanding how ad-evoked emotional responses influence advertising responses (e.g. Aaker *et al.* 1986; Batra and Ray 1986; Brown and Stayman 1992; Burke and Edell 1989; Edell and Burke 1987). Research on emotional responses to advertising grew largely from the extensive research on attitude toward the ad (A_{ad}) which was empirically reviewed by Brown and Stayman (1992). The effects of ad-evoked feelings on A_{ad} are considered to be direct (e.g. Burke and Edell 1989), whereas the effects of feelings on brand attitude have been found to be primarily indirect and mediated by A_{ad} (e.g. Stayman and Aaker 1988). Most recently, Brown *et al.* (1998) used meta-analysis to conduct a systematic, quantitative analysis of the strength and generalisability of ad-evoked feeling effects. Perhaps most directly related to the study reported here is Koslow *et al.*'s (1994) investigation of US Hispanics' emotional responses to monolingual Spanish, bilingual Spanish/English, bilingual English/Spanish and monolingual English print advertisements. Their results suggest that positive emotional responses to both the monolingual Spanish and bilingual versions did lead to increased liking of the advertisement, which, in turn, increased liking of the brand and increased purchase intent.[2]

2.2. Tension between Anglos and immigrants

This study investigates this issue from the opposite perspective, seeking to determine Anglos' reactions to monolingual Spanish versus bilingual advertisements. Much evidence points to an increase in tensions between English speakers and non-English speakers in the US. For example, over the last decade, twenty-two states have passed English-only legislation. In California, school districts are fighting the State Board of Education's mandate that non-English-speaking children be taught in bilingual education programmes. A popular initiative is even being prepared for the June 1998 ballot, which would curtail bilingual education throughout the state (Anderson 1997: A3). Based on these examples, it does indeed seem that 'a campaign to make English the nation's official language is gathering strength' (Headden 1995: 38).

The reasons behind this tension are myriad. Nelde (1987) claims that tension between language groups in contact is inevitable. His assertion that language contact invariably leads to language conflict is now referred to as Nelde's Law. With the increasing mobility of our societies, language groups will come into contact with other language groups. If Nelde's Law is indeed the case, perhaps there are ways to mitigate the inevitable language conflict. Perhaps bilingual, rather than monolingual languages – other-than-English signage, would be one way to accomplish this; several recent conflicts suggest this may be the answer. In the late 1980s, English speakers coming into contact with languages-other-than-English on business signage did indeed lead to language conflict in several southern California communities. In the early 1980s, many Anglo residents of Monterey Park, California, a suburb of Greater Los Angeles, lobbied against business signage in languages other than English, interpreting these 'Chinese signs as a bold symbol of the takeover of American business and the decline of the English language' (Horton 1995: 94). While some residents were pacified by a voluntary compliance with a city ordinance requesting Chinese business people to provide signage with at least 50 per cent English, others would not be satisfied until English became the only visible language in Monterey Park. Frank Arcuri, a local resident, wrote in his letter to the editor of the *Monterey Park Progress*:

> They have signs that are in a language that the majority of citizens cannot read. They are in Chinese with just a sprinkling of English. . . . Stores that post signs that are 80 per cent Chinese characters make us feel like strangers in our own land. These signs make Americans feel like foreigners living in a Chinese city. . . . I will go a step further than the proposed law and say that all signs must be completely in English.
> (Arcuri 1985 in Fong 1992: 313–14)

Garden Grove, California, another suburb of Greater Los Angeles, experienced similar turmoil over non-English language signage, in this case, Korean signage. In 1989, a commission voted to have at least one word in English describing the nature of the business on Korean signs (Lai 1989). The Planning Commission later changed this regulation to a voluntary suggestion. Brody (1987: B1) describes the conflict:

> it is the foreign-language signs that make the biggest impression on many residents. Most of the business signs in Little Seoul are printed in Korean characters, with English translations printed in small letters below. John Perrot, the owner of a carpet and linoleum shop on Brookhurst Street near Little Seoul, said the Koreans should reverse the dimensions of their signs. Perrot wants the large letters to be printed in English and the small letters printed in Korean.

In this case, it appears that bilingual signage is not sufficient; English must occupy the dominant position on the sign.

While the conflicts in Monterey Park and Garden Grove concerned local business signage, it does appear that Spanish-language billboard advertising – which, it should be noted, is in practice always monolingual Spanish advertising – also causes language conflicts. Karl Kravetz, president of Cruz/Kravetz: Ideas in Los Angeles, explained: 'When an advertiser does outdoor ads in Spanish, it is not uncommon to get complaints from Anglos' (Fisher 1994: S6). Several industry experts interviewed specifically for this study concurred. Maryann Dougherty, Account Supervisor at En Lace Communications which handles Hispanic advertising for TBWA Chiat/ Day in Venice Beach, California, claims that of the three largest Hispanic markets in the United States, Los Angeles is the least tolerant of Spanish-language billboards. She has received many complaints from residents of communities in which Dougherty's agency placed billboards, arguing that the neighbourhoods are not Spanish-speaking. Shery Baumann, sales assistant at Outdoor Systems Advertising in Los Angeles, agreed, as did Kevin Ford, Director of Marketing at Eller Media, who recounted that his company had pulled down a Hispanic billboard once because 'so many Anglos kept calling in, complaining it was out-of-place'. Although these companies claim to have perfected the art of placement of ethnic outdoor advertising using geodemographics, it appears that many Anglos are exposed to them and are upset enough by them to lodge complaints.

2.3. Advertising's role in stereotyping

While the use of monolingual Spanish billboards may have negative consequences for the brand and the advertiser, this study also investigates the role of monolingual Spanish billboard advertising in creating an inaccurate image of US Hispanics' language usage.[3] Much has been written about how the media, and specifically advertising, create and perpetuate stereotypes of women (Courtney and Whipple 1980), African-Americans (Stearns et al. 1987; Stevenson 1991) and Hispanics (Wilkes and Valencia 1989). Just as all women are not homemakers and all African-Americans are not entertainers or sports figures, all US Hispanics are not Spanish-monolingual or even Spanish-dependent. Data from the 1990 US Census of Population and Housing show very clearly that the Hispanic immigrants of this wave of immigration are very similar in their language usage and assimilation patterns to immigrants during the other major immigration waves: the immigrant generation is initially fairly dependent on their native language, but gradually becomes more bilingual as the years progress. Their children, however, are usually functionally bilingual, if not English-dominant or English-monolingual. By the third generation, the use of the heritage language has been replaced by English monolingualism (Marin and Marin 1991; Veltman 1991). From these statistics, it would appear that monolingual Spanish advertising is not an accurate representation of the language usage and assimilation patterns of US Hispanics. Rodriguez (1997: M1) argues that advertising agencies which specialise in the Hispanic market perpetuate the myth of generational Spanish dependence and monolingualism to ensure the survival of their speciality: if much of the US Hispanic market could be effectively reached in English, there would be less need for their services. Rodriguez states: 'neither Spanish-geared Hispanic ad agencies or Spanish-language television networks are strongly motivated to counter the idea that the Latino population is linguistically unidimensional'. He continues, claiming that a Los Angeles Hispanic ad agency informs its clients that 'only 4 per cent of US Latinos prefer to use English, that 15 per cent are bilingual and 47 per cent are Spanish-dependent'. The Census data indicate, however, that 55 per cent of US Latinos are bilingual.

2.4. Hispanic advertising agencies as language planners

In the field of language planning, most research has concentrated on language planning efforts at the governmental and even national level. This does not mean that non-governmental, individual organisations do not engage in micro-language planning behaviour, however. De Cluver (1991: 48) states specifically that 'the role of non-governmental agencies such as the mass media and trade and industry [in language planning] *has largely been ignored'* [emphasis added]. Grin, too, recognises the potent role of the media in language planning: 'Language use in the workplace, in contracts, in advertising . . . *can powerfully enhance or undermine language planning efforts'* (1994: 271; emphasis added).[4]

3. METHODOLOGY

3.1. Video stimulus

In order to make the experiment as ecologically valid as possible, a video stimulus was created which simulated an abbreviated work commute in the Los Angeles area consisting of drive-time on both freeways and surface streets. The duration of the video was 2 minutes and 50 seconds.

Through the video, subjects were exposed to six billboard advertisements for mass-appeal products. Three of the billboards were in English-only in each treatment; the language usage on the other three varied to create the four treatments: English only, English dominant/Spanish secondary, Spanish dominant/English secondary, and Spanish only. In each treatment, subjects were exposed to three manipulated billboards based on the 'three exposure hypothesis' – a generally accepted hypothesis in the advertising industry which states that three is the minimum number of exposures needed to make an impact (Krugman 1972). The billboard advertisements were actual advertisements which were running at the time of the study. As three of the billboards needed to have their language usage manipulated and since there were no bilingual billboards in existence, photographs of English-only and Spanish-only billboards were manipulated using a computer graphics program to create the four different language usage scenarios for each of the three billboards. The advertisements[5] were shown in the following order for a duration of 10 seconds with approximately 10 seconds of drive-time in between each exposure.

1. McDonald's Big Breakfast — Always in English-only
2. Lucky Supermarkets Rewards Program — Varied according to treatment
3. The Disney Channel Sunday Night Movies — Always in English-only
4. McIlhenny's Tabasco Sauce Condiment — Varied according to treatment
5. Baskin-Robbins Ice Cream — Always in English-only
6. Nike Baseball Shoes — Varied according to treatment

3.2. Selection of the site

The experiment was conducted in Long Beach, California – a suburb considered part of Greater Los Angeles. Long Beach was chosen for its diversity, with 49.5 per cent of the population self-reporting as Caucasian/White, 23.6 per cent as Hispanic, 13.2 per cent as Black/African-American, 12.9 per cent as Asian or Pacific Islander and 0.7 per cent as American Indian or Other. For the language spoken at home, Long Beach is also quite diverse, with 70 per cent of the population English-speaking, 20 per cent Spanish-speaking, 3 per cent Tagalog-speaking, 3 per cent Hmong-speaking and 1 per cent Vietnamese-speaking (Department of Commerce, Bureau of the Census 1991).

3.3. Administration of the experiment and discussion of measured constructs

Researchers sought out a convenience sample of participants at a city beach festival and at an outdoor mall over several weekends. The original stimulus and questionnaire were piloted on a sample of 40, which led to significant changes in both. For the final experiment, the total sample was 220. After indicating their prior impressions of the advertised brands (i.e. Brand Attitudes, measured via 9-point dislike/like scales) and viewing the videotape stimulus, subjects completed the questionnaire containing the measures of the key constructs (i.e. those measuring Brand Attitudes; Alienation; Anger; Racism; Target of the ad; and Threat; and those measuring the creation of the misperception of US Hispanics as Spanish mono-lingual Linguistic Assimilation and Social Assimilation). Respondents indicated their level of agreement with each of the statements in Table 11.1 via a 9-point rating scale (1 = 'strongly disagree' and

Table 11.1:   Measurement of the key underlying constructs

Ad-induced emotions and attitudes

Alienation (r = .60)*

These ads make me feel like a stranger in my own country.

I felt uncomfortable seeing these ads.

Anger (= .74)

Hispanic immigrants are using too many government services without paying for them through taxes.

The government should eliminate all forms of public assistance for Hispanic immigrants.

Hispanic immigrants are taking away available jobs from Americans.

Racism (r = .47)

Personally, I don't feel comfortable with marriages between Hispanics and members of my own race.

I prefer to socialise with those of my own race.

Target of the ad (= .51)

The billboard ads were aimed at people like me.

These ads aren't directed at me.

The advertiser wrote these ads to focus on me.

Threat (= .73)

Sometimes, I think there are people in this country who would like to make Spanish the official language.

There is a serious threat that Spanish may become the dominant language of the United States.

At the rate things are going, English speakers will soon be a minority in the United States.

Stereotyping

Linguistic assimilation (= .80)

Hispanic immigrants don't want to learn English.

Most Hispanic immigrants don't try hard to learn English.

Hispanic immigrants should be forced to speak English or leave the US.

Social assimilation (= .77)

Hispanics who immigrate should act like Americans.

Hispanics who immigrate to the United States don't try very hard to fit into the American culture.

Hispanic immigrants don't seem to want to assimilate.

---

* Pearson correlations (r) are reported for two-item indices.

9 = 'strongly agree'). In addition to the above measures, respondents provided a variety of demographic information (e.g. age, gender, income, education and so on).

Because of sample size limitations, factor analysis was not utilised as a scale development or reliability assessment mechanism. Construct measures and associated internal consistencies (i.e. coefficient alphas) are presented in Table 11.1. The fact that the measures of each construct were interspersed throughout the questionnaire and were not presented as individual batteries, may partly explain why some of the internal consistencies are lower than we would have desired.

4. RESULTS

4.1. Overview of the data analysis

In order to test the guiding hypotheses, one-way ANCOVAs were performed for each of the scales created by summing the individual items for each construct presented in Table 11.1. To account for potential differences across treatments in subjects' age, level of education, gender and household income, these four factors were incorporated as covariates.

4.2. Tests of the guiding hypotheses: ad-induced emotions and attitudes

To test the impact of the language used in the billboard advertisements on attitudes towards the advertised brands, difference variables were created by subtracting prior brand attitudes from the brand attitude measures collected after exposure to the videotape. The language used in the billboard advertisements only influenced subjects' attitudes towards McDonald's (F(3,206) = 4.19, p < .01), one of the English-only advertisements which was interspersed among the monolingual Spanish and bilingual advertisements. *Post hoc* comparisons of the individual cell means revealed that the English-only ad had a significantly greater effect on brand attitudes (mean difference = 1.54) relative to the other language alternatives (mean differences = 0.86, 0.63 and 0.06). It should be noted that none of the covariates was significant in the ANCOVA analysis for this variable. This unexpected finding may be an artefact of the less-than-satisfactory method of testing the effects of advertising on brand image. Since advertising is assumed to have cumulative, long-term effects on brand image, perhaps the impact of one advertisement simply cannot be measured accurately.

The hypothesis that exposure to monolingual Spanish billboard advertisements would lead to greater levels of alienation than the bilingual versions was borne out. The Spanish-only (mean = 4.31) and bilingual ads (means = 3.41 and 3.30) resulted in increased levels of alienation compared to the English-only ads (mean = 2.69) after accounting for the covariates (F(3,199) = 5.94, p = .001). The two forms of bilingual ads were not significantly different from each other. The threat measure showed directional support (p = .12) with the monolingual and bilingual Spanish versions (Spanish-only mean = 4.43, Spanish/English mean = 4.35, English/Spanish mean = 4.34) being perceived as more threatening than the English-only version (mean = 3.65).

The language used in the billboard advertisements also had an effect on respondents' racism-related attitudes (F(3,203) = 2.54, p = .057), but not exactly as hypothesised. Those who viewed the Spanish-only (mean = 3.02) and English–Spanish versions (mean = 3.25) expressed more racist attitudes than those viewing the Spanish–English (mean = 2.55) and English-only (mean = 2.54) versions after accounting for the covariates (age, education and gender being significant). Perhaps this result can be explained in that the dominant position of English in the English–Spanish version reinforced the image of English as the superior language.

Subjects who saw the English-only billboards (mean = 5.27) were also most likely to indicate that they believed the ads were directed at them (F(3,199) = 5.04, p < .01). The other patterns of results behaved as expected with the Spanish-only ads (mean = 3.90) having the lowest 'targeted to me' score, followed by the Spanish–English (mean = 4.65) and English–Spanish (mean = 4.93) billboards. It should be noted that particular negative emotions elicited by the Spanish versions of the billboards did not translate directly into negative attitudes towards the brand.

4.3.   Stereotyping effects

The results did not confirm that exposure to Spanish monolingual or bilingual versions of billboard advertisements lead to increased attributions of non-assimilation, either linguistic or social.

5. DISCUSSION AND FUTURE RESEARCH

The reactions of non-Hispanic consumers to Spanish language bill-boards appear to be much more complex than first considered. As would be expected, non-Hispanic viewers of Spanish-language bill-boards did not believe the advertisements were directed at them. However, this is not to say that Spanish-language billboards had no effect on them. When non-Hispanics are exposed to Spanish mono-lingual or bilingual billboard advertisements, they are more likely to feel alienated from their community. Spanish-language bill-board advertising may indeed increase racist attitudes among non-Hispanics, although the effect may be more complex and require a more subtle survey instrument than the one created for and used in our research. Combined, these two effects suggest that there may be a serious backlash among Anglos to Spanish-language billboard advertising.

Some of the complexity of results may be due to the fact that this study used blatant measures of racism, anger towards Hispanics and perceived threat rather than more subtle ones. Several authors (e.g. Meertens and Pettygrew 1997; Sears et al. 1997) have com-mented on a new form or expression of racism that is typically more covert than traditional racism. Referred to as subtle prejudice, symbolic, modern or aversive racism, these measures use scales that allow subjects to express views disparaging an ethnic group's values or culture. In a highly racially charged environment like Los Angeles, hardened racists may be covering up their attitudes and therefore may only express their true attitudes in an indirect manner.

The study also showed that some of this backlash can be directed at the products that are associated with Spanish-language advertis-ing; however, in this case, it was found that it was a control advert-isement which was always presented in English which bore the brunt of the backlash. This advertisement was always presented in English first in the simulated drive, and for this effect to hap-pen there may be some competitive interference (see Burke and Srull 1988) occurring in subjects' memories. McDonald's is a large Spanish-language advertiser in Los Angeles, and subjects may be re-membering McDonald's Spanish-language billboard advertisements outside the study rather than the actual advertisement presented in the experiment. It may also be the case that because the McDonald's advertisement came first in the experiment, it was later misiden-tified as a Spanish-language advertisement in the Spanish-language treatments. These issues bring up some concerns about the appropriateness of ecological validity in the current study.

This study sought high ecological validity by using actual billboard advertisements in treatments, which may have reduced the internal validity of the study. For example, the billboard advertisements used in the study had few words in them, and the authors did not use a later check to confirm which advertisements subjects thought were in Spanish. Also, to add to the realism of the study, the authors used three English-only billboards as controls, but this may have reduced the size of the effects observed by limiting the repetitive effect of Spanish-language exposure.

In terms of future research, the authors encourage more studies of micro-language planning, language planning at the non-governmental, organisational level which has rarely served as the focus of research. Since corporations are arguably one of the most important institutions in our society and often have assets rivalling those of many government organisations, their effects on society in general must be investigated (Deetz 1992). This is clearly of particular relevance in the use of promotional business texts created with the aim of influencing consumers' behaviour.

While Cooper (1989: 41) describes much corporate language planning as 'haphazard, unplanned and uncoordinated', Haarmann (1986) describes it as incomplete, in that the consequences of promoting minority languages for minority and majority language speakers are not considered. He explains:

> prestige planning should function as a kind of control for corpus and status planning activities in order to keep up a balanced planning level (thus neither unilaterally promoting a minority language nor unilaterally fixing the status of a dominant language in terms of prestige). Ideally, prestige planning in a setting of contact between a minority language and a dominant language is balanced so that the potential circumstances of ethnic friction and conflict can be reduced to a minimum. . . . As most planning activities tend to be partial (in unilaterally promoting the language the planning is focusing on), the planning process often carries the risk of creating new sources of friction in the future between the members of the promoted community and members of other communities.
>
> (Haarmann 1986: 89)

From this study, it appears that advertisers are engaging in 'incomplete' language planning. If advertisers want to use Spanish in media attended to by Anglos, there may be an unintended backlash.

This backlash may take the form of increased feelings of alienation, or the flaring-up of racist attitudes, or the current fight to end bilingual education. It may also affect brand attitudes. Although advertisers do not want to engender alienation among members of the general public, neither do they want to acquiesce with racist attitudes by avoiding strategic use of Spanish-language advertising. Thus there is no straightforward solution to this dilemma.

NOTES

1. The authors would like to acknowledge Dr Touchstone's Spring 1997 Marketing Research class at California State University, Long Beach (CSULB), for their role as junior researchers on the project. Class members included James Achten, Jerry Aschoff, Kim Bishop, Jeff Buchanan, Jean Chu, Laurie Fonnet, Bridgette Hecht, Tong Hoang, Angela Kocsis, Lisa Kreske, Jonathan Lopes, Matthew McKellar, Shane Medoff, Ryan Miller, Richard (Chuck) Moore, David Pasienski, Russ Peters, Rick Pinkerman, Steven Quan, Anthony Rodriguez, Edward Savre, Ray Smith, Justin Ward, and Kyle Wilson. Pamela Homer acknowledges the support of the CSULB Scholarly and Creative Activities Committee. The authors also appreciate the assistance of Bob Rodgers of the Multimedia Department at CSULB in the development of the video stimuli. This research was funded by a research grant awarded to the third author, from the University of Waikato, New Zealand.

2. See also Van Nus (this volume) for the relationship between the marketing environment and text, and Vandermeeren (this volume) for the influence of the consumer relationship on language choices, i.e. code, in promotional documents.

3. See the Introduction to this volume for a discussion of the principles of structuration and the reciprocal relationship between context and text.

4. See Nickerson (this volume) for a discussion of the impact of corporate language policy on the use of English in internal written communication between Dutch employees.

5. The researchers chose products which have mass appeal and which are not targeted only or mainly at Hispanics. This was necessary to ensure that participants would also consider themselves part of the target market of the product. Also, in discussing this issue, we realised that there are very few products nowadays with the popularity of ethnic foods that are targeted exclusively at Hispanics. We also chose products which are typical for mass appeal and Hispanic-targeted outdoor advertising based upon an audit of billboard advertisements which were in place at the time of the study. Pictures of these billboards were

provided by the major outdoor media companies in the Greater Los Angeles area.

REFERENCES

Aaker, David A., Stayman, Douglas M. and Hagerty, Michael R. (1986) Warmth in advertising: measurement, impact, and sequence effects. *Journal of Consumer Research* 12 (March): 365–81.

Anderson, Nick (1997) Judge oks district's attempt to curb bilingual education. *Los Angeles Times* (September 11), A3, A18.

Arcuri, Frank (1985) English on signs. *Monterey Park Progress* (May 29): A10.

Baldauf, Richard B., Jr (1994) 'Unplanned' language policy and planning. In W. Grabe *et al.* (eds), *Annual Review of Applied Linguistics* 14. New York: Cambridge University Press, pp. 82–92.

Batra, Rajeev and Ray, Michael L. (1986) Affective responses mediating acceptance of advertising. *Journal of Consumer Research* 13 (September): 234–49.

Baumann, Shery (1997) Personal communication.

Brody, Jeffrey (1987) Little Seoul and neighbors edge toward better relations. *The Orange County Register* (10 May): B1.

Brown, Steven P., Homer, Pamela M. and Inman, J. Jeffrey (1998) A meta-analysis of relationships between ad-evoked feelings and advertising responses. *Journal of Marketing Research* 35 (February): 114–26.

Brown, Steven P. and Stayman, Douglas M. (1992) Antecedents and consequences of attitude toward the ad: a meta-analysis. *Journal of Consumer Research* 19 (June): 34–51.

Burke, Marian Chapman and Edell, Julie A. (1989) The impact of feelings on ad-based affect and cognition. *Journal of Marketing Research* 26 (February): 69–83.

Burke, Raymond R. and Srull, Thomas K. (1988) Competitive interference and consumer memory for advertising. *Journal of Consumer Research* 15 (June): 55–68.

Byrne, D. (1971) *The Attraction Paradigm.* New York: Academic Press.

Cooper, Robert L. (1989) *Language Planning and Social Change.* Cambridge: Cambridge University Press.

Courtney, Alice E. and Whipple, Thomas W. (1980) Sex stereotyping in America: an annotated bibliography. Marketing Science Institute Report No. 8–100 (February).

Davis, Riccardo A. (1994) Patrick Media eyes Hispanics. *Advertising Age* (17 January): 71.

De Cluver, August D. (1991) A systems approach to language planning: the case of Namibia. *Language Problems & Language Planning* 15 (1): 43–64.

Deetz, Stanley A. (1992) *Democracy in an Age of Corporate Colonization*. Albany, NY: State University of New York Press.

Department of Commerce, Bureau of the Census (1991) *The 1990 Census of Population and Housing*. Washington, DC: US Government Printing Office.

Dougherty, Maryann (1997) Personal communication.

Edell, Julie A. and Burke, Marian C. (1987) The power of feelings in understanding advertising effects. *Journal of Consumer Research* 14 (December): 421–33.

Elliott, Stuart (1996) Big, bold, outside and in fashion. *New York Times*. (11 July): D1, D6.

Fisher, Christy (1994) Hispanic media see siesta ending. *Advertising Age* (24 January): S1, S6.

Fong, Timothy P. (1992) The unique convergence. Doctoral dissertation, University of California at Berkeley.

Ford, Kevin (1997) Personal communication.

Frank, Vicki (1997) Personal communication.

Giles, Howard, Taylor, D. M. and Bourhis, R. Y. (1973) Toward a theory of interpersonal accommodation through speech accommodation: some Canadian data. *Language in Society* 2 (August): 177–92.

Grin, François (1994) The bilingual advertising decision. *Journal of Multilingual and Multicultural Development* 15 (2 & 3): 269–92.

Haarmann, Harald (1986) *Language in Ethnicity: a View of Basic Ecological Relations*. Berlin: Mouton de Gruyter & Co.

Headden, Susan (1995) One nation, one language? *US News & World Report* (25 September): 38–42.

Hernandez, Sigfredo A. and Newman, Larry M. (1992) Choice of English vs. Spanish language in advertising to Hispanics. *Journal of Current Issues and Research in Advertising* 14 (Fall): 35–45.

Horton, John. (1995) *The Politics of Diversity: Immigration, Resistance, and Change in Monterey Park, California*. Philadelphia: Temple University Press.

Koslow, Scott, Shamdasani, Prem N. and Touchstone, Ellen E. (1994) Exploring language effects in ethnic advertising: a sociological perspective. *Journal of Consumer Research* 20 (4): 575–85.

Krugman, Herbert E. (1972) Why three exposures may be enough. *Journal of Advertising Research* 12 (6): 11–14.

Lai, Thanhha (1989) Garden Grove planners vote not to require English signs. *The Orange County Register* (20 December): B1.

Marin, Gerardo and Marin, Barbara V. (1991) *Research with Hispanic Populations*. Newbury Park, CA: Sage.

Meertens, Roel W. and Pettigrew, Thomas F. (1997) Is subtle prejudice really prejudice? *Public Opinion Quarterly* 61 (Spring): 54–71.

Nelde, Peter (1987) Language contact means language conflict. *Journal of Multilingual and Multicultural Development* 8 (1–2): 33–42.

Outdoor Advertising Association of America (1997) www.oaaa.org/np/ht/whatbb.htm

Rodriguez, Gregory (1997) The rising language of latino media: English. *Los Angeles Times* (Sunday, 3 May): M1, M3.

Sears, David O., Van Laar, Colette, Carrillo, Mary and Kosterman, Rick (1997) Is it really racism? *Public Opinion Quarterly* 61 (Spring): 16–53.

Stayman, Douglas M. and Aaker, David A. (1988) Are all the effects of ad-induced feelings mediated by Aad? *Journal of Consumer Research* 15 (December): 368–73.

Stearns, James, Unger, Lynette S. and Luebkeman, Steven G. (1987) The portrayal of blacks in magazine and television advertising. In S. P. Douglas and M. R. Solomon (eds), *AMA Educator's Proceedings*. Chicago: American Marketing Association.

Stevenson, Thomas H. (1991) How are blacks portrayed in business ads? *Industrial Marketing Management* 20: 193–9.

Veltman, Calvin (1991) Theory and method in the study of language shift. In J. R. Dow (ed.), *Language and Ethnicity: Focusschrift in honor of Joshua A. Fishman III*. Philadelphia: John Benjamins Publishing Co., III, pp. 145–68.

Whitehill King, Karen and Tinkham, Spencer F. (1989/1990) The learning and retention of outdoor advertising. *Journal of Advertising Research* (December 1989/January 1990): 47–51.

Wilkes, Robert E. and Valencia, Humberto (1989) Hispanics and blacks in television commercials. *Journal of Advertising* 18 (1): 19–26.

Zbar, Jeffrey D. (1996) Marketing to hispanics. *Advertising Age* (18 March): 27–28.

TWELVE

English as a lingua franca in written corporate communication: findings from a European survey

Sonja Vandermeeren

1. INTRODUCTION

This chapter reports on some of the findings of a research project[1] entitled 'Foreign language use in European business', set up at the University of Duisburg (Germany) to measure foreign language use in selected companies located in Germany, France, the Netherlands, Portugal and Hungary. The objectives of the project were as follows:

1. to analyse, compare and contrast patterns of language use by these companies with foreign trading partners;
2. to identify the factors which shape these patterns of language use;
3. to determine whether there is a statistically significant correlation between foreign language use and export performance;
4. to investigate attitudes held by export and sales managers *vis-à-vis* the use of certain languages, such as the awareness of foreign language skills as a prerequisite for successful exporting, and the desirability of English as an extensively used lingua franca;
5. to identify foreign language needs and to explore the issue of unmet needs;
6. to look at the implementation of strategies to improve foreign language proficiency in these companies.

The findings presented in this chapter focus on the use of English[2] as a medium of written communication between German and French companies and between German and Dutch companies. These findings cast light on the following aspects of foreign language use:

(a) the frequency of use of English by German companies as a medium for correspondence with French and Dutch businesses;

(b) the frequency of use of English by French and Dutch companies as a medium for correspondence with German companies;

(c) the number of German companies which send documents (offers, catalogues, advertising brochures, technical documentation, contracts, confirmations of order, invoices) in English, either on its own or in combination with another language, to their French and Dutch customers;

(d) the number of French and Dutch companies which send documents in English to their German customers;

(e) the presence of a statistically significant correlation between the variable 'written English language use' and company variables (size, sector and percentage of goods exported to the countries in question).

The remainder of this chapter is organised into five sections. Section 2 introduces the concept of lingua franca and discusses it in relation to English in business. Sections 3 and 4 present and discuss the methodology and selected findings of the project, respectively. The results of the survey are then summarised in section 5.

2. LINGUA FRANCA USE IN BUSINESS

A lingua franca is a language that non-native speakers of that language use with other non-native speakers. It is therefore a foreign language for all parties concerned. The term 'lingua franca' is applicable to both natural and artificial languages, which may be mixed and/or simplified. It is used to describe a natural mixed language made up of elements of several other natural languages, e.g. the language known as *sabir*, which was used from the thirteenth century to the eighteenth century in the Mediterranean basin by seamen and merchants. Sabir was based on Italian dialects and included elements from Spanish, French, Portuguese, Arabic, Turkish, Greek and Persian (Samarin 1987: 371ff.). Another example of a lingua franca is pidgin, a trade language which emerged in the nineteenth century during the period of contact between the English and Chinese. Sabir and pidgin are examples of mixed natural languages with a specialised use as a contact language. Their constructions are simple and their vocabulary is limited. On the same principle languages such as Esperanto or Volapük were artificially created to be used as lingua francas, and existing natural languages such as Arabic, Chinese, German, English, French, Russian and Spanish can also function in the same way. On a daily basis English is used among non-native speakers in a multiplicity of domains: tourism, trade, diplomacy, journalism, science, technology and politics. Not only do companies from smaller countries such as the Netherlands make use of English as a lingua franca, but also those from larger ones such as France or Germany.

A lingua franca, then, is a language used among people for whom it is a foreign language. It can have numerous variants resulting from the synergetic influences of different first languages and cultures, and of differences in pronunciation, constructions and vocabulary. Empirical research on lingua franca communication is still relatively undeveloped. Among other issues, one that is relevant to this study is the process of the integration of elements from the individual national languages into the lingua franca. On this subject, Beneke (1981: 8) writes: 'We will have to find out, for instance, how Italian speakers of English interpret Japanese or Arab variants, and there is more to it than accents and intonation. Kinesics, proxemics as well as cultural routines and even conversational maxims will have to be reconsidered.'

Often lingua franca use in business interaction is affected by limited socio-linguistic and pragmatic knowledge. Non-native speakers tend to interact in accordance with the socio-cultural norms which govern the use of their own first language. In order to make sure that their communicative intentions are not misunderstood, business interactants must negotiate with their interlocutors as to which rules govern the conversation between them. In this way, a convergence of norms is achieved (Beneke 1991: 60ff.). Business representatives belonging to a certain network (e.g. car components manufacturers and car manufacturers), who regularly meet and use a lingua franca on these occasions are perfectly able to negotiate a conversational style acceptable to all members. Over the course of regular (written and oral) communications within a network, a style becomes established which transcends cultural and linguistic boundaries (see also Firth 1991, 1995 for further discussion, and Pogner, this volume).

In this chapter, the use of English as a lingua franca in business settings is referred to as 'standardisation' and the use of the first language of the trading partner is called 'adaptation', as opposed to 'non-adaptation', which is the use of one's own first language.[3] 'Standardisation' and 'adaptation' are not 'all or nothing' phenomena. Most companies mix their strategies of language choice. The problem is one of defining 'degrees' of 'standardisation' and 'adaptation'. Hagen (1993: 10) states that 'at the micro-level of companies, transactions are frequently carried out in a mixture of several languages'. In fact, a business interaction is rarely a monolingual event. In addition, at the macro-level of international business communication, certain languages are more commonly used than others, a phenomenon that seems determined by factors such as the number of people who speak them, their potential as a lingua franca, or the purchasing power of their native speakers. For instance, 'adaptation' is more often pursued with countries which have a high involvement in international business activities as producers and purchasers of finished goods and/or providers of services (Holden 1989). Companies may conduct cost/benefit analyses regarding their language use with a certain market. For example, if the market in question is small and the use of its language is not widespread, the benefit from learning its language, or paying for translations, would not exceed the costs involved. On the other hand, when a company believes that using the language of a certain market will decisively optimise their profits, they may decide to do so.

3. METHODOLOGY

The instrument developed for the original survey was a questionnaire in eight versions: four in German for German companies exporting to France, the Netherlands, Portugal and Hungary, one in French for French companies exporting to Germany, one in Dutch for Dutch companies exporting to Germany, one in Portuguese for Portuguese companies exporting to Germany, and one in Hungarian for Hungarian companies exporting to Germany. The questionnaire consisted mainly of closed questions. Content validity was checked by submitting the questionnaire to a pre-test which resulted in the re-formulation of some questions. The material sent to the companies comprised the questionnaire, a return envelope and an introductory letter addressed to the export/sales manager which explained that the survey was simultaneously being carried out in five European countries and which outlined the objectives of the project.

The questionnaire was not only designed to elicit information on language use, needs, attitudes and the policies of the companies which completed it, but also on their profiles, by sector, number of employees and goods exported to particular markets as a percentage of total sales. By means of chi-square-tests, it was possible to identify those company variables which correlated with variables relating to the use of certain languages, such as English, German and French.

The target sample was not only restricted to geographical location but also to sector (car components and the electrical and electronics industry). A total of 1560 companies were selected and two repeat mailshots were carried out between March 1993 and May 1994. The total number of questionnaires returned was 415, i.e. a response rate of 27 per cent: 143 from Germany, 83 from France, 81 from the Netherlands, 60 from Portugal and 48 from Hungary. An SPSS database with 415 entries, each with 231 variables, was set up.

4. FINDINGS

4.1. Profile of the respondents

Of the total number of questionnaires returned by German companies (143), 64 were in the target sample of the companies exporting to France and 43 in the target sample of the companies exporting to the Netherlands. Eighty-three questionnaires were completed by French companies and 81 by Dutch companies. All but two of the French and Dutch companies export to Germany. The field of car components manufacturing is represented by about 30 per cent of the German sample, and the electrical and electronics field by about 70 per cent. In the Dutch sample, 40 per cent of the respondents are in the electrical and electronics sector and 60 per cent in the car components industry. Half the companies in the French sample are involved in car components manufacturing and the other half in the electrical and electronics industry (see Table 12.1).

Table 12.2 presents a breakdown of the companies by size. Three size classes are distinguished according to number of employees: 50 or fewer employees, between 50 and 150 employees and over 150 employees. Of the German sample 50 per cent have fewer than 50 employees, 30 per cent are in the 50–150 employee bracket and

Table 12.1:   Breakdown of companies by sector and country

Sectors	Germany	France	Netherlands
Electrical and electronics	71.3	49.4	39.5
Car components	28.7	50.6	60.5

Table 12.2:   Breakdown of companies by size

No. of employees	Germany	France	Netherlands
50 or fewer	50.0	18.5	50.0
50–150	30.1	21.2	26.4
Above 150	19.9	60.3	23.6

20 per cent employ more than 150 people. The three categories contain similar percentages for the Dutch sample. The French sample, however, has the highest number in the category with over 150 employees (60 per cent), which suggests that French companies in these two sectors are generally larger than the German and Dutch ones.

As shown in Table 12.3, about 30 per cent of the French and Dutch companies export more than 20 per cent of their goods to Germany. In contrast, less than 5 per cent of the German respondents export more than 20 per cent of their goods to France or the Netherlands.

Table 12.3:   Breakdown of companies by % of export to Germany

Goods exported to the German market as a % of total sales	France	Netherlands
Less than 5 %	27.1	28.8
5–20 %	42.9	39.5
20–40 %	21.4	22.7
40–60 %	5.7	3.0
Above 60 %	2.9	6.0

4.2. English as a medium of written communication between German and French companies

Figure 12.1 represents the percentages of German companies which use English in correspondence with French companies. These percentages are compared with the percentages for French and German. (Only respondents who report having dealings with France are included.) When asked to express the frequency of use of English with French companies, about 30 per cent of the German respondents reported that their company (almost) always uses English and about 20 per cent that English is regularly used. About 30 per cent indicate that they rarely use English and about 20 per cent claim that they never use it. English is used slightly more often than French (by about 7 per cent more companies at the 'nearly always' level). German, however, is used far less frequently: only about 10 per cent almost always use it and about 20 per cent regularly.

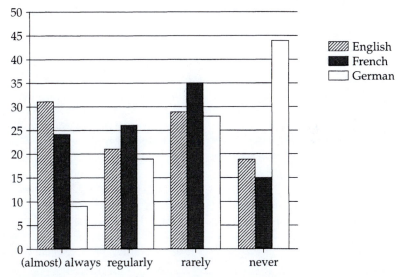

Figure 12.1: Language use of German companies: correspondence with French companies

Figure 12.2 represents the language use of French companies in correspondence with German companies. When the managers of French companies were asked how often their companies use English for correspondence with German companies, 30 per cent

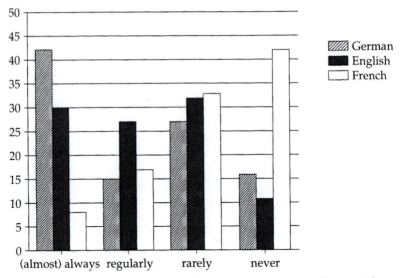

Figure 12.2:   Language use of French companies: correspondence with German companies

responded that English is almost always used and 27 per cent that it is regularly used. English is rarely used by 32 per cent and never used by 11 per cent. The use of English appears to be a little lower than the use of German (about 42 per cent of the companies reported using German 'almost always'). French, however, is almost always used by only 8 per cent of the respondents.

On the basis of these findings, it is possible to conclude that in German–French written business interaction English does not dominate as a lingua franca. French and German companies do not primarily correspond in English. In fact, two strategies of language choice compete with each other: the use of English as a lingua franca and the use of the first language of the business partner. In addition, the level of German language use by French companies seems to be higher than the level of French language use by German companies.

The next question relates to the use of English in different kinds of written texts. The results of the analysis of the written use of English by German companies with their French clients are given in Table 12.4. About 40 per cent of the German companies draw up contracts with French companies in English, about 35 per cent write confirmations of orders in English and about 30 per cent do the

Table 12.4: Languages used in German documents sent to French companies (percentages)

Document type	English	English– French	English– German	English– French– German	German	French	German– French
Offers	22.5	17.5	7.5	2.5	12.5	30.0	7.5
Catalogues	22.5	5.0	15.0	2.5	22.5	30.0	2.5
Advertising brochures	15.0	10.0	17.5	7.5	15.0	30.0	5.0
Technical document.	25.0	10.0	7.5	2.5	22.5	27.5	5.0
Contracts	40.0	2.5	7.5		15.0	30.0	5.0
Order conf.	35.0	2.5	10.0	2.5	22.5	22.5	5.0
Invoices	30.0	5.0	7.5	2.5	30.0	20.0	5.0

same with invoices. Invoices are as frequently issued in German (30 per cent). About 30 per cent of the German companies send offers, catalogues and advertising brochures in French to their French clients; and about 30 per cent also draw up contracts in French. It is no coincidence that pre-sale documents (e.g. advertising catalogues and offers) are more frequently written in French than post-sale documents (e.g. confirmations of order and invoices). Companies seem to be aware of the fact that using the client's language helps in closing the deal.

French companies seem to use English in written documentation almost as frequently as German companies do (see Table 12.5). About

Table 12.5: Languages used in French documents sent to German companies (percentages)

Document type	English	English– French	English– German	English– French– German	German	French	German– French
Offers	27.5	5.0	15.0		47.0	5.0	
Catalogues	15.0	7.5	15.0	7.5	42.5	10.0	2.5
Advertising brochures	17.5	7.5	10.0	5.0	42.5	12.5	5.0
Technical document.	25.0	2.5	15.0	2.5	42.5	10.0	2.5
Contracts	27.5	5.0	10.0		47.5	7.5	2.5
Order conf.	25.0	5.0	5.0		42.5	20.0	2.5
Invoices	32.5	5.0			30.0	27.5	5.0

27.5 per cent of the French companies write offers, technical documentation, contracts and confirmations of orders in English, and 32.5 per cent issue invoices in English. However, French companies use German even more often for these same documents (42.5 to 47.5 per cent), with the exception of invoices (30 per cent). As noted above, it appears that there are more French companies using only German with German companies than there are German companies using only French with French companies.

4.3. English as a medium of written communication between German and Dutch companies

In German–Dutch business activities, the use of English is completely different. Only about 5 per cent of the German companies use English 'almost always' for correspondence with Dutch companies. English is regularly used in about 22.5 per cent of the companies, rarely in about 25 per cent, and 47.5 per cent of the respondents never make use of it at all. In contrast, the 'almost always' use of German rises dramatically to 62 per cent. It appears that German companies in general use German when doing business with Dutch companies (see Figure 12.3).

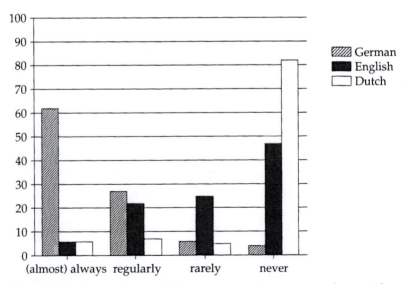

Figure 12.3: Language use of German companies: correspondence with Dutch companies

Finally, the Dutch managers report a similar pattern of language use, represented in Figure 12.4. About 10 per cent of the Dutch companies almost always use English for correspondence with German companies, 20 per cent use it regularly, 25 per cent rarely and 45 per cent never. Of the Dutch companies 50 per cent almost always use German and 30 per cent use it regularly. There is no doubt that German is more frequently used than English.

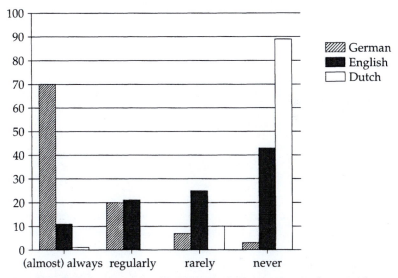

Figure 12.4: Language use of Dutch companies: correspondence with German companies

A comparison of the frequency of use of English with the frequency of use of German shows that there is a very significant difference. For both Dutch and German companies the percentage of those using German greatly exceeds the percentage of companies using English. The explanation for this is that most Dutch companies are competent in German and that the use of German as a business language clearly dominates that of Dutch, a fact which is also accepted by the Dutch-speaking companies. In contrast, German is not often used in German–French business dealings, because the French in general are not as fluent in German as the Dutch are, and because German is no more dominant than French in its use as a business language. In other words, German and French tend to have equal status in international business whereas Dutch does not. Consequently, in German–French interaction, both sides either use English as a neutral lingua franca, or they use the language of their business counterpart, in a process of 'reciprocal adaptation'. As shown in Table 12.6, the overwhelming majority of the German respondents (between 60 per cent and 70 per cent) send their documents in German to their Dutch companies. Dutch customers seem to allow for a very extensive use of German in written documentation, while English as a lingua franca is only rarely used.

Table 12.6:   Languages used in German documents to Dutch companies

Document type	English	English–Dutch	English–German	English–French–German	German	Dutch	German–Dutch
Offers	15.0		10.0		67.5	7.5	
Catalogues	12.5		15.0		62.5	5.0	5.0
Advertising brochures	10.0	2.5	10.0		60.0	10.0	7.5
Technical document.	10.0		10.0		70.0	7.5	2.5
Contracts	12.5		7.5		72.5	7.5	
Order conf.	15.0		7.5		70.0	7.5	
Invoices	12.5		5.0		72.5	10.0	

As expected, Dutch companies primarily send documents in German to their German customers (50 to 67.5 per cent), and the frequency with which they use English only (15 to 22.5 per cent) with German companies is slightly higher than the frequency with which German companies use English with them (10 to 15 per cent) (see Table 12.7).

Table 12.7:   Languages used in Dutch documents to German companies

Document type	English	English–Dutch	English–German	English–French–German–Dutch	German	Dutch	German–Dutch
Offers	15.0		15.0		67.5		2.5
Catalogues	22.5		15.0	2.5	50.0	7.5	2.5
Advertising brochures	17.5	2.5	15.0	2.5	55.0	7.5	
Technical document.	17.5		17.5		60.0	5.0	
Contracts	20.0		20.0		57.5	2.5	
Order conf.	15.0		10.0		65.0	5.0	5.0
Invoices	20.0		10.0		55.0	12.5	2.5

4.4.   Correlations between written language use and company profile

Several questions arise in relation to written language use and company profile. For example, how often do those French companies which export more than 20 per cent of their goods to Germany correspond in English with German companies? Furthermore, do they use English as often as companies which export less than 20 per cent of their goods to Germany? By means of a chi-square-test the answers from the two groups of companies were compared. The difference between them was in fact greater than the difference that would have been picked up by random sampling. French respondents reported lower frequencies of English language use when their turnover in the German market was higher than 20 per cent of their total turnover. They were more likely to report their English language use with German companies as high if they export less than 20 per cent of their goods to Germany (see Table 12.8). This suggests that export performance has a direct bearing on English language use. It is also possible to hypothesise that the opposite is true and that it is language use which influences export performance. If one considers language use as a factor influencing export performance, Table 12.8 may be read vertically instead of horizontally. Half of the French companies which never or rarely use English export more than 20 per cent of their goods to Germany, whereas only just under a quarter of the companies which regularly or almost exclusively use English export more than 20 per cent of their goods to Germany. In short, the companies which use English frequently also export less.

Table 12.8:   French exports to Germany and English language use

% of French goods exported to Germany	English-language use of French companies with German companies (correspondence)		Significance
	Never/rarely	*Regularly/(almost) exclusively*	
Less than 20 %	14	34	
			.05279
20 % or more	12	9	

As far as Dutch companies are concerned, there appears to be no close relationship between the level of English language use and the percentage of goods exported to Germany. There is, however, a statistically significant correlation between the level of English language use and the variables 'sector' and 'size'. Dutch companies in the electrical and electronics business use more written English with German companies than Dutch companies representing the car components industry (see Table 12.9). It is also worth noting that Dutch companies which have more than 50 employees use more English than companies which employ fewer than 50 people (see Table 12.10).

Table 12.9: English language use in Dutch companies trading with Germany (by sector)

Sector	English language use of Dutch companies with German companies (correspondence)		
	Never/seldom	*Regularly/(almost) exclusively*	*Significance*
Electrical and electronics	17	15	
			.01468
Car components	39	9	

Table 12.10: English language use in Dutch companies trading with Germany (by company size)

Number of employees	English language use of Dutch companies with German companies (correspondence)		
	Never/seldom	*Regularly/(almost) exclusively*	*Significance*
Fewer than 50	34	7	
			.01395
50 or more	19	16	

In contrast, sector and size do not correlate with the English language use of French and German companies. Since almost all German companies in the sample export less than 20 per cent of their goods to France or the Netherlands, it was also impossible to

Table 12.11: English language use in French companies trading with Germany

% of French goods exported to Germany	German language use of French companies with German companies (correspondence)		Significance
	Never/seldom	Regularly (almost) exclusively	
Less than 20 %	23	25	
			n.s.*
20 % or more	7	15	

* Due to the small sample, however, it was not possible to prove that the relationship between German language use and export performance in the German market is statistically significant.

look for correlations between turnover in the markets in question and language use. Although the search for correlations could have benefited from a larger sample, it seems clear that French companies with a high percentage of business with Germany correspond less often in English than those with a low percentage. Because the use of languages is likely to be complementary, this suggests that the former would use more German than the latter, and this was confirmed by the findings of the survey. Two out of three of the companies which export more than 20 per cent of their goods to Germany regularly or almost exclusively use German, whereas only half the companies which export less than 20 per cent of their goods to Germany do the same (see Table 12.11).

Table 12.11 also shows that less than one-quarter of the French companies which never or rarely use German with German companies export 20 per cent or more to Germany, whereas over one-third of the French companies which regularly or almost exclusively use German export 20 per cent or more. This indicates that French companies which often respond in an 'adaptive' way to companies in Germany, export higher percentages of their goods than those companies which adapt less often. 'Adaptation' therefore seems to contribute to export success.

. It is impossible to isolate the language factor from the other factors which may influence export performance, and correlations do not always represent causalities. There is sufficient evidence, however, to suggest that French companies which 'standardise' to a high degree when corresponding with German companies – i.e. which use English as a lingua franca – also seem to export low percentages of their goods to Germany. This leads to the somewhat alarming conclusion that 'standardisation' has a negative effect on export performance.

5. CONCLUSION

There is a general consensus among linguists and non-linguists (e.g. Emmans 1974; King 1984; Hagen 1988; Holden 1989; Pearce 1991) about the positive effect of 'adaptation' on export performance, and because language use is complementary this could mean that 'standardisation' has a corresponding negative effect. This is supported by the survey 'Foreign language use in European business', selected findings of which have been reported and analysed in this chapter. Alarmingly, French companies which standardise to a high degree when corresponding with German companies export lower percentages of their goods to Germany than companies which standardise less often. The picture of language use between German and Dutch companies is very different. Both groups usually write in German, and only 28 per cent of the German companies correspond almost always, or regularly, in English with Dutch companies, as do only 32 per cent of Dutch companies with German companies. In addition, there appears to be a clear correlation between the use of English by Dutch companies and both company size and sector. Dutch companies in the electrical and electronics sector use more English with German companies than companies from the car components industry, and Dutch companies which have more than 50 employees use more English than companies which employ fewer than 50 people.

German is prominently used in German–Dutch business dealings because most Dutch companies are competent in German and the use of German as a business language clearly dominates that of Dutch. Dutch companies linguistically respond in an 'adaptive' manner to German companies which in return use their own first language, i.e. non-adaptation. As far as French–German business dealings are concerned, both sides use English as a lingua franca or they use the language of the other side, i.e. 'reciprocal adaptation'.

One explanation for this is that unlike Dutch and German, French and German are considered as having equal status in business settings. To use one's own first language as a French or German speaker would challenge this equality. German companies either use English as a lingua franca ('standardisation') or French ('adaptation') when corresponding with French companies. French companies either use German ('adaptation') or English ('standardisation') when corresponding with German ones. In short, the two strategies of language choice compete with each other: the use of English as a lingua franca and the use of the first language of the business partner – see Herrlitz and Loos (1994) for further discussion on this point. A more detailed examination of their language use reveals that the level of German language use by French companies is slightly higher than the level of French language use by German companies. Interestingly, adaptation is more frequently pursued when writing before-sale documents, such as advertising brochures and catalogues, than when writing after-sale documents, such as confirmations of orders and invoices. Companies do seem, therefore, to be aware of the fact that using the customer's language helps in closing the deal.

The question remains as to whether there is sufficient awareness of foreign language use as a prerequisite for successful exporting. Managers who dismiss the negative consequences of insufficient language skills as a marginal issue may not realise that a company's linguistic adaptation to its clients can make the difference between failure and success in establishing and maintaining a business relationship.

NOTES

1. The author was responsible for the project which was carried out at the University of Duisburg (Germany) between 1992 and 1996, originally under the title 'Die Stellung der deutschen Sprache in der europäischen Wirtschaft' (The status of German in European business). The project was instigated by Professor Ulrich Ammon (German Department) and financed by the Deutsche Forschungsgemeinschaft.
2. In order to set the numerical findings relative to English language use within the wider context of the original survey (Vandermeeren 1998), figures for French, German and Dutch language use have also been provided in this chapter.

3. 'Standardisation' and 'adaptation' are terms also used in international marketing. The latter refers to the company strategy of responding in an 'adaptive' manner to national markets (different products, brands, prices, qualities, advertising campaigns, etc. for different markets), the former to the strategy of 'standardising' marketing practices (one product, one brand, etc. for all markets) (Boddewyn *et al.* 1986).

REFERENCES

Beneke, Jürgen (1981) Cultural monsters, mimicry and English as an international language. In Reinhold Freudenstein, Jürgen Beneke and Helmut Pönisch (eds), *Language Incorporated: Teaching Foreign Languages in Industry*. London: Pergamon Press, pp. 73–93.

Beneke, Jürgen (1991) Englisch als lingua franca oder als Medium interkultureller Kommunikation? In Renate Grebing (ed.), *Grenzenloses Sprachenlernen*. Berlin: Cornelsen, and Oxford: Oxford University Press, pp. 54–66.

Boddewyn, Jean, Soehl, Robin and Picard, Jacques (1986) Standardization in international marketing: is Ted Levitt in fact right? *Business Horizons* (November–December) 29: 69–75.

Emmans, Keith, Hawkins, Eric and Westoby, Adam (1974) The use of foreign language in the private sector of industry and commerce. York: Language Teaching Centre, University of York.

Firth, Alan (1991) 'Lingua franca' negotiations: towards an interactional approach. *World Englishes* 9 (3): 269–80.

Firth, Alan (ed.) (1995) *The Language of Negotiation*. Berlin: Mouton de Gruyter.

Hagen, Stephen (ed.) (1988) Languages in British business: an analysis of current needs. Newcastle upon Tyne: Newcastle upon Tyne Polytechnic Products Ltd/CILT.

Hagen, S. (1993) *Languages in European Business: a Regional Survey of Small and Medium-sized Companies*. London: CTC Trust/CILT.

Herrlitz, Wolfang and Loos, Eugène F. (1994) Taal en taalgebruik in de internationale bedrijfscommunicatie: Een taalwetenschappelijk perspectief. In M&O. 48.2.144–160, Alphen aan de Rijn: Samsom Bedrijfsinformatie.

Holden, Nigel (1989) Toward a functional typology of languages in international business. *Language Problems and Language Planning* 13 (1): 1–7.

King, Tony (1984) The role of foreign languages in the Jaguar success story. *The Incorporated Linguist* 24 (3/4): 154–9.

Pearce, Gillian (1991) Bonjour Europe: languages and the British manager. Corby, Northants: British Institute of Management.

Samarin, William J. (1987) Lingua franca. In Ulrich Ammon, Norbert Dittmar and Klaus J. Mattheier (eds), *Sociolinguistica: an International Handbook of the Science of Language and Society*. Berlin and New York: Walter de Gruyter, pp. 371–4.

Vandermeeren, Sonja (1998) *Fremdsprachen in europäischen Unternehmen. Untersuchungen zu Bestand und Bedarf im Geschäftsalltag mit Empfehlungen für Sprachenpolitik und Sprachunterricht*. Waldsteinberg: Heidrun Popp Verlag.

THIRTEEN

Exploring aspects of context: selected findings from the Effective Writing for Management project

Florence Davies, Gail Forey and David Hyatt

1. INTRODUCTION

In recent years the study of language has become increasingly char-acterised by a commitment to the analysis of 'attested, authentic instances of use, not as intuitive invented sentences' but as 'whole texts' (Stubbs 1993). This concern with real language in real use reflects a recognition of the need to locate such research within the context of the social and organisational settings in which it is pro-duced and received, and for linguists to collaborate with key players in the workplace to investigate language use in organisational set-tings (Brown and Herndl 1986; Carter 1990; Davies and Scott 1992; Swales and Rogers 1995; Stainton 1996; Nickerson 1998). There is thus now a growing body of research into the language of the work-place, and in particular of the written language which both shapes and reflects organisational goals and organisational culture.

Within the context of education, there is a long-established infra-structure for research which underpins the teaching of writing at all levels from primary to tertiary education and a representative col-lection of examples of effective and less effective writing which is directly accessible to teachers (Grabe and Kaplan 1996). But in sharp contrast to education, the research base for writing in the workplace is limited and access to examples of effective and less effective writ-ing typically severely restricted. That the research base for writing in the workplace is limited is suggested by the bibliography of re-search on language and communication in business (Kennedy *et al.* 1993).[1]

With respect to training for writing in the workplace, it appears that two fundamentally competing sources of training are widely available to British organisations: either in-house apprenticeship over a long period of time, and/or the quick/sharp short courses lasting from one to three days currently offered by external agencies, such as the ninety-five listed in the National Training Index (1996). In the EFL sector, evidence of global demand for training in Business English comes not only from the expansion of courses in this area, but also from publishing lists; of the twenty-four new course books in English for Specific Purposes in 1996, twenty-one were in the area of Business English (St John 1996). To date, however, there appear to be no formal mechanisms for assessing the relative effectiveness of these various forms of training. In sum, in contrast with education, training for writing in the workplace is characterised by diverse and divergent forms of provision and diverse and possibly competing mechanisms for the assessment of quality.

Against this background, and the sheer breadth and diversity of organisational settings, researchers have courageously responded to the challenge of investigating the language of the workplace, and are currently committed to the collection of data about what is written in the workplace, and why and how it is written. The primary goals are to delineate the relationship between text and context and to discover what contributes to effective writing. In pursuing these goals, current research utilises a wide range of methodologies and instruments and there is a wide range of interpretations of the concept of context.

2. LINGUISTIC APPROACHES

Following a long-established and respected tradition in linguistics and Halliday's emphasis on the relationship between context and text, for many linguists the text itself is the source of interpretation of context (Halliday 1994; Hasan 1989; Ghadessy 1993; Hyatt 1994). Within this tradition, the analysis of specific linguistic choices – e.g. the element selected as grammatical subject or as theme, or aspects of transitivity, is seen as the starting point for exploring aspects of context, and as having the potential for evaluating the relative effectiveness of writing. Thus Berry (1989), analysing student writing within the broad genre of tourist guides, shows how the relative distribution of 'interactive' and 'topical' themes can be used as an index of success in writing; Davies (1994a and b), analysing published texts within the same field, illustrates the potential of theme analysis for identifying the different roles which writers adopt as they seek to maintain a balance between 'organising' the text, 'interacting with readers' and 'presenting information'. In the context of organisational culture, Thompson and Ramos (1995) undertake an analysis of ergativity, or cause and effect relationships, to show how writers of 'public face' texts such as annual reports select from within the system of ergativity in order to present the company in a positive light: 'The image presented through ergativity choices, of positive control of the company in adverse conditions, in fact runs through the whole text, gaining strength and emerging more visibly as the text proceeds' (Thompson and Ramos 1995: 20). In a further study of the genre of advertising, Thompson and Thetala (1995) start with the analysis of transitivity roles and speech acts to reveal the way in which writers of such materials manipulate the role relationship between writer and readers.

Studies undertaken within the tradition of rhetoric are represented by Couture (1992), who presents an argument for the rhetorical categorisation of professional discourse, specifically the rhetoric of engineering, administration and technical writers. In an elicitation task, representatives of each of these groups of writers were asked to select from pairs of sentences in alternative wordings those which they were most likely to use. Couture's analysis shows how values promoted within each profession are reflected in the way in which authority is assigned or assumed and hence in distinct messages.

3. ETHNOGRAPHICALLY ORIENTATED STUDIES

In contrast to linguistic analysis and rhetoric, case studies with an ethnographic orientation do not rely on linguistic analysis and/or analysts' intuitions about context, but extend the notion of context through observation and/or participation in the organisational setting under study. In one way or another they combine linguistic analysis with visits to the source of the writing under study and typically make use of specialist informants. Thus in their now classic ethnographic study, Brown and Herndl (1986) interviewed manager/writers and manager/editors in order to explore organisational factors which might help to explain the difference between effective and less effective writers and they also obtained access to documents written by 'good' and 'less good' writers. While the linguistic analysis focused on two (discouraged) features of writing, nomin-alisation and narrative style, the interviews revealed two social parameters which were influential: writer status and writer anxiety.

Rogers and Swales (1990) undertook an initial analysis of the mission statement of a single company, Dana, and then sought the reactions of three or four members of Dana's Policy Committee who wrote it. The linguistic analysis focused principally on ele-ments chosen as grammatical subject as evidence of the presenta-tion of the company persona. The interviews with members of the Policy Committee filled out more pertinent aspects of organisational context. They revealed evidence of the wide-ranging power of the members as it was disseminated through the written word in a company fervently committed to oral, rather than written commun-ication and to the cultivation of a 'paper-free' organisation. In a further study, Swales and Rogers (1995) extend the concept of con-text to take account of the history of the organisation: 'We have gone beyond the surface of the text to explore the framing context. With this aim we have studied company history/ collected a wide range of documents, searched the business press, made site visits and talked to key players' (Swales and Rogers 1995: 236).

In a study which involved informants more directly, Stainton (1996) has sought to evaluate the effectiveness of the writing repres-enting the genre of technical writing. From the start she sought the views of participants in the workplace in identifying a genre which was regarded as important, and having collected a substantial corpus, then asked twenty informants to rate the texts. Linguistic analysis of two features hypothesised to be discriminators of effective writing – metalanguage and theme choice – followed.

4. SURVEYS

In contrast to studies based on linguistic analyses of texts, or case studies based within a single or related organisation(s), recent surveys have sought to gain a picture of the broader parameters of the con-text of organisational writing by surveying practices across relatively large numbers of organisations within a particular geographical con-text, typically using questionnaires and/or interviews. Thus Davies and Scott (1992) in the Liverpool/São Paulo DIRECT project used structured interviews to undertake a survey of the 'communications skills needs' of 155 public and private sector organisations in the Merseyside region.

As a follow-up to this study, Barbara *et al.* (1996), representing the São Paulo branch of the DIRECT project, used a questionnaire to survey the relation between type of organisation, language and document type required in 200 São Paulo-based organisations, many of which are internationally based. In a survey of the subsidiary companies of British organisations based in the Netherlands, Nickerson (1998) surveyed 305 corporations in an investigation of the corporate culture. She proposes a model of corporate culture which accommodates communication patterns, corporate activities, language used (i.e. English/ Dutch or other), and position of respondents within the organisation. Currently, the CPW project (Nunan and Forey 1996) is analysing data collected through a questionnaire based on the EWM project (see below) from more than 1000 accountants working in Hong Kong.

5. THE EFFECTIVE WRITING FOR MANAGEMENT PROJECT

It is against the background of such studies that the EWM (Effective Writing for Management project, Davies and Forey 1996) was set. Like many of the studies reported above, the project was restricted to the study of written genres; like others, it was located within organisational settings in which the majority of participants, though not all, are native speakers of English. The project sought to build upon and extend previous work by surveying a sample of the population representative of managers at the national level, and by focusing on aspects of context relating to the daily demands of writing in an organisational context in the high-risk situation of work. The project was based at Bristol University School of Education during the academic year 1994–95. Following extensive piloting of the research instruments, a questionnaire was distributed and completed by a 'convenience' sample of 202 managers following MBA courses on a part-time basis at British universities, and interviews with 28 of the questionnaire respondents were conducted.

The present chapter reports the principal findings of the questionnaire-based survey and discusses these through reference to selected interviews. Space does not permit a more detailed analysis of interviews or of the corpus of texts collected during interviews.

These are the topics of papers in preparation. The aspects of writing which the questionnaire sought to explore with managers related to the importance of writing within the context of management, the amount of time invested in writing, managers' experience of the process of writing, their perceptions of the demands of writing, their feelings about their own writing, the different types of documents written and the nature of support available for writing. The interviews sought to probe these issues in greater depth. Data on these aspects of writing, we believe, will help to flesh out earlier surveys by contributing to our understanding of the day-to-day context of writing in the workplace.

5.1.   Writing perceived as a central part of management

The findings provide clear evidence of the role which is served by writing and of the importance managers assign to writing; 82.4 per cent of respondents agreed with the statement 'writing is an essential part of the organisation' and 'it is an opportunity to impress'. The interview data add strong support to the findings of the questionnaire. Writing is regarded as 'oil for the project to keep it running successfully'. With respect to the paperless office, one manager summarised the general view that, 'despite the advent of computers etc. it is as important as it ever has been. In many ways it is more important I think.'

As Brown and Herndl have shown, the capacity to write effectively is closely connected with status and with high status: 'as I move up the management ladder it will become more and more important'. It is clearly important for middle managers to 'prove' themselves to those in higher positions: 'it will go to all board members; it has to be some communication to each one in writing'. However, writing is not only important for the presentation of self within the company, but is also critical in meeting the needs of clients:

> When I'm letting contracts; when I'm writing specifications . . . when I'm talking about terms and conditions of contracts, I have to be very precise. So it has to be a very good style that's understandable and very clear to the research contractor. Cost must also be calculated so it probably costs us for a large bid 3 quarters of a million pounds so if we don't get that job we have lost £750,000 . . . there is no return of money lost.

[Happily there are managers who find writing, if not a pleasure, then at least satisfying.]

... it can be quite interesting – I find it can be quite creative.

At the practical level, the simple potential of the written word to communicate with a large number of people is widely recognised: 'there is such a wide range of people we have to deal with to actually get the message across ... you can't physically go and talk to everyone ... [it's] probably the major form of communication in the organisation'.

The findings also confirm Swales and Rogers' (1995) observation that writing shapes, as well as generates, culture change and that a major change is the shift from a hierarchical management structure to a more democratic mode of working. Thus writing is 'crucial because I am involved in culture change programme'. Teamwork is critical:

> The whole style of the way we work has changed enormously because our business is more about being in teams and partnering and being more open and having trust. Now we have a range of people in our organisation that are well educated and that are strong minded and they need to be persuaded so when we write to them saying what we are doing, what their part will be in it, writing this clearly, forcefully and persuasively is critical.

The global shift from manufacturing industries to service industries is also evident: 'the only asset we have is people – we don't make anything – and therefore employing and training and hiring and firing is right at the heart of the company's income producing streams and cost base'. For many managers globalisation has been a fact of life for some time and brings with it special demands: 'we have got a lot of companies working around the world ... so we need a global culture; we need to work as a team to terms and conditions that are quite onerous'. Changes within management clearly also impact on writing practice within the organisation, for better or for worse: 'but whereas the last managing director wanted to know all the information about the key issues and the detail that backed it up, the new managing director doesn't ... all he wants to know is what the key issues are and not the supporting detail'.

5.1.1. Substantial amount of time spent on writing by managers

In view of these findings it is not surprising that the data on time spent on writing reveal that the managers in the sample appear to spend a great deal of time on writing during the working week. Over half the sample (51.5 per cent), spend 15 hours or more writing and 33.6 per cent spend a substantial part of the working week on writing – over 20 hours.

The data from the open-ended question exploring respondents' feelings about writing reveal serious concerns about finding time to write and research; 62.5 per cent are concerned about finding the time to write; 48.5 per cent are concerned about the amount of research required:

> When I am actually writing business proposals to set up new parts of our business, . . . if I want to go up on the new project in a new area I basically put a business plan together to build that case up and then I do need to bring figures in from the industry, looking things up in the library, get things from finance, get things from outside sources and to bring those in that is very much where I have to do the writing – so it is not just data that is brought in, it is data that I have to think about and regurgitate. And that I find difficult; that takes me a lot of time.

5.2.   Most frequently written document types: letters, memos and reports

In order to investigate the range of writing demands for managers, they were presented with a list of twenty-seven different types of document which had been identified by managers in a pilot study as examples of writing required in their own organisations, and asked to indicate those which they write in the course of their work. The data further confirm the picture of the demands of managerial writing and provide clear evidence that the range of different documents written by individuals is considerable: 86.0 per cent write eleven or more different types of documents and 49.5 per cent write more than sixteen different types of documents. The extent of the range is further underlined by the fact that 37.1 per cent write between sixteen and twenty and 11.4 per cent write from twenty-one to twenty-five different types of documents.

The most frequently written documents types are either 'interactive' documents such as *letters* (formal letters 96.5 per cent; informal, 90.9 per cent) and *memos* (95.5 per cent) or 'reporting' documents: *ad-hoc reports* (91.4 per cent), *presentations* (88.4 per cent) and *progress-related reports* (84.7 per cent). Included in the list of twenty-seven document types were two media of communication: *faxes* and *e-mail*. The very high frequency for the writing of *faxes* (95.5 per cent) and the fact that over half of the sample use *e-mail* (58.0 per cent) provided evidence for the increasing exploitation of technology and electronic means of communication. From the interviews it became clear that while faxes are pretty well accepted as a way of life, e-mail, with its widely acknowledged advantages, has brought a number of serious problems, which space does not allow us to discuss here (but see Mulholland, this volume).

In order to discover whether certain types of documents are perceived as being more demanding to write than others, we asked respondents to identify three of the twenty-seven different types of document they find most demanding. Despite the high frequency of writing for *reports*, reports are most frequently cited (37.6 per cent), followed by *business /strategy plans* (31.1 per cent) and *formal letters* (19.4 per cent). When asked in a further open-ended question to give reasons for writing being demanding, the most frequently cited reason was identifying audience: 'not identifiable audience (sometimes)', 'trying to find a balance to convey the good with the bad for all readers', 'unsure of readers' requirements', 'difficult to be brief and cover all relevant points and keep their interest'. This suggests that knowledge, or lack of knowledge, of audience is perceived to be critical but that it is not always readily accessible, a point to which we return below.

5.2.1.   Most frequently written documents are also among the most demanding to write

The findings relating to most frequently written documents are not surprising; they confirm our intuitions and also the findings of previous surveys (Davies and Scott 1992; Barbara *et al.* 1996; Nunan and Forey 1996). However, the finding that documents cited as most demanding are written by over 60 per cent of the sample and that reports are written by over 90 per cent raises fundamental questions about the nature of training and the nature of reports. They suggest either that current training programmes such as those offered in the National Training Index, which almost without exception focus on report writing, are less than effective and/or that such courses do not and cannot address the problems of the diverse range of different types of report required by different organisations and different audiences. Just as Stainton (1996) found that the label 'memo' is consistently used in an engineering firm to refer to technical reports of 15–40 pages, the term 'report' appears to be used to refer to different generic categories within and across organisations.

5.2.2. Wide range of reports: internal and external audiences

Our interviews revealed managers' awareness of a wide range of different types of report, and managers made clear distinctions between internal reports and external reports. For internal reports the audience is typically known, but so too, is the writer, for whom status depends on getting the report right. Reports 'will go to the most senior people in this building' and 'will be dealt with at very high levels. So if the report is going up there you have to be absolutely spot on in terms of dates and facts, both engineering as well as legal.'

With respect to external reports, the audience varies from those at the client end to those at the providing end. At the client end, reports may well be a response to a problem:

> Reports are written when either there are problems or the client specifically requests it. It's a reactive thing rather than proactive. . . .
> For example [there was] a budget estimate that was quite a long way out so we had to write a report to at least try to ascertain why that had happened and what action we can take to solve the problem.

In some cases the line between document types such as report and a presentation may be represented as a cline, rather than a discrete point:

> 'And in fact what we did with this report was to present a file to the client at a client meeting so it was the basis of a formal presentation'.

[However a spoken presentation can lead to further writing.]

> 'And you often get them saying I came to the presentation but I didn't quite get what you were saying and I find I follow up with report saying this is what I am really saying to clarify the situation.'

5.2.3. Managers' concern with conciseness and structure

In addition to audience as a factor in writing demand, many respondents identified the need to be concise as a major preoccupation. It seems that the managers in this sample want to produce a document which is 'to the point', including relevant detail, but is still 'concise'. The observation that it is 'difficult to be brief and cover all relevant points and keep their interest' demonstrates that there may be a tension between wanting to be sure that readers have all the relevant information and not burdening them with too much to absorb. This tension was perceived to be particularly acute with respect to the writing of *business plans* and *formal letters*. *Letters* were seen as demanding because 'they have to be structured well because a client or prospective client will be reading the letter'; the 'right tone' is important when writing letters.

5.3.   The process of writing

With respect to the actual process of writing, the findings reveal that collaborative writing is widely practised, with 82.2 per cent of the sample reporting being involved in collaborative writing and 52.0 per cent reporting that a colleague is involved in the editing of their documents (in 39.1 per cent of cases in addition to someone 'senior'). The data from the interviews allowed us to explore the nature of the collaborative process in greater depth.

5.3.1.   *A reactive model of preparation for writing*

There was little evidence of what we call 'proactive' preparation for collaborative writing, such as establishing parameters of audience in advance, examining previous documents or agreeing on structure or style. Overwhelmingly, the pattern which emerged was of 'reactive' collaboration and/or editing, involving either a key writer or editor, and a team of three to eight players, each taking responsibility for a particular contribution, followed by meetings and/or final editing. That this process can be somewhat *ad hoc* and that it is very costly in terms of time was evident from most interviews:

> There was an inter-directorate, inter-departmental group that were involved in this work and . . . various people wrote various parts of the document and then someone went through it to make sure that it flowed. . . . Everybody did a bit and then the whole thing was put together, and the person who chaired the group worked through the proof, tweaked it a little bit and out came the document.

> Well there's a draft base, you combine that with somebody else's writing, put it together, and then we reviewed the whole thing, and it went through that stage or that process probably seven or eight times, if not more, until we came to the final version.

In some cases the document is referred to a 'reviewer' within the organisation, but the review process is clearly also *ad hoc*:

> The other thing is getting someone who is not involved in the project to get the proof reading, I think that is quite important. Test it with other people, just try and say what do you think of this. I don't know, preparing and structuring and writing usually tend to merge into one actually and the reviewing sometimes is fairly *ad hoc*.

The problem of synthesising different styles is clearly a major one, especially in large teams:

> All of us round the board table would have an input to that . . . as you would imagine eight people writing a different piece it doesn't hang together well, it needs to be synthesised so collaboration there is very important so that the thing is seamless and shall we say the document then reads like a Beethoven symphony because what happens when eight individuals write their documents, they are all very well written but when you put them together they don't gel so it's like an orchestra playing out of tune.

Evidence of a reliance on individuals within the organisation perceived to be good communicators also emerged from interviews:

> Well because people think that I have got good communication skills and very good writing skills what I tend to get is the task of leading this collaborative approach.

> Yes we know within the office who has the best written work so if I want to write and it is going to go to an internal office I actually give it to one of my supervisors because her written work is ten times better than mine.

That this role inevitably involves editing and makes an important contribution to in-house training, or apprenticeship, is also evident:

> It may often lead to me rewriting other people's material but in the way that we work now my task would be more of in fact taking other people through their own material and other people's material and showing them how as they have written it doesn't enhance the whole and suggesting to them how they would rewrite it to fit it together.

For the key writer or editor, there is the further problem of allowing the individual voice to speak or imposing a more coherent form on the document: 'So the dilemma is do you change it so it is a more formal . . . more standardised method report or do you leave it as it is. . . . That is the biggest problem you know that I have, I don't know what is right.'

5.3.2. *The potential of talk and of templates*

The potential of 'talking through' the writing of a particular document and of a corpus of examples of effective writing as a source of
'templates' is suggested by one manager:

> I need to have either a template to work from or somebody to talk to.
> So I spend my life collecting best practice examples so that I can
> compare with the specifications, for example, other contracts or other
> minutes. So I do it that way. I evaluate the work myself. I very often
> ask other people to comment. I'm not afraid, I think, of asking my
> immediate manager to say what she thinks of this particular effort.
> I also ask colleagues at my level to comment on my written work
> at times. Obviously that all depends on how confident I feel of their
> response.

The interviews also revealed an urgent need for feedback, but for
feedback which is constructive and understandable:

> The most frustrating thing I used to find with my boss and I told him
> to stop was that he would just change things. And then I had to sit
> down and try to work out just exactly why he had changed it. And
> often you are talking about subtle changes, use of a different word or
> an extra word in a sentence or taking a sentence out. And if it is a
> long document, trying to find those changes can be a time-consuming
> process.

Overall the interviews provided clear evidence that writing both reflects and shapes organisational policy and daily practice. Documents
do not exist in isolation but are generated by activity sequences and
in turn generate further activity sequences: memos, meetings, proposals, minutes of meetings, site visits, external meetings, project
reports, technical reports, situation reports and visit reports.

5.4. The manager as a writer

In order to find out more about how managers feel about writing
and what they regard as their strengths and weaknesses, we first
asked them to indicate their agreement with certain positive and
negative statements which were spontaneous statements generated
by respondents in the pilot study. In general, the findings suggest
that most managers are positive about writing. Of the respondents
94 per cent were 'confident about the purpose' and had a clear idea
of the 'audience'. Over 80 per cent of the sample population believed

that writing was an 'essential part of their organisation', and over 88.9 per cent did not believe writing was a distraction nor that the size of the task was cause for panicking. Over 76 per cent of the respondents in the sample believed that writing a document was exciting and allowed them the 'opportunity to impress and/or shape policy'.

However, responses to negative statements and to the question asking respondents about their strengths in writing reveal quite marked inconsistencies. In response to the open-ended question asking them to evaluate their strengths and weaknesses in writing, only 12.9 per cent cited audience. In response to our question about the focus of initial draft only 17.1 per cent cited audience, against 57.0 per cent citing content. We did not have the opportunity to ask whether or not the 17.1 per cent are the 'good writers', but we may speculate that this may be the case. Overall, the questions relating to both feelings about writing and actual practice indicate that both positive and negative feelings about writing can co-exist and that there are discrepancies between respondents' beliefs and what they actually do. There is also the problem of interpreting data from simple questions; with respect to audience, respondents were asked to agree or disagree with the statement: 'have a definite idea about audience'. Clearly, 'having a definite idea', like knowing the person or company, which may be taken for granted, is very different from predicting precisely how that audience will respond to aspects of either content or language.

The interview data certainly suggested that the managers in our sample spend a great deal of time actually agonising over audience, and are sharply aware of the importance of audience. For one manager parameters of audience are clear:

> I try to tailor the letters to the circumstances of the individual, their seniority, what they are doing, what are the special circumstances, obviously you would be dealing with things like location, salary, pensions and so on, so there would be some generic features in there but all the letters that I write, I am writing to very senior people, as opposed to my colleagues who are hiring engineers and do them somewhat on the assembly line, so they have written proformas in their offers. Every letter that I write is a bespoke letter but it covers some of the same ground.

That the question of audience on occasions involves ethical decisions and decisions about the level of risk a manager is willing to settle for was also evident:

You have to be careful what you put – sometimes it pays to put your head above the parapet and be counted. Sometimes it doesn't .You see you have to pick your audience, pick your time depending on the report – your writing – cater it so that it actually gives the right message at the same time maintaining a balance between what is morally right and what the company would like to hear.

5.4.1. Evidence of lack of confidence in choosing appropriate language

In addition to uncertainty about audience, the findings suggest that a substantial proportion of the managers in this sample are less than confident about their competence in making appropriate language choices: only 22.3 per cent of the sample cited language as a strength, and language was the most frequently cited area of weakness, with 29.7 per cent citations; 22.3 per cent cited conciseness as a weakness.

The findings from the questions relating to strengths and weaknesses in writing gain further salience when related to the findings from the question asking respondents which aspects of writing they wished to improve. For this question, respondents were presented with a closed set of five aspects of writing, three of which referred to features of product – 'grammar', 'linking sections' and the 'structure' of the document – and two to aspects of process – 'ways of redrafting' and 'collaboration'. With respect to the features of product, the figures for grammar, with 44 per cent, the highest frequency, wishing to improve, and for structure, 31.8 per cent wishing to improve, are not inconsistent with those derived from the strengths and weaknesses question.

The interview data confirmed this concern with grammar and structure; but the question of just how competence is achieved is an open question. Obviously, a long-term apprenticeship helps but whether it is the most efficient route is another question.

> But just in terms of the basics – it has been 16 years since I had any kind of English lesson. If you said to me tell me about sentence construction I couldn't do it. I know it has got a verb in there somewhere and that kind of things, but I couldn't sit and tell you theoretically how it should look. You just look at something and think that sounds right.

The issue of differences between more or less spoken and more or less written modes which has long been of interest to linguists is something that some managers are also aware of: 'One of them [the writers] has the most amazing style of talking and as he talks he writes, so the way if you read his report you could imagine him speaking but it is all right when you are talking but it is not so good when it is on the written paper.'

5.4.2. The physical process of writing

Despite the evidence above of the demands of writing, there is no doubt that modern technology has brought positive benefits for the process of writing. The findings from the question about the physical process of writing reveal that 77.7 per cent of the managers in the sample write directly onto a PC, and that this is welcomed:

> I personally think word processors are fantastic, I much prefer it to write straight onto the screen, seeing the thing as it will be finished. I think that is a great way of overcoming and tackling some of the problems that we have mentioned about presentation and so on. You are able to highlight things and see how it would be, come out on the finished coat and I think it is a great leap forward. I always remember years ago although I have never been trained to type I developed the skill and I am quite comfortable with a typewriter.

However, the need to become competent at using non-textual facilities of PCs and to integrate these effectively with one's own and others' texts is also important: 'Effective writing relies more and more on the inclusion of graphs, tables, figures and diagrams to communicate a message.'

The changing face of managerial writing is further reflected in the figures for dictation: 11.9 per cent dictate to a recording device for typing by a secretary and only 6.4 per cent dictate to a secretary. The implication of these findings for the current role of secretaries is not one we were able to pursue in this chapter, but it clearly impacts on modern organisations.

6.   CONCLUSION

In this chapter we have sought to provide an in-depth picture of the day-to-day context of organisational writing. The findings suggest that this context is complex and dynamic. They also indicate that, within and across organisations, writing does not occur in a vacuum nor as a set of discrete products. Rather it is produced in response to, and shapes, organisational goals, which in turn lead to sequences of organisational activities which may be unique. The findings also provide evidence that managers are sensitive to the criteria for effective writing, but lack on the one hand operational definitions of such concepts as conciseness and structure, and on the other, organisational support for writing. What is clear is that short external courses cannot be a substitute for in-house support. The evidence indicates that such support could be provided through the establishment of an infrastructure for writing and through the adoption of a more pro-active approach towards writing. That organisations would benefit from having access to a corpus of examples of effective writing is a possibility worth investigating. That they would benefit from linguistic analysis of the features of language associated with effective writing is also clear. Thus the need for continuing research employing different research perspectives, linguistic, ethnographic, and survey research, is established.

NOTE

1. In a search of 60 journals, 27 of which are language orientated and 33 business orientated, only 234 papers are listed. Of these papers 113, almost exclusively from business-orientated journals, were non-investigative, geared towards solving problems through 'tips' and the traditional template model of training for writing. And while there is a growing body of research aimed at exploring the relationship between the context of the workplace and writing, through the analysis of small, closed collections or corpora of texts, there is as yet no accessible collection of representative examples of effective writing in the workplace. Apart from secondary documents, such as reports drawn from newspapers and journals, the language of the workplace is not represented in either the COBUILD corpus of 320 million words, nor the British National Corpus of 100 million words.

REFERENCES

Barbara, Leila, Celani, Antonieta A., Collins, Heloisa and Scott, Mike (1996) A survey of communication patterns in the Brazilian business context. *English for Specific Purposes* 15 (1): 57–71.

Berry, Margaret (1989) Thematic options and success in writing. In C. S. Butler, R. A. Cartwell and J. Channel (eds), *Language and Literature: Theory and Practice – A Tribute to Walter Grauberg*. Nottingham: University of Nottingham, pp. 62–80.

Bhatia, Vijay K. (1993) *Analysing Genre: Language Use in Professional Settings.* London: Longman.

Brown, Robert J. and Herndl, Carl G. (1986) An ethnographic study of corporate writing: job status as reflected in written text. In Barbara Couture (ed.), *Functional Approaches to Writing: Research Perspectives*. London: Frances Pinter, pp. 11–28.

Carter, Ronald A. (1990) When is a report not a report? Observations from academic and non-academic settings. In W. Nash (ed.), *The Writing Scholar: Studies in Academic Writing*. London: Sage Publications, pp. 171–91.

Couture, Barbara (1992) Categorizing professional discourse: engineering, administrative and technical/professional writing. *Journal of Business and Technical Communication* 6 (7): 5–37.

Davies, Florence (1994a) *Introducing Applied Linguistics: Introducing Reading.* Harmondsworth: Penguin English.

Davies, Florence (1994b) From writer roles to elements of text. In L. Barbara and M. Scott (eds), *Reflections on Language Learning*. Clevedon: Multilingual Matters, pp. 170–83.

Davies, Florence and Forey, Gail (1996) *The Effective Writing for Management Project: Report to the Advisory Board*. Bristol: Bristol University School of Education.

Davies, Florence and Scott, Mike (1992) An aspect of training: report of the Survey of Communication Skills Needs in Local Organisations. Liverpool: English Language Unit, Liverpool University.

Ghadessy, Mohsen (ed.) (1993) *Register Analysis: Theory and Practice.* London: Printer Publishers.

Grabe, Walter and Kaplan, Robert B. (1996) *Theory and Practice of Writing.* London: Longman.

Halliday, Michael A. K. (1994) *An Introduction to Functional Grammar.* London: Edward Arnold.

Halliday, Michael A. K. and Hasan, Ruqaiya (1985/89) *Language, Context and Text: Aspects of Language in a Social-semiotic Perspective*. Oxford: Oxford University Press.

Hasan, Ruqaiya (1989) The Structure of a Text. In M. A. K. Halliday and R. Hasan (eds.), *Language, Context and Text: Aspects of Language in a Social-semiotic Perspective*. Oxford: Oxford University Press.

Hyatt, David (1994) The discourse of advertising. *Forum for Education* 11: 19–29, Bristol: University School of Education.

Kennedy, Christopher, Dudas, Juliana and Hewings, Martin (1993) *Research on Language and Communication in Business: Bibliography*. Birmingham:

Birmingham Centre for English Language Studies, University of Birmingham.

National Training Index (1996) 4 Burlington Place, London W1X 2HX.

Nickerson, Catherine (1998) Corporate culture and the use of written English within British subsidiaries in the Netherlands. *English for Specific Purposes*, pp. 52–69.

Nunan, David and Forey, Gail (1996) CPW Communication in the Professional Workplace project. Phase 1: Research report. Hong Kong: University of Hong Kong.

Rogers, Priscilla and Swales, John (1990) We the people? An analysis of the Dana Corporation Policies document. *The Journal of Business Communication* 23 (3): 293–313.

St John, Maggie Jo (1996) Business is booming: Business English in the 1990s. *English for Specific Purposes* 15 (1): 3–18.

Stainton, Caroline (1996) The Technical Review as a Genre. Nottingham Working Papers, no. 3. Nottingham: Department of English Studies, Nottingham University.

Stubbs, Michael (1993) British traditions in text analysis – from Firth to Sinclair. In Mona Baker, Francis Gill and Elena Tognini-Bonelli (eds), *Text and Technology, in Honour of John Sinclair*. Amsterdam: John Benjamins, pp. 1–33.

Swales, John (1981) Aspects of article introductions. Aston Research Report, No. 1, Birmingham: University of Aston.

Swales, John (1990) *Genre Analysis: English in Academic and Research Settings*. Cambridge: Cambridge University Press.

Swales, John and Rogers, Priscilla (1995) Discourse and the projection of culture: the mission statement. *Discourse and Society* 6 (2): 223–42.

Thompson, Geoff and Ramos, Rosinda (1995) Ergativity in the analysis of business texts, DIRECT Working Paper no. 21, Liverpool: CEPRIL / Applied English Language Studies, Liverpool University.

Thompson, Geoff and Thetala, Puleng (1995) The sound of one hand clapping: the management of interaction in written discourse. *Text* 15 (1): 103–27.

EPILOGUE

AT THE INTERSECTION BETWEEN WRITING AND SPEAKING

FOURTEEN

Intertextual networks in organisations: the use of written and oral business discourse in relation to context

Eugène Loos

1. INTRODUCTION

How do actors in an organisation succeed in sharing meaning? In many communication handbooks authors present an overview of all the ways in which an organisation's employees can communicate with each other and their clients. Keuning (1991: 213–21), for example, considers that actors can communicate internally and externally, and use written and oral media. He also explains the difference between horizontal, vertical and lateral communication. It is curious to see, however, that much of this work remains anecdotal and little empirical evidence has been collected on how actors really communicate. Of course, it is difficult for researchers to get permission from companies to investigate actual communication inside their organisation, and as Firth (1991) suggests, the main reasons for companies for refusing to collaborate are lack of time, no interest in the research and fear of intrusion into internal practices. To gain an insight into the complex and dynamic process of business communication as a whole, it is, however, of vital importance to refer to a corpus of actual business discourse, and it is also necessary that the corpus consists of both written and oral communication. This is because actors communicating with each other construct an intertextual network which is based on a sequence of actions and which consists of both written and oral texts. They do this by using the two intertextual dimensions, 'tyings' (Firth 1991, 1995) and 'cues' (Gumperz 1978, 1982) that are explored in this article. 'Tyings' are utterances actors use to link their current text to prior and future written and oral texts in order to create what may be referred to as 'sequential context' (Loos 1997: 48–52). 'Cues' are signals – for example, intonation in oral texts and underlining in written texts – that enable actors to create what may be referred to as 'cultural context' (Loos 1997: 53–7) in order to inform each other of what is going on. Considering their discourse from an intertextual angle allows the reconstruction of the ways in which actors in organisations use written and oral texts to share meaning.

Section 2 shows how 'tyings' and 'cues' enable actors to construct an intertextual network. Two case studies (Firth 1991, 1995; Loos 1997), in which written documents and audio-recorded data from international companies are analysed, will be used in section 3 to illustrate the 'management of meaning'[1] by actors communicating in an organisation. In section 4 some conclusions are drawn and the implications for future research are outlined.

2.   CONSTRUCTING AN INTERTEXTUAL NETWORK

2.1.   Actor perspective

To analyse the use of written and oral business discourse in relation to context, it is necessary to adopt an actor perspective. This is because it is human (inter)action that is the object of study in the investigation of business communication. Boden (1994: 56) stresses that:

> Organizations do not *act* or *do* anything, people do. If we accept, at least as a working assumption, that organizations *are* the people who comprise them, then what we need is a far finer grasp of human action. Human activity is exclusively, and one may say irreducibly available through human action.

Actors construct meaning by producing and interpreting texts. A micro-level analysis of text can therefore lead to a reconstruction of the ways in which actors use language to share meaning. Conversation Analysis (CA) can be usefully applied to accomplish this task. As Boden (1994: 203) suggests: 'Conversation analysis provides an unambiguous method for careful observation . . . since the intersubjective accomplishment of meaning in interaction is readily available at the level of talk.' CA originally focused on the turn-taking system in conversations representing a finely geared 'machinery' (Psathas 1995: 2), and institutional settings were therefore not included. Recently, however, more researchers taking a CA approach have been interested in talk-based work activities (Firth 1991, 1995; Boden 1994; Koole and Ten Thije 1994; Loos 1996, 1997, 1998). In section 3.1 a CA perspective is adopted in the reconstruction of intertextual networks in organisations.

2.2.   'Tying' and 'cues' as intertextual dimensions

2.2.1.   Producing and interpreting written and oral business texts

If one wants to understand business discourse, it is necessary to focus on the patterns of actions that are constructed and followed by actors who interact by producing and interpreting written and oral texts in a specific situation. This view is supported by Fairclough (1992: 3) who suggests that 'This sense of "discourse" emphasizes interaction between speaker and addressee or between writer and reader, and therefore processes of producing and interpreting speech and writing, as well as the situational context of language use.' By adopting an intertextual perspective, as Fairclough suggests, it is possible to reconstruct how actors realise chains of speech communication by referring to both prior (already produced) and future (going to be produced) written and oral texts. Fairclough (1992: 101–2) draws on Bakhtin (1986) in order to make clear how actors constitute a text by using elements of other texts:

> Bakhtin points to the relative neglect of the communicative functions of language within mainstream linguistics, and more specifically to the neglect of ways in which texts and utterances are shaped by prior texts that they are 'responding' to, and by subsequent texts that they 'anticipate'. For Bakhtin, all utterances, both spoken and written, from the briefest of turns in a conversation to a scientific paper or a novel, are demarcated by a change of speaker (or writer), and are oriented retrospectively to the utterances of previous speakers (be they turns, scientific articles, or novels) and prospectively to the anticipated utterances of the next speakers. Thus 'each utterance is a link in the chain of speech communication' (Bakhtin 1986: 89). That is, utterances – 'texts' in my terms – are inherently intertextual, constituted by elements of other texts.

Giddens (1979: 43) stresses that texts are constructed by 'acting subjects', and he considers organisations as social systems that enable them to 'bracket time and space' (Giddens 1987: 153; see also Boden 1994: 17). The systematic structuring of temporal and spatial dimensions can be seen as anchored in and articulated through oral texts, constructed in meetings and telephone calls, and in and through written texts, such as letters and faxes. Section 2.2.2 explains how actors in organisations succeed in bracketing time and space by using 'tyings'. Section 2.2.3 argues that 'tyings' alone are not sufficient to share meaning, and that actors also need 'cues'.

2.2.2. Use of 'tyings' to create sequential context

In section 3.1 Firth's corpus is used to demonstrate that actors create sequential context by actions which explicitly 'tie' the printed mode (e.g. letters and faxes) to the current spoken mode (e.g. face-to-face and telephone conversations) and vice versa. For this reason Firth (1991: 95) calls these actions 'tyings'. 'Tyings' like 'Thank you for the fax you sent me' and 'Can you send us a fax to confirm this?', refer to prior and future written texts, and 'We refer to your phone call of last Friday', and 'Please call tomorrow at 10 a.m.' refer to prior and future oral texts. These 'tyings' are examples of ways in which actors link their discourse to texts *outside* the current text in order to create sequential context (Loos 1997: 48–52).

Actors also create sequential context *inside* the text that they are producing by turn-taking. As Boden and Zimmerman (1991: 10) argue:

> It bears repeating that what is at issue for the achievement of mutual understanding and coordinated action is not resolved by reference to shared symbol systems which encode and decode the meaning and import of the talk. Instead, the resources for mutual understanding are found in the fundamental nature of sequencing – that the elements of interaction are not merely serially realized as 'once and for all' but are rather actions that are *shaped* and *reshaped* over the course of the talk. The initiation of an action and the response to it create the immediate sequential context of these events, and occasions as well exhibit the participants' analysis and understanding of the unfolding course of the interaction. Mutual understanding is thus a methodical *achievement* employing the resources provided by the mechanisms of conversational interaction. See Garfinkel (1967: 38–42) and Heritage (1984: 259).

This sequencing of action means that the utterance of one actor is followed by that of another actor. The first utterance establishes the context for the second and the second confirms the meaning of the first (Goffman 1971: 149; Saville-Troike 1989: 153). 'Tyings' enable actors to create sequential context. While 'tyings' represent an important intertextual dimension that enables actors to share meaning, 'cues' provide another.

2.2.3. Use of 'cues' to create cultural context

According to Gumperz (1982: 131), 'cues' are all those features of linguistic form that contribute to the signalling of contextual presuppositions. He stresses that actors who want to share meaning need 'cues'[2] as signals to explain to each other what is going on:

> Channelling of interpretation is effected by conversational implicatures based on conventionalized co-occurrence expectations between content and surface style. That is, constellations of surface features of message form are the means by which speakers signal and listeners interpret what the activity is, how semantic content is to be understood and *how* each sentence relates to what precedes or follows.
>
> (Gumperz 1982: 131)

Gumperz (1978: 29) also adds that 'These contextualization phenomena tend to go unnoticed in everyday situations although their effect is constantly felt. They are learned in the course of previous interactive experience.'

Gumperz (1978: 23–4) lists the following as examples of 'cues' in oral texts: paralinguistic and prosodic cues, e.g. rhythm, pitch register, loudness and tone grouping, tonic or nuclear placement and tune, and deictic pronouns, which are those pronouns only interpretable by reference to preceding utterances and interjections, such as 'yes' and 'no', all of which are used by listeners to signal their reactions to what has been said.

Loos (1997: 56) suggests that in written texts 'cues' can also be identified in the use of italics, underlining, lower-case letters and capital letters, which allow writers to stress certain words or parts of a text. By using 'cues' actors refer to knowledge within a cultural model and create cultural context (Loos 1997: 53–7). This knowledge is continuously transmitted, for example, through dialogues with parents, brothers and sisters, friends, teachers, students and colleagues that take place at home, school and work. In other words, people acquire knowledge by experience, which is then passed on in the course of dialogues and stored as 'co-texts' in a cultural model (Loos 1997: 17, 53). Actors need such cultural models to know how to behave and communicate. Minsky (1975: 212) refers to these cultural models as 'frames', and explains them as follows:

A *frame* is a 'data-structure' for representing a stereotyped situation, like being in a certain kind of living room, or going to a child's birthday party. Attached to each frame are several kinds of information. Some of this information is about how to use the frame. Some is about what one can expect to happen next. Some is about what to do if these expectations are not confirmed.

The term 'frame' was first introduced by Bateson (1955). It is also used by Hymes (1974), Goffman (1974) and Frake (1977). Bartlett (1932), Chafe (1977a, 1977b), Rumelhart (1975) and Bobrow and Norman (1975) use 'schema', and Schank and Abelson (1977) use 'script'. Despite the use of different terms Tannen (1979: 138–9) explains that:

> All these complex terms and approaches amount to the simple concept of what R. N. Ross (1975) calls 'structures of expectations', that is, that, based on one's experience of the world in a given culture (or combination of cultures), one organizes knowledge about the world and uses this knowledge to predict interpretations and relationships regarding new information, events and experiences.

'Cues' allow actors to signal contextual presuppositions to each other by referring to knowledge in their common cultural model, enabling them to share meaning. It is important to stress that the knowledge in the cultural model to which actors refer does not prescribe the way they have to act; it delimits a range of options rather than specifying a single rigid pattern (Fairclough 1992: 127). Using 'cues' to refer to this kind of knowledge allows actors to foreground certain aspects of background knowledge and underplay others, in order to construct meaning (Gumperz 1982: 131). Giddens (1984: 86) observes that this construction of meaning by actors happens in situated interaction. He proposes the concept of 'duality of structure' (1979: 53), which means that action and structure presuppose one another i.e. structure is both constraining and enabling.

3. DATA PRESENTATION AND DISCUSSION[3]

3.1. Discourse at work during international negotiations by telex, fax and phone

The examples analysed in this section are taken from Firth's corpus, which consists of written and oral texts that were produced and interpreted by business partners in Denmark and Saudi Arabia (Firth 1991, 1995). While Firth sets out to demonstrate how these actors use 'tyings' to refer to written documents like faxes and telexes as mutual reference points during their negotiations by telephone, therefore constituting a 'purchasing sequence of actions', his corpus will be used in this section to show how actors construct an intertextual network by using 'tyings' and 'cues' to create sequential and cultural context respectively, enabling them to share meaning. The analysis concentrates on a telex from Guptah (an importer working for the Saudi Royal Import Export Company in Saudi Arabia) to Hansen (an exporter from Melko Dairies in Denmark) and their subsequent conversation one day later by telephone (Firth 1995).

Guptah sends his business partner Hansen a telex to let him know that he cannot agree with the selling prices Hansen has offered him in a previous message.

[1]   6749 ROYAL SAUDI, JEDDAH
      DATED 20.3.90
      MSG. NO. 976/90
      ATT: MR. MICHAEL HANSEN

      WE REFER TO YOUR TLX NO. PA077 DTD 16.3.90 AND
      VERY SORRY TO
      INFORM YOU THAT CHEDDAR WHITE/YELLOW PRICES
      QUOTED BY YOU ARE
      HIGHER THAN SELLING PRICES OF OTHER LOCAL
      IMPORTERS. WE THEREFORE
      REQUEST YOU TO PLS RECHECK ALL YOUR PRICES
      AND INFORM US BY RTN TLX
      SO THAT WE CAN CONFIRM OUR ORDER.

      BEST REGARDS
      7658 GUPTAH

By using a 'tying' ('WE REFER TO YOUR TLX NO. PA077 DTD 16.3.90'), Guptah links a telex to a preceding one in which Hansen offered him certain prices for the cheese he wants to buy. He explains to Hansen that he cannot accept his offer because his prices are higher than the prices offered by other local importers and he therefore asks him to recheck all his prices. Loos (1997: 37) suggests that while Firth convincingly demonstrates how these actors use 'tyings' to refer to written texts like fax and telex as mutual reference points, he makes little reference to the use of 'cues'. The sentence 'INFORM US BY RTN TLX', for example, is not only a 'tying' through which Guptah refers to a future text and creates sequential context, it is also a 'cue' that creates cultural context. This 'cue' refers to knowledge of the organisation as part of a cultural model that they share, and makes clear to Hansen that Guptah still wants to continue the negotiation. Firth explains that the business partners use 'a set of inferential expectancy principles' (1991: 75) in order to understand each other:

> The sender's selection of the telex to convey this message – coupled with his stipulation that the response should be made via 'return telex' – is an indication that price revision is regarded as a relatively straightforward undertaking. Moreover, it is being seen as an *intra*-organizational undertaking, where the buyer's participation in the price-revision process is unnecessary. In implying that the resolution of the issue is an intra-organizational matter it may be argued that Guptah is attempting to minimalize his non-alignment with the preceding offer; this he does by communicating his rejection of the offer via telex.
>
> (Firth 1991: 93)

It is interesting to see how Hansen reacts to this telex. Although Guptah asks him to answer by telex, he uses the telephone. Firth (1991: 93) suggests that the selection of the telephone mode over the printed mode occurs when one of the actors believes that a 'conflict threshold' has been reached in the relationship and that direct *inter*-organisational activity is therefore necessary to avoid a breakdown in their negotiation. In other words, social and strategic utility of communicative mode selection helps the actors to share meaning.

The transcript of the telephone call, reproduced below, contains several examples of the use of 'tyings' and 'cues' in an oral text.

[2] 1 A ello?
    2 H yes hello er saudi royal import export
    3   company:?
    4 A ye:s
    5 H it's er michael hansen er melko dairies
    6   speaking. (0.8 sec.) could I speak to mister guptah
    7   please?
    8 A moment
    9   (17.0 sec.)
  10 B allo:?
  11 H yes hello er michael hansen melko dairies

```
12      speaking
13  B   one minute
14      (4.0 sec.)
15  G   hello?
16  H   hello mister guptah (.) how are you?
17  G   fine. (.) how're you?
18  H   fine than' you (0.6 sec.) know now the summer
19      time has come to denmark as well
20  G   ((laughing)) huh hh:eh heh ::hh
21  H   so for: the:- us here in denmark it's hot
22      (.) it's twenty five degree, but for you it
23      will be- it would be cold (.) I think
24  G   no, here in this er: forty- forty two
25  H   yes?
26      (1.0 sec.)
27  G   yes
28  H   well I prefer twenty five. (.) it's better to
29      me
30      (0.9 sec.)
31  G   yeah
32      (1.1 sec.)
33  H   GOOD er- I got a telex for er- from you
34      (1.3 sec.)
35  G   yeah
36  H   you don' er: (.) accept our prices.
37      (1.2 sec.)
38  G   for this cheddar
[continues]
```

Firth (1991: 97) shows how Hansen (H) in Denmark succeeds in making contact with Guptah (G) in Saudi Arabia. Hansen undertakes a series of what Firth calls 'pre-tyings'. In lines 2–3 he seeks confirmation that he has reached the Saudi Royal Import Export Company. In lines 5–6 he identifies himself to employee (A) and in lines 6–7 there is a switchboard request. In lines 11–12 Hansen again identifies himself, this time to employee (B). In lines 16 and 18–19 there is some social talk. Firth (1991: 94) refers to Durkheim (1926) to explain that small-talk can be considered as 'positive rituals', and he explains that these rituals are:

> the interpersonal gratification rites which affirm and support the social relationship between interactants. Such 'rites' or 'rituals' – which are

largely omitted from the telex and telefax communications in the corpus – are most clearly identifiable as 'small-talk' in telephone communications, and prototypically include exchanges on the topics of vacations, the weather, health and family.

The 'pre-tyings' in lines 2–3, 5–6, 6–7, 11–12, 16 and 18–19 finally allow Hansen to undertake the 'tying' in line 33. Loos (1997: 38) suggests that the sentence 'GOOD er- I got a telex for er- from you' not only allows him to link his current text to the preceding telex Guptah had sent him, it is also a 'cue' for his business partner. Hansen makes clear that he wants to get down to business. The metalinguistic marker GOOD that is preceded by a pause (1.1 sec.) and is enunciated stressed with falling intonation (Firth 1991: 97–8) is also a 'cue'; it is a signal for the hearer that important information will follow.

3.2. Dutch–German communication at Parador

Loos (1997) reports on the reconstruction of an intertextual network of the communication between Dutch and German employees and guests at Parador, a Dutch holiday centre. The study is based on a period of several days spent at the company's headquarters in Amsterdam and a week spent at one of the holiday centres in Germany in December 1994. Fifty conversations were recorded at the Reservation Department in Amsterdam where Dutch employees interact by telephone with German guests to make reservations at a holiday centre, and at the reception of a holiday centre in Germany where Dutch and German employees interact with German and Dutch guests.

Loos's research focuses on the management of meaning by the Dutch and German employees and guests at Parador. Transcripts of actual oral communication are referred to in conjunction with relevant written documents, to reconstruct the intertextual network that employees and guests construct together, by using 'tyings' and 'cues', in order to share meaning. The findings show that Dutch and German actors construct and follow sequences of actions which are part of a chain of actions related to the event 'staying in a holiday centre'. A guest telephones Parador's Reservation Department in Amsterdam (oral text), the telephonist inputs data into the computer to make a reservation (written text), an invoice (written text) is sent to the guest who, after having paid, receives a receipt (written text), which they then show at the reception desk in the holiday park (where the interaction is oral) in order to check in. Complaining, asking for information and finally checking out are other activities which are carried out by producing oral texts.

The example given below is the transcript of a phone conversation between a Dutch female telephonist (DTf) at the Reservation Department in Amsterdam and a German male guest (GGm) in Germany who wants to change his reservation. They start their conversation as follows.

[3]

1DTf   Guten Morgen Par- guten Morgen Parador Reserverungen. Sie spechen mit
1GGm

2DTf   Maria de Wit.   Guten Morgen.
2GGm   Ja Karl Schneider, guten Morgen. Ich hab' ne

3DTf   Ja
3GGm   Frage und zwar ich habe eh Harz   am dritten

4DTf   Hmhm
4GGm   dritten gebucht. Wollen Sie meine Reservierungsnummer

5DTf   Ja gerne. Ja.   Ein-   ein
5GGm   haben?   Neun eins   drei acht

6DTf   Moment bitte   Neun eins .   drei acht ja
6GGm   also   Ja . drei acht   drei zwei

7DTf   Ja   acht drei . ja und Sie haben eine Frage darüber?
7GGm   acht drei.

The Dutch telephonist and the German guest identify themselves and greet each other in lines 1–2 in German.[4] Then the German tells her in lines 2–4 that he wants to ask her something about a reservation in the Harz that he has made for the 3rd: 'Ich hab' ne Frage und zwar ich habe eh Harz am dritten dritten gebucht.' This utterance is a 'tying', which enables him implicitly to link one *oral* text (a prior telephone call), which he had made to make a reservation for a residential bungalow in the holiday centre in the Harz, to another *oral* text (their current conversation). In lines 4–5 the guest asks if the telephonist needs his reservation number: 'Wollen Sie meine Reservierungsnummer haben?' The utterance illustrates the way in which actors are able to create sequential and cultural context by using 'tyings' and 'cues' as intertextual dimensions. By asking her this question this utterance is another 'tying' which links the preceding *written* text (the booking that has already been made) to the *oral* text (their conversation) that they are producing together. Once this prior text as part of the chain of actions related to the event 'staying in a holiday centre' is activated by the 'tying', it is also a 'cue' for the telephonist that the guest wishes to cancel or change his reservation. This demonstrates that 'cues' are not only constituted by signals like intonation, but are also provided by utterances that refer to common knowledge related to the organisation, stored as 'co-texts' in a common cultural model. In line 5 the Dutch telephonist tells the guest that she in fact needs his reservation number ('Ja gerne. Ja.'), which he then provides in lines 5–7. This allows her to find the data related to his reservation on the computer. She then asks him in line 7 what he wants to know and he tells her that he would like to change his booking and arrive one week later.

[4]   8DTf
      8GGm   Ja, ich wollte fragen, ob ich 'ne Woche später
                kommen könnte.

      9DTf   Eh eine Woche später? Oder, oder was?
      9GGm   Geht das?   Ja.

      10DTf   Ich
      10GGm   Eine Woche. Also am zehnten wär's ja dann, ne?

      11DTf   werd's mal sehen.   Ein
      11GGm   Vom zehnten bis zum siebzehnten.

      12DTf   Moment hoor . ein Harz für zwei Personen.
      12GGm   Hm hm.

      13DTf   Hmhm . . ehm . . das ist kein . Problem . .
      13GGm

In line 9 the Dutch telephonist checks if she has understood him by asking if he wants to arrive one week later: 'Eh eine Woche später? Oder, oder was?' The German guest answers in line 9 that this is the case ('Ja') and asks her in lines 10–11 if he is right that the new date will be from the 10th to the 17th: 'Eine Woche. Also am zehnten wär's ja dann, ne? Vom zehnten bis zum siebzehnten.' This implicit reference to a written text (a calendar) is also a 'tying'. The telephonist tells him in lines 10–12 that she will look ('Ich werd's mal sehen.') if there is accommodation available for two people at the holiday centre. While the Dutch telephonist checks this in her computer, the German guest lets her know by 'back-channelling'[5] ('Hm hm.') in line 12 that he understands her. In line 13 she tells him that there is no problem ('Hmhm . . ehm . . das ist kein . Problem . .'). Finally, the German guest checks the new reservation.

[5] 14DTf   Ja. Sie bekommen
     14GGm Krieg' ich dann 'n neues Schreiben von Ihnen?

     15DTf ein- eine neue Bestätigung.
     15GGm   Also vom zehnten bis

     16DTf   Ja.   Stimmt, ja.
     16GGm zum siebzehnten wär' das.   Alles klar.

     17DTf OK?   Tschüß.
     17GGm   Viel'n Dank . . Tschüß.

In line 14 the German guest creates sequential context for the Dutch telephonist by asking her if he can receive a new invoice. He uses a 'tying' to refer to the future *written* text ('n neues Schreiben') that he wishes to receive, and in doing so he activates a text for the telephonist, which is part of the chain of actions related to the event 'staying in a holiday centre'. This activated text is also a 'cue'; the German guest refers to knowledge of the organisation as part of their common cultural model. The telephonist understands that he wants confirmation of the new reservation and promises him a 'neue Bestätigung' in lines 14–15. Finally the German guest checks the new reservation one last time in lines 15–16: 'Also vom zehnten bis zum siebzehnten wär' das.'. The telephonist confirms this in line 16 ('Ja. Stimmt, ja.') and the German guest lets her know in lines 16–17 that he is satisfied and thanks her. They close their conversation by saying 'Tschüß' to each other.

During the reservation exchange, the telephone allows the telephonist and the guest located at different places to speak directly to each other. This procedure also enables them to co-ordinate their actions in order to make sure that the guest will be in his residential bungalow in the right place at the right time, i.e. at the right holiday centre. Thus, by using 'tyings' and 'cues' as intertextual dimensions in the production of both written and oral texts, the actors have 'bracketed time and space'[6] simultaneously in two different ways.

4. CONCLUSIONS AND IMPLICATIONS FOR FUTURE RESEARCH

Firth's example clearly illustrates that 'tyings' enable actors to create sequential context. They refer to prior and future written texts that are seen as mutual reference points which 'can be located or orientated to in order that the parties can inform each other of their state of progress, or, more generally, of their interactional *"whereabouts"'* (Firth 1991: 100–1).

In contrast to the findings reported by Firth (1991, 1995), in the second case-study (Loos 1997) actors do not only refer to prior and future written texts, but also to oral texts. As a result, both written and oral texts can be viewed as mutual reference points, which actors use in order to inform each other of their 'interactional whereabouts'. A second finding not reported by Firth is that actors do not only refer to texts which they produce themselves, but they also link texts produced by others (such as the calendar used to check a date for a reservation) to their current conversation. A third difference between the two case-studies is that in Loos (1997), in addition to 'tyings', actors also use 'cues', where these 'cues' can be viewed as signals; i.e. they refer to knowledge stored as 'co-texts' in their shared cultural model, through which they create the cultural context that helps them to predict how to interpret each other's utterances in a specific interaction.

To conclude, then, actors construct and follow sequences of actions; by using 'tyings' and 'cues' as intertextual dimensions in their production of oral and written texts they create sequential and cultural contexts, respectively. Constructing their intertextual network in this way allows them to share meaning. To gain more insight into this management of meaning requires further research based on authentic documents, focusing on the reconstruction of the process involved. Recent empirical studies such as Boden (1994) show that actors share meaning in the course of interaction. In Boden's (1994: 18) words:

> Meanings, most importantly, do not occur as isolated cognitive
> phenomena in the heads of atomized individuals; they are constructed
> *interactively* and under quite pressing conditions of time and space.
> The 'need to know' has a for-the-moment quality that is irreducible to
> individual cognition; nor can it be abstracted away from the concrete
> actions and treated as an independent system.

It would be interesting to investigate further how actors succeed in sharing meaning despite different cultural backgrounds and languages and to analyse the ways in which they use 'tyings' and 'cues' during their production and interpretation of both written and oral business texts in the mutual construction of an intertextual network.

NOTES

1. Gastelaars and Hagelstein (1996) report on research from the Centre of Policy and Management Studies of Utrecht University (the Netherlands) which concentrates on 'management of meaning'.
2. Gumperz (1978: 23–4) calls them 'contextualization cues', and shows how actors with different cultural backgrounds use 'cues' differently.
3. All names have been replaced by pseudonyms.
4. See Firth (1990), Herrlitz and Loos (1994), Hoogenboezem *et al.* (1997), Loos (1997) and Loos (1998) for a discussion on language choice by actors in international organisations.
5. 'Backchannelling . . . gives the speaker an indication that the hearer(s) is (are) still listening. It is intended to keep up the communication by confirming or reacting to a preceding statement . . . and can be regarded as a "positive interruption", in fact as an encouragement for turn maintenance' (Clyne 1994: 110).
6. See also Giddens (1987: 153) and Boden (1994: 17) in section 2.2.1.

REFERENCES

Bakhtin, Mikhael (1986) *Speech Genres and Other Late Essays.* C. Emerson and M. Holmquist (eds), V. W. McGee (trans.). Austin: University of Texas Press.

Bartlett, Frederic C. (1932) *Remembering: A Study in Experimental and Social Psychology.* Cambridge: Cambridge University Press.

Bateson, Gregory (1955) A theory of play and phantasy. In *Psychiatric Research Reports: Approaches to the Study of Human Personality* 39–51. Washington, DC: American Psychiatric Association.

Bobrow, Daniel G. and Norman, Donald A. (1975) Some principles of memory schemata. In D. G. Bobrow and A. Collins (eds), *Representation and Understanding: Studies in Cognitive Science.* London, New York: Academic Press, pp. 131–49.

Boden, Deirdre (1994) *The Business of Talk: Organizations in Action*. Cambridge: Polity Press.

Boden, Deirdre and Zimmerman, Don H. (eds) (1991) *Talk and Social Structure: Studies in Ethnomethodology and Conversation Analysis*. Cambridge: Polity Press.

Chafe, Wallace (1977a) The recall and verbalization of past experience. In R. O. Freedle (ed.), *New Directions in Discourse Processing*. Norwood, NJ: Ablex, pp. 41–55.

Chafe, Wallace (1977b) The recall and verbalization of past experience. In R. W. Cole (ed.), *Current Issues in Linguistic Theory*. Bloomington: Indiana University Press, pp. 215–46.

Clyne, Michael (1994) *Intercultural Communication at Work*. Cambridge: Cambridge University Press.

Durkheim, Emile (1926) *The Elementary Forms of the Religious Life*. London: Allen & Unwin.

Fairclough, Norman (1992) *Discourse and Social Change*. Cambridge: Polity Press.

Firth, Alan (1990) 'Lingua franca' negotiations: towards an interactional approach. *World Englishes* 9 (3): 269–80.

Firth, Alan (1991) Discourse at work: negotiating by telex, fax and 'phone. Unpublished PhD dissertation. Aalborg: Aalborg University, Faculty of Humanities, Department of Intercultural Studies.

Firth, Alan (1995) Multiple mode, single activity: telenegotiating as a social accomplishment. In Paul ten Have and George Psathas (eds), *Situated Order: Studies in the Social Organization of Talk and Embodied Activities*. Washington, DC: University Press of America, pp. 151–72.

Frake, Charles O. (1977) Plying frames can be dangerous: some reflections on methodology in cognitive anthropology. *The Quarterly Newsletter of the Institute for Comparative Human Development*. Rockefeller University, I: 1–7.

Garfinkel, Harold (1967) *Studies in Ethnomethodology*. Englewood Cliffs, NJ: Prentice-Hall.

Gastelaars, Marja and Gerrit Hagelstein (eds) (1996) *Management of meaning: besturen en organiseren als processen van betekenisgeving*. Utrecht: ISOR.

Giddens, Anthony (1979) *Central Problems in Social Theory: Action, Structure and Contradiction in Social Analysis*. London, Basingstoke: Macmillan Press.

Giddens, Anthony (1984) *The Constitution of Society: Outline of the Theory of Structuration*. Cambridge: Polity Press.

Giddens, Anthony (1987) Time and social organization. In A. Giddens, *Social Theory and Modern Sociology*. Cambridge: Polity Press.

Goffman, Erving (1971) *Relations in Public: Micro Studies of the Public Order*. New York: Harper & Row.

Goffman, Erving (1974) *Frame Analysis: An Essay on the Organization of Experience*. New York: Harper & Row.

Gumperz, John J. (1978) The conversational analysis of interethnic communication. In E. L. Ross (ed.), *Interethnic Communication*. Athens, GA: Georgia University Press, pp. 14–31.

Gumperz, John J. (1982) *Discourse Strategies*. Cambridge: Cambridge University Press.

Heritage, John (1984) *Garfinkel and Ethnomethodology*. Cambridge: Polity Press.

Herrlitz, Wolfgang and Loos, Eugène F. (1994) Taal en taalgebruik in de internationale bedrijfs-communicatie: Een taalwetenschappelijk perspectief. In *M&O* (1994) 48 (2): 144–60. Alphen aan den Rijn: Samsom Bedrijfsinformatie.

Hoogenboezem, Karien, Ijgosse, Hester J. and Le Loux-Schuringa, Jetske (1997) Taalkeuze binnen multinationals: Improvisatie of beleid? In *M&O* (1997) 51 (6): 35–49. Alphen aan den Rijn: Samsom Bedrijfsinformatie.

Hymes, Dell (1974) Ways of speaking. In R. Bauman and J. Sherzer (eds), *Explorations in the Ethnography of Speaking*. Cambridge: Cambridge University Press.

Keuning, Doede (1991) *Organiseren en leiding geven*. Leiden/Antwerp: Stenfert Kroese.

Koole, Tom and Jan ten Thije (1994) *The Construction of Intercultural Discourse: Team Discussions of Educational Advisers*. Utrecht Studies in Language and Communication, PhD dissertation, Utrecht University. Amsterdam, Atlanta, GA: Rodopi.

Loos, Eugène F. (1996) Mensen in (inter)actie: onderzoek naar de relatie tussen dialoog en context in organisaties. In Marja Gastelaars and Gerrit Hagelstein (eds), *Management of meaning: Besturen en organiseren als processen van betekenisgeving*. Utrecht: ISOR, pp. 71–88.

Loos, Eugène F. (1997) Internationale bedrijfscommunicatie: een reconstructief onderzoek naar het intertekstuele netwerk van Nederlandse en Duitse actoren in een bungalowpark. PhD dissertation, Utrecht: Utrecht University.

Loos, Eugène F. (1998) Language choice at work: implications of language policy for management of meaning at a Dutch holiday centre in Germany. In: Marja Gastelaars & Arie de Ruijter (eds), *A United Europe. The Quest for a Multifaceted Identity*. Maastricht: Shaker Publishing, pp. 101–25.

Minsky, Marvin L. (1975) A framework for representing knowledge. In P. H. Winston (ed.), *The Psychology of Computer Vision*. New York: McGraw-Hill.

Psathas, George (1995) *Conversation Analysis: The Study of Talk-in-Interaction*, Qualitative Research Methods Series, 35. Thousand Oaks, London, New Delhi: Sage.

Ross, Robert N. (1975) Ellipsis and structure of expectation. In *San José State Occasional Papers in Linguistics* I: 183–91.

Rumelhart, David E. (1975) Notes on a schema for stories. In Daniel G. Brobow and Allard Collins (eds), *Representations and Understanding: Studies in Cognitive Science*. London, New York: Academic Press, pp. 211–36.

Saville-Troike, Muriel (1989) *The Ethnography of Communication*. Oxford, New York: Blackwell.

Schank, Roger C. and Robert P. Abelson (1977) Scripts, plans and knowledge. In *Advance Papers of the Fourth Interactional Joint Conference on Artificial Intelligence, Tbilisi, Georgia, USSR*, vol. I, pp. 151–57. Cambridge, MA: Artificial Intelligence Lab.

Tannen, Deborah (1979) What's in a frame? Surface evidence for underlying expectations. In Roy O. Freedle (ed.), *New Directions in Discourse Processing*. Norwood, NJ: Ablex, pp. 137–81.

General Index

adaptation (language) in business, 275–6, 287–9

billboard advertisements,
  and corporate language planning, 262, 268
  and cultural stereotyping, 261, 266
  bilingual vs monolingual, 257
  emotional response to, 258, 265–6
  in multicultural contexts, 259–60

Communication Research Institute of Australia, 87, 92
context,
  a model of corporate context, 184
  contextual influences on writing, 46–8, 63–9, 181–2, 305, 309
  contextualisation, 130, 133
  contextualising, 3
  'cues' in cultural context, 316, 319–20, 328
  of writing, 133–4
  'tyings' in sequential context, 315, 318, 328
corporate language planning, 268–9
  in billboard advertising, 257, 261–2
  in business interaction, 276, 288–9
  in business signage, 259–60

culture,
  corporate culture, 115–16, 159–60
  influences on professional writing, 113–14, 137–48
  national culture, 113–14

direct mail, 207–8
  as part of marketing campaign, 185–7
  features of, 181
  functional analysis of, 190–1, 198–201
  selection of, 185–7
  structure of, 188–90, 193–4
DIRECT Project, 252 note 1, 296–7
discourse,
  business, 1–2, 40, 317
  institutional, 1, 17
  professional, 1–2, 112, 137–48
discourse community, 7–8, 102–4
  writing engineers, 103–4
  writing managers, 305–8

Effective Writing for Management Project, 297–8
electronic communication,
  as a new genre, 58–9
  efficiency of, 63, 81
  features of layout in, 49–51, 70–3
  historical development, 59–60
  influence of context on, 46–8, 63–9

Name Index

Agar, M., 1
Akar, D., 27, 224
Auer, P., 133, 149

Bakhtin, M., 8–12, 22, 27, 57, 59, 216, 317
Barabas, C., 2, 5, 7
Barbara, L., 35, 39, 297, 301
Bargiela-Chiappini, F., 1, 2, 133, 229
Bauman, R., 130–1, 134
Bazerman, C., 8, 12, 13, 27, 130
Berkenkotter, C., 8, 27, 103
Beneke, J., 275
Berry, M., 294
Bhatia, V. K., 3, 42, 52, 181, 183, 185, 188, 190, 201, 210, 212
Bizzell, P., 101–2
Boden, D., 15, 53, 316–17, 318, 328–9
Briggs, C. L., 130–1, 134
Brown, P., 63, 72, 166
Brown, R., 293, 295, 298
Bruffee, K., 4

Campbell, K. K., 154, 158–9
Chafe, W., 218–20, 320
Charles, M., 15
Chin, E., 134, 149
Clyne, M., 124, 229, 329
Connor, U., 124, 189, 208–9
Cook-Gumperz, J., 133

Cooper, R. L., 268
Couture, B., 104, 295
Crawford, M., 157, 167
Crismore, A., 196, 203

Daft, R. L., 37–8
David, C., 155, 157, 166, 168
Davies, F., 293, 294, 296, 297, 301
Deetz, S. A., 268
Devitt, A. J., 6, 8, 11–12, 27, 28, 130, 183
Douglas, M., 134
Driskill, L. P., 28, 181, 184

Faigley, L., 16
Fairclough, N., 8–11, 14, 22, 183, 185, 216, 220, 317, 320
Firth, A., 26, 124, 208, 275, 315–18, 321–4, 328, 329

Giddens, A., 12, 13–14, 26, 52, 317, 320, 329
Goffman, E., 59, 73, 318, 320
Goswami, D., 16, 101
Grabe, W., 4, 8, 293
Graham, M. B., 155, 157, 166, 168
Grin, F., 262
Gumperz, J., 26, 130, 133, 315, 319–20, 329
Gunnarsson, B-L., 1, 11, 124, 130, 183, 198